QUIT

The Hypnotists Handbook To Running
Effective Stop-Smoking Sessions

Sarah Carson

Shawn Carson

Jess Marion

We would like to dedicate this book to everyone who will achieve a smoke free life through hypnosis and to the hypnotists who help them get there.

Acknowledgments

We would like to take a few moments to thank everyone who has helped us to realize the dream of writing and publishing this book. We would like to begin by extending a very special thank you to John Overdurf, the co-creator of HNLP. Through his mentorship we have grown as trainers, coaches, and change workers. Thanks to his friendship we continue to explore the depths of human potential. He continues to inspire us to seek out all that is beyond everything we thought was possible.

Our deepest thanks to Igor Ledochowski who continues to inspire us to find new and innovative ways of teaching and doing deeply transformative hypnosis. He is a long time friend and mentor without whom this book would not have been possible.

We could devote an entire chapter of thanks to Melissa Tiers. Your encouragement, teaching, friendship, unwavering support and positive energy lifts us all to greater heights than ever and we thank you for everything that you are and everything you will be.

In addition to our personal teachers and friends we would like to thank the founders of the various fields that are contain within this book. First we offer a special thanks to Milton Erickson for laying the foundations of conversational hypnosis, the cornerstone of our approach to change work.

Richard Bandler and John Grinder, the founders of the field of Neuro-Linguistic Programming. Their curiosity into the ways in which the mind creates experience has opened the door for us to create powerful patterns for change.

Frank Farelly, the creator of Provocative Therapy. His elegantly constructed system allows us to challenge a client's deeply held beliefs in ways that keeps rapport and produces the space for change.

Gary Craig, the creator of EFT for his contribution to the field of change work and for providing us with one of the most powerful, easy and remarkable techniques we know.

In addition we would each like to offer personal thanks to those not acknowledged above who have played an important role in this work.

Shawn Carson

To my co-authors Sarah and Jess who did all the work.

To my Mum Dorothy who enjoyed every cigarette she smoked even as she tried to Quit!

Sarah Carson

A special thank you to Jess for her endless positivity and ever deepening friendship.

My love and deep thanks goes to Shawn for opening the door into the wonderful world of NLP and Hypnosis and for helping me find my "authentic swing."

An especially big thank you to Mum and Dad for teaching me to live with an open mind, learn from every experience and to love with a big heart.

Jess Marion

I would like to deeply thank Shawn and Sarah without whom I would not be who I am today. Their continued love, support, and friendship have made this possible. I am beyond fortunate to have them in my life.

I would also like to personally thank Igor Ledochowski for setting my feet firmly on this path.

A very special thank you to my sister Lindsey Churchill who has been with me every step of the way supporting, encouraging, and laughing with me. She continues to inspire me to reach higher.

Finally thank you to my mom and younger brother Shaughn, who have done more things than I can count to make this possible.

The three of us would like to thank our talented editor Kristin Prevallet who has worked hard to transform our messy manuscript into a beautiful book.

Finally we want to thank all our students including those who participated in this workshop. Their continued support, enquiring minds, transformations and enthusiasm made this book possible and continues to inspire us to learn and grow.

Table of Contents

FOREWORD

I believe that hypnotherapists are a tremendous force for good in the world. We help others find it inside themselves to lead richer, happier and more rewarding lives. Sometimes the person just needs a little nudge and sometimes they need someone to parachute into the hell they find themselves in to show them the way out. Not all hypnotherapists can work at both ends of this range. Fewer still have lived it long enough to teach others how to follow in their footsteps. Finding a teacher like this is a rare gem. I believe that Sarah, Shawn & Jess are three such gems, rarer still for the fact that they have found each other and are now sharing their experiences with the world.

We hypnotherapists are in the healing profession. Creating more healers in a world where people are still suffering in too great a number is a great thing. So you would expect that any healer with the skills of a competent hypnotherapist should become inundated with clients the moment they hung up their shingle. Sadly this is not the case. Far too many hypnotherapists cannot make a living from their craft and are forced to abandon it or spend most of their time doing other things to feed their family, reserving only a few precious moments to work their calling.

This is a terrible state of affairs, especially given how things need NOT be so!

It is my experience that there are so many people seeking aid like ours that every competent hypnotherapist could have a practice that is overflowing with clients, helping them make the transformations they so desperately want. It is no secret that some 90% of people that turn to hypnosis as a field for help are initially drawn to it to help them stop smoking or lose weight. Many of these people start here, but then go on to make even more profound life changing transformations — either as a result of these sessions or because their initial success inspired them to take the risk to face other issues that were considered to be "hopeless" before.

It is therefore a wise hypnotist that will master the intricacies of running a Stop Smoking or Weight Loss program in order to both keep their practice afloat and to leave the door ajar for the wide range of issues that hypnotherapy has proven to have a practical, fast and effective solution to offer.

I remember my first days as a hypnotherapist in London (England). I remember wracking my brains as to how I might work with the smokers that approached me. I remember the failures, the frustrated feeling of a clumsy caveman trying to figure out how to make a wheel. I also remember the elation when a more experienced hypnotist offered to share his method and show me the way. That was the turning point in my own career.

And now it is your turn.

Sarah, Shawn and Jess have done a tremendous job in writing this book. And they have given you a gift: the gift of knowledge. Instead of forcing you to explore an unknown landscape, they have given you a detailed map not just of the territory, but also of the best routes to navigate through it. With this precious map you will be able to guide anyone that is sincere about making the journey to the "promised land" of freedom on the other side. This map is so detailed that you will be able to pick the best route for each client, whether they are a "sightseer" that wants to take the gentle scenic route or a "pragmatist" that just wants to get there as fast as possible, even if that means climbing a few mountains along the way!

If you follow the advice in this book, you will be in very good hands. Even if I did not know Shawn, Sarah and Jess personally or had not seen their work first hand to know just how impressive it really is, I would still be recommending the book in your hands right now to you without any reservations. The contents speak for themselves. As a hypnotist of some accomplishments myself, I always know quality when I see it… and I see an abundance of quality in this book!

I hope it brings you as much elation and success as a knowhow similar to this brought me when I most needed it.

Igor Ledochowski
Author of *The Power Of Conversational Hypnosis*
www.HypnosisTrainingAcademy.com

PREFACE

As Hypnotists we see many clients who want to quit smoking. In fact it is probably the most common issue that people come to see a hypnotist for help with.

In this book we outline a complete protocol for Hypnotists and Change Workers to use with clients. The protocol is based on hundreds of hours working with quit-smoking clients to find out what works and what doesn't.

In describing the protocol, we will lead you all the way through from the initial phone call to the moment when your client leaves your office as a new non-smoker. You will learn how to elicit clients' hidden motivation to create the leverage that will make the change easy for them. And you will learn how to lock the change in place by easily dealing with issues of secondary gain. You will discover easy techniques to help your client deal with cravings, change their identity to one of a non-smoker, create an unconscious aversion to cigarettes, and find new ways of dealing with the stresses that may have caused them to smoke in the past.

We utilize techniques from Neuro Linguistic Programming (NLP), Humanistic Neuro Linguistic Programming (HNLP), traditional hypnosis, Erickson Hypnosis, Conversational Hypnosis and the Emotional Freedom Techniques (EFT); and we present three totally new and unique patterns for transformation. All the patterns are laid out in a simple-to-follow unified process that leads to success for you and your clients.

This work is trance-scribed from our four-day workshop and it is a wonderful opportunity for you to become one of the students in the class with us. You will join in with other Hypnotists, NLPers, social workers, health coaches and lifestyle coaches in making a difference in the lives of others.

Whether you are a "start on page 1" person or someone who prefers to dip in to "whatever catches your fancy," we suggest that you read this book in the best way for you. As our friend and teacher John Overdurf likes to say, "either way is better."

Day 1

INTRODUCTION

Sarah: Welcome everybody to the "Quit" Workshop for Hypnotists and Change Workers. I'd like to congratulate each and everyone of you and thank you for taking the time to come here today because the more of us who are doing positive work to help smokers quit, the more lives are benefitting each and every day and I think that's fantastic.

Jess: This workshop is specifically designed to give you the optimal opportunity to have success with helping your clients to stop smoking. Over the next four days you will learn how to handle the initial phone call, what to be listening for, and questions to be asking. You will learn how to to leverage change by working with the client's individual presuppositions and internal programming.

We have "craving buster" techniques to share and three completely new patterns built into the program. We will be sharing how to deal with secondary gain issues and we will be giving you ways to effect change on the unconscious level either conversationally or through direct trance. It is a very thorough and complete protocol that will take you from the moment you pick up the phone with a potential client all the way through to the end of the sessions when your client will be dumping their cigarettes and saying "I'm done!" And there is no greater thrill, at least for me, than at the end of the session when I offer the client their pack of cigarettes back and they won't touch them, not even to throw them out.

This protocol is designed specifically to give you the optimal opportunity to have success with your clients. As you know, working with any client is a fluid process, a dance, and a negotiation. With smokers there are particular presuppositions, ideas, and techniques we have found that work particularly well to help them quit.

Sarah: Because every smoker is a unique individual and will be "doing" their problem in their own unique and individual way, there are choice points, options, and alternative routes built into this program. What is so lovely is that it will become clear which road to take with your client because you will know how to "read" each person differently. You will have all the signposts showing you the best way to go in order to help them change quickly and effectively.

This is a very thorough protocol and to effect change we usually recommend an initial 2 hour session and then a week later, a one-hour follow up session.

Jess: How many of you are already seeing clients for Stop Smoking sessions? How many of you plan to start soon?

(*Students raising hands*)

Jess: Each and everyone of you is here because you want to help people quit smoking, which means that you are saving lives. What you do when you are coaching someone in your office, in your clinic, or in a group setting, is helping them to save their own life.

Sarah: The Center for Disease Control and Prevention says that there are more than 43 million cigarette smokers in the USA. Although it is the leading preventable cause of death, one in five deaths are attributed to smoking. That's huge, isn't it? And the CDC says that smoking claims 438,000 lives per year. So the work that we do is necessary and powerful.

It's a good idea to have some research and statistics to back up the work that we do. If you go online you can easily find studies that demonstrate the effectiveness of using hypnosis to help someone quit smoking cigarettes. For example, a 2001 University of Washington School of Medicine study stated a 90% success rate in patients using Hypnosis.

In a large scientific comparison study of the different methods to help people stop smoking, researchers at the University of Iowa found hypnosis to be three times more effective than any nicotine replacement, and fifteen times more effective than relying only on willpower.

We suggest that you do your own research and have some ideas of the research that backs up what we are doing.

Out of interest, is anyone here a smoker? Just one. Anybody and ex-smoker? Alright, quite a few people. Anyone never smoked, or just tried a few?

Mercedes: I was cute!(*laughter*) I liked the way the cigarette looked in my hand and drew attention to my hand and my nails.

Sarah: It was all about the nails!

Mercedes: My boyfriend told me to just stop with the cigarettes! (*laughter*).

Sarah: I've never really been a smoker. I tried it a couple of times when I was younger but never really liked it, so I count myself kind of fortunate because I know that for some people it's a tough habit to break...and I also know that hypnosis is incredibly powerful and highly effective in helping someone quit.

Shawn: I used to smoke very occasionally at University because it made the alcohol cheaper! It opens up the capillaries in the brain, so the alcohol is able to get to your brain faster (*laughter*).

Lawrence: A good scientific reason! (*laughter*)

Shawn: Yeah absolutely! But that was maybe one cigarette a week so I was never really a smoker. Oh and remember, I went to school in the UK where it is perfectly legal to drink from the age of 18!

Jess: I have not ever smoked cigarettes but I see lots of people who do. They come into my office and I sniff the air and think to myself, "No." The smell just seems to permeate the air.

Sarah: So that's enough about us. Now just take a couple of moments to go around and meet everybody in the class, introduce yourself and if you'd like, share a little bit about your own smoking history or non-smoking history. So put your things down and get yourselves up!

Shawn: So everybody meet everybody? Did anybody meet nobody?

Mark: I was looking for him!! (*laughter*)

HOLDING THE SPACE

Jess: Great...Hopefully you are all feeling happy, excited and curious about what you are going to be learning with us here. As you may know, the foundation of hypnosis is state elicitation and state control.

When we work with any client, smokers included, it is very important for us to go into the Coaching State and to "Hold The Space." The way we do this is through eliciting our own positive state and understanding that as change workers, we have all of the tools and resources we need to help the client get in touch with the tools, resources and strategies they need to make the change. And because of your experience as coaches, mentors, trainers, change workers and hypnotists you have lots of experience and the knowledge to help your client reach their goal. Lets practice "Holding the Space" by building it in three easy steps.

Step 1: Peripheral Vision

I would like for everyone to find some point in front of you, somewhere where you can focus your gaze...and as you find that point...you can find the tiniest spot within that point...so maybe it's the edge of something or a change of color on the wall; perhaps it's somewhere where shadow and light touch...and as you focus your gaze on that point...I'd like for you to begin to notice any tiny changes in color, noticing the differences in light and dark...in fact it's almost as if you were to look closely enough, you would be able to see the tiniest molecules that make up that point. And then when you have a sense of that...allow your gaze to relax...so you can still see that point and you can see the rest of the

19

wall...you can still see that point and you can begin to have an awareness of what's to your left and what's to your right...sensing any movement to your sides...noticing the wall to your right...the window to the left and as you see that point and sense that movement...you can have an awareness of the space between you and that point...the space behind you...you can have an awareness that you're sitting on a chair that's comfortably supported by a floor...attached to a building...resting on planet earth...and sensing that movement and seeing that point...you can hear the sounds that are to your left and to your right. And then when you're ready allow your vision to return to normal, bring your awareness to the here and now.

Jess: How was that everyone?

Group: Cool...trancy...great!

Shawn: So what is actually happening here is that when we go into peripheral vision, we relax our gaze and become aware of everything around us.

Let me ask you this...what happened to the chatter in your mind?

Group: It was quiet!

Shawn: Yes, that usually happens. We are opening our sensory channels and the chatter and voices in our heads just seem to go away. Think of how useful that is when you are coaching or doing hypnosis! No more talking to yourself and taking yourself away from the client. This is all about heightened attention and when we have this we are able to see every little micro movement, pick up every hesitation or sigh or change in voice tone. Our calibration skills go through the roof.

Karen: I just felt all tranced out....how can I help the client if I am looking like a zombie? *(laughing)*

Jess: Right…thank you for that…remember we said there were a few steps to this?

Step 2: Bring it around

The second step is to gather that open awareness and bring it around the client…almost like you are creating a "bubble" between you and them.

Lets get into pairs and I will lead you through this. One at a time, be the hypnotist and go into the state.

> *Find a spot near your partner where you can focus your gaze…look very closely and notice every detail about the spot…maybe where the light and dark meet…or where one color crosses over to another…now soften your gaze and slowly begin to expand it out…so you can see more and more of whatever you are looking at…maybe as you continue to expand, you can see the corners of the wall…or become aware of the other students in the class. Become aware of all the sounds in the room and outside of the room…the sound of the heater…the traffic in the street…the sound of your own breathing and as you do so…become aware of all the space in front of you…all the space behind you…all the space above you and all the space beneath you …and as you continue to have an awareness of all the space and energy around you…you can begin to gather it and wrap it around your partner in front of you… so opening your vision, your hearing, your energy and your awareness and begin wrapping it around the person in front of you…creating a bubble of energy, or if you like, of openness and total awareness. And when you are ready, coming all the way back to the here and now.*

Jess: How was that? More focus..less zombie?

Karen: Yeah much better…but I still feel a bit trancy.

Sarah: Well of course you do...this is hypnosis after all...and we know that we have to "go first" into the trance state in order to lead our client there. Also, we are giving you "training wheels" here in order to practice going into this state. That involves leading you through a hypnotic experience and as you are all trance junkies...you fall right in! You will find that with practice this becomes so much easier to access without having to stare at a spot on the wall first...that would look weird right? Your clients would really be wondering, "what I have I gotten myself into?" (*laughing*)

Jess: Yeah Sarah is right...these are practices and you will be so used to this by the end of this course that it just becomes second nature and you will look perfectly normal and be able to hold conversations with your clients and be in the coaching state all the time.

Step 3: Holding a Positive Image

After you have gone into peripheral vision and wrapped your 'bubble' around your client we want you to imagine them as already having quit...that they have all the resources they need to make this change and that you see them as already successful. You can do this by holding this to be true, or by making an image of them, or by sending them positive energy...or anything else that works for you.

So sit with your partner and let's go into peripheral vision again. This time, go a little faster.

Begin to focus on a spot on the wall or somewhere in the room...allow your gaze to soften...and begin to expand so you can see the entire wall while looking at the same spot...you can notice any movement around you...the sounds in the room and outside of the room..the traffic...the sound of your own heartbeat...and you can become aware of the space in front of you and behind you...above you and below you...and as you have expanded your awareness out...now expand it around the person in front of you...creating your own energetic bubble with them...because you know that you have a client sitting there in front of you and hypnosis is an incredibly powerful tool for creating this change...and that client in front of you has every resource they need...a lifetime of knowingness...experiences...perhaps even successful times of quitting in the past...only they forgot about it later on...and they have all the resources they need to make this change and you know because you want something good for them...and that you will do everything you can...use every skill that you have to help them create this change. And then when you're ready allow your vision to return to normal, bring your awareness to the here and now.

How was that?

Karen: Great...it was easier to get into it this time and because it was faster, and I wasn't so trancy.

Jess: Now what we would like you to do is to get into groups of three, and label yourselves A, B and C. Each person is going to have an awesome role and we will all get a chance to switch roles too. Person A: your role is to expand your awareness, get in touch with your peripheral vision and wrap that energy around person B, knowing that they are an incredibly resourceful person and you are an incredibly resourceful change worker, and that they can achieve their goal. Simply holding the state and holding those beliefs.

Person B: your role is to enjoy what happens, to simply "be" and to allow the hypnotist to hold the space for you.

Person C: sit where you can observe both A and B. Your role is to simply notice the space in between and observe what happens.

Lets have two minutes per person and we will chime the bell to let you know it is time to switch roles.

(*Students do exercise*)

Sarah: So welcome back everyone, how was that?

Kathy: As "being" person B, within about 10 seconds, by just looking at me while in the coaching state, Karen miraculously put me into a trance (*laughter*)... I could just feel myself going into trance. It was really fast... I wasn't expecting that.

Sarah: So you caught her trance!

Jess: States are contagious!

Sarah: And there is an elegant art to it. You don't want to stare someone down, and you don't want to look at them as though you are in love with them. It's that fine line which communicates, "I am open and I am here for you."

As hypnotists, we go into this state of awareness. We widen our peripheral vision and then wrap that energy, that open feeling, around the person in front of you to create a bubble - an energetic space. And that is what we mean by "holding the space."

So you are completely open because you've left all your own-ness aside. Does that make sense? (*agreement from class*) You're seeing the person in front of you as complete, not broken or challenged, or having a difficulty. You're seeing them as if they already made positive changes, and that they have all the resources they could possibly need.

All of these things go into creating this state, the Coaching state. And when you feel it... You'll feel it.

Jess: And it's a powerful thing for the clients to experience, and you do feel it. When a smoker comes in for the first session, after the initial phone consultation, in my mind I already see them as a non-smoker. As hypnotists we have to be bigger than whatever the clients' problems and behaviors are.

One of the ways to do this is to connect with them as a complete person who has overcome anything from the past, and has now made an awesome change in their life.

When the person decides to either throw out their cigarettes, or even if they haven't smoked for a couple of hours before the session - in my mind they are already a non-smoker. They've quit... it's done. Now when they come in for the session, we are reinforcing a decision that they have already made.

Yuval: We all found it easy to go into this state, but what happens if you get someone who is really nervous?

Sarah: Has it ever happened to you that you've worked with someone and they were really nervous? No? Okay. So part of creating this state, the bubble if you like, is that the hypnotist goes into it before the client arrives in the office. And as we saw with Karen and Kathy, states are contagious.

Now your client may be feeling somewhat nervous or cautious because perhaps they don't know what's going to be happening. Maybe it's their first time going into hypnosis...so it's really important for us to step into and maintain our coaching state. And the curious thing is that they begin to pick it up.

Jess: If a smoker comes in and it's the first time they are doing hypnosis not only are they changing something about a part of them, a part of their life that's been with them for X number of years, they are taking that step into the unknown - and they're doing it in a way that is unfamiliar.

So from time to time you may have that client who is nervous or unsure and as you hold the space and hold the state, your physiology automatically communicates the message "Hey... it's fine" and they'll catch it. It's contagious.

Sarah: Anyone else before we move on? Mark?

Mark: I've had a few clients who start go into hypnosis and then they suddenly come out of trance. They break the state and start talking.

Sarah: That's Ok. I have had that too, and if we remember that hypnosis is very easy to move into we can just as easily suggest that they go back inside. Talking is allowed; in fact, we like our clients to talk because otherwise we don't know exactly where we are in a session. As hypnotists we like to be able to dip into a hypnotic state but at just the right level so that we can still communicate, talk, observe, and calibrate everything that we need to about our clients.

Maybe you remember when you first learned peripheral vision and maybe you felt very trancy and thought to yourself "how am I supposed to do work now?" (*Laughter*). It's that fine balance between going into this state and still appearing quite normal... You don't want to completely freak out your clients by appearing glazed and totally out of it. It's about having the ability to converse and helping them to converse about what's going on while still maintaining the state and holding the space.

So it absolutely is a hypnotic state, but it's not so deep that you're the one who has gone deeply into trance. It's a balance.

THE TELEPHONE CONVERSATION AND INITIAL CONSULTATION.

Sarah: I have a question for you: when does the session start?

Mark: At birth!

Sarah: "At birth!"… Good answer! When does the session start?

Kathy: At the phone conversation.

Sarah: Yes! Most clients will phone up. If they email I usually want to have a phone consultation with them. This is when the entire process begins. So what do we do on the phone? What do you do now when someone calls up and is interested in quitting smoking?

Kristina: Ask "what stops you?"

Sarah: Yes.

Rita: I would find out if they really want to stop or if someone else wants them to stop.

Sarah: How would you know?

Rita: I would ask them.

Sarah: Yes…any thing else about that?

Rita: Umm…not sure.

Sarah: OK, we are going to talk in a moment about that.

Kristina: Have they tried before?

Sarah: Yes…and "What else have you tried?"

Lawrence: Why they want to quit and where they want to be afterwards.

Sarah: This is great, everyone is heading in the right direction with this. We are definitely going to be asking these kinds of questions and we are going to be listening very carefully to how they answer. We are going to be listening for the energy behind their answers.

First of all, I'm always going to ask "is this for you or for someone else?" I have had people call up and say "I'm interested in your quit smoking program" and at first I assumed it was for the person calling, but no, they were calling up on behalf of someone else. So now I will always ask "is this for you or someone else?"

I will also check if this is to stop smoking cigarettes. I have had people half way through our conversation mention that they are inquiring about giving up smoking marijuana and of course that issue is going to be slightly different. This workshop is about helping someone to quit smoking cigarettes.

One of the big questions that you are always going to ask is "why do you want to quit?" I'm guessing that this is a question they are expecting to be asked, so along with their verbal answer what else am I listening for?

Yuval: Motivation?

Sarah: Yes, I'm absolutely listening for their level of motivation. That's what I mean about listening for the energy behind what they're saying.

Mark: Contradiction?

Sarah: What do you mean by that?

Mark: Like a double message. Something like, "on the one hand I want to quit but on the other hand…" This could be in the hesitancy or the length they take to answer a question. Or something in their attitude.

Sarah: Exactly. And what's going to help us tremendously to pick up all of those things?

Mark: Listening?

Sarah: Yes, and going into the coaching state. Right? Even though the person isn't sitting right there in front of you, going into the coaching state helps you to be able to hear all of these things -the subtle nuances, the hesitancy, the energy.

So I'll ask, "is this for you or someone else?" "Is this for cigarettes?" "Why do you want to quit?"

If they begin to say, "well... my doctor said I need to quit" or "my daughter won't let me hold the baby," then I'm going to probe even more. And depending what they say I'm likely to say, "I'm not entirely certain that you are completely ready for this."Because if they are quitting for someone else, what is their real motivation? It's somebody else's motivation.

We really want the client themselves to be completely committed to and motivated for this change. So we are really listening extremely carefully to how they answer those questions. Is there any hesitancy, do they take a long time to answer, or are they truly self-motivated? I may also ask if they tried before, what methods they used, and what worked before.

If it's their first time quitting, I'll ask whether they've been hypnotized before just to get a little bit more information. This telephone conversation is vital, because it really determines whether I'll be taking them on as a client or not.

Jess: Another important question — especially if you're going the route of social couponing — is "why now?" "Why at this moment have you decided that it's time to make a change?" And if the answer is "well, because I saw the coupon" then you have to dig a bit deeper. The "why now?" question will also get to the heart of whether this change is for them, or whether it is because their wife or their doctor wants them to change. In those cases it tends to be the people in their life who have the problem with the behavior, and not the smoker. In which case their energy may not be strong enough to propel them through to being a non-smoker.

Lawrence: So you've got someone on the phone and discovered their motivations are not their own and you decline to take them on as a client. That's not something they're expecting to hear. How do you finish off the conversation?

Shawn: Well you're not turning them down as a client, you're turning them down as a client NOW.

Sarah: There are a couple of ways to do this. One way is to push them even more, play hard ball with them and say something like, "have you not seen all the evidence that points to how bad smoking is? You've known this for years… are you telling me that you're only just coming to this realization?" So they might start to back off and consider more what their motivation is. And they may self-select at this point because I'm pushing. Of course there are softer ways to get them to examine their motivation as well.

Lawrence: So you can stop them there and say, "so why don't you take some time to examine your motivation and…"

Sarah: Yes, that's a nicer way to do it.

Shawn: Basically you're saying, "come back when you're ready to quit not when someone else wants you to quit." So you're not pushing them away you're just saying "not now." This comes also to Jess's point on the social couponing. If someone calls having already purchased a session then you've already got a client and you can't turn them away. You have to decide how to deal with that person given that perhaps you feel that they don't have the motivation to quit.

Lawrence: But then you can use the session to help them get in touch with their own motivation.

Sarah: Exactly!

Shawn: Absolutely!

Lawrence: And then book them for a second session for smoking cessation.

Shawn: Yes and you always spend time in the session getting leverage, because no one is going to come to see you completely ready to quit. If they were ready to quit they would've quit by themselves and they wouldn't need to see you. Some part of your job is to actually help them build the leverage they need against cigarettes.

Jess: If you do go the social couponing route one way to negotiate is to spend the session using a pattern to help build motivation. I would probably say, "look, I get a sense that this isn't really the change you want, how would you like to use the session?" And if they still insist on doing the smoking cessation then we will take it one step at a time and start building the motivation.

One lady called me up with a voucher because she and her husband wanted to come for smoking cessation. I could tell from talking to her that she didn't want to stop smoking so I asked up front "do you really want this" and she stopped for a moment and then said, "no you're right. I want to use the session for something else." So people will self-select as well.

Sarah: Sometimes I say to a potential client; "convince me, convince me that you're ready" or "why should I take you as a client?" You can do that in a really soft way or in a hard way depending on the energy that you've got with them.

Shawn: What you have to bear in mind is that one in five deaths are caused by smoking. These guys are literally playing Russian roulette, and taking an enormous risk. That's a huge motivation to quit.

Sarah: And I think we also have to bear in mind that we are not the Smoking Police. It is not our job to go out and convince everyone that they should quit. If people want to smoke then they can smoke. It's up to them. It really is up to the individual but if they want to quit and they are ready to quit then we are here to help them.

And smokers often have a hard time with that idea. If I'm out and about and I tell people that I'm a hypnotist and I help people quit smoking, sometimes smokers will say to me, "don't make me quit… You can't make me quit." It makes me smile because why would I do that? And sometimes they have a hard time when I say "go ahead smoke…it's up to you." It's got nothing to do with me. It's their life, their choice.

So with all that in mind we would like you to get into pairs and role-play having a telephone conversation. One person is calling up as a potential client wanting to book a session, and the other being the hypnotist. As the potential client you can decide what you will say, what your motivations will be, and your reasons for wanting to quit. Hypnotists: you will go into the coaching state and see what you come up with. Cool? So we'll give you three or four minutes each. Have fun.

(*Students do exercise*)

Jess: So how was that everyone?

Group: "Great/good."

Jess: Ok. So we will add just a few more things into the initial phone session. Once I have agreed to take the client and have set up an appointment time I always ask my clients to have their last cigarette a few hours before the session and to bring their pack of cigarettes with them. This way I am already gaining compliance and seeing if they will follow instructions. Sarah, I know you ask them for something a bit different.

Sarah: Yeah. I tell them to have their last cigarette the night before they come in to see me. That way when they wake up in the morning they are already 6-8 hours into being a non-smoker. Their body is already beginning to change as their blood pressure decreases, their CO_2 level is diminishing and there is more oxygen in the blood. This is a big motivator for lots people.

Yuval: So what happens if they don't? I mean, what if that appointment is very late in the day and they may have to wait for hours.

Sarah: Yes that's right and sometimes they will smoke. Sometimes they'll sneak a cigarette sometime during the day and even just before coming in to see me. And they think I won't be able to smell it on them? (*Laughing*) So if they have smoked some time that day I would explain that it might take a bit longer for them to quit.

Shawn: And sometimes it works the opposite way. A colleague of ours once had a client who she was having a hard time with because he believed that he was totally out of control –he believed that the cigarettes owned him. So she referred him to me and told him not to smoke the day of the appointment. When I asked, "did you smoke?" he said, "No."

I looked at him and said, "but I thought you were totally out of control?" And he said, "well Nina told me not to smoke...so I didn't smoke." I smiled and said, "and what would happen if Nina told you to quit?" And he said, "I'd quit!" So I told Nina to put him into a deep trance and tell him to quit...that was it , he just wanted someone to tell him not to smoke.

Yuval: So he can say, "someone made me quit."

Shawn: Yeah... he wanted to be made to comply.

Shawn: The problem is that if they smoke just before coming in to see you, then they don't have the craving so you can't do the Craving Buster. And that's a big piece of what we do as you'll find out later in this workshop.

Jess: If they have called up and I'm not quite certain that they're ready to quit, I like to have an 'in person' consultation with my potential quit-smoking clients. That way I can calibrate to their gestures, any changes in breathing or color in their skin tone and really see what is going on when they talk about the issue. Plus if I have some doubts, it's a compliance test. If they show up for the consultation, that says a lot about them being ready to make this change. If they don't show up for the consultation then I know exactly where they are at, and it was better off that I didn't take them on as a client right away anyway. So there is no hard rule, and I like to do both.

Rita: When someone calls you to do a session do you say it will take one session...? What is the expectation?

Sarah: We normally sell a package of three 1 hour sessions.

Rita: What if they ask, "What if I quit after the first session?"

Sarah: You say "Great! And you probably will. And we use the follow-up sessions for reinforcement." The first session is a double session - that's two hours. Then a follow-up session is one hour. Three hours in total.

Jess: You can also suggest that they give the follow-up session as a gift to a friend or family member if they don't need it. That's a way to generate a new lead.

Sarah: Another thing that I usually do with any client is to ask for payment in advance, particularly if it is the first time that I will be seeing them. This shows commitment from them and it ensures that I will get paid for my time. When I first started out I didn't do this and there were quite a few times when I sat in the office and the client didn't show up and I had essentially wasted my time.

Jess: And if you're going to go the free consultation route I suggest that you set the time of your availability for when you are going to be in the office anyway because you will have people who don't show up and there's no sense in going all the way to your office if you're not going to have a client.

CLIENT PRESUPPOSITIONS

Shawn: Ok so lets move forward and begin to think about what is going on with the client. If we think about the client and the smoking habit as a game of Russian Roulette, then we can see that this person is taking an enormous risk with their life. To take that risk they would need to have built up an amazing map of the world that in some way justifies how they can be doing this to themselves. If they didn't have some amazing justification then they just wouldn't smoke.

Smoking is such a ridiculous thing to do. No offense to the smokers in the room but in terms of health, in terms of cost, in terms of all sorts of other things - especially in New York when it gets cold in winter and these guys are all huddled outside the office smoking away in subzero temperatures...

Yuval: It's a way to have a break from work, to socialize for a bit.

Shawn: See, here's the justification... Because there is no way you could possibly take a break and not smoke (*laughing*). The non-smokers in the room - you never take breaks right? (*Laughing*) Right?

Because you'd have nothing to do, and apparently you can only take a break with a cigarette (*laughing*). So here you see how smokers create an amazing map of the world that will be something like, "I can only take a break if I have a cigarette" or "I need it in order to calm down" or "I smoke because it's cool." So there's an amazing map that they've built to overcome the fact that they are gambling with their life. Each cigarette takes 10 minutes off your life, so they say.

Yuval: Per cigarette?

Shawn: Yeah… Not in total! (*Laughing.*) So the structure of this map is what we are calling the "presuppositions of the client." As hypnotists we hold certain presuppositions about our clients: the fact that your client is totally resourceful, the fact that they can go into trance, etc.

But the client also has their presuppositions, and we have to understand what these are. You have all worked with smokers, right? So, what are some typical presuppositions that a smoker holds that allows them to smoke?

Karen: I know that for me it was, "I have something to do with my hands."

Kathy: I couldn't write unless I was smoking.

Shawn: Right, I can't do X without a cigarette.

Mark: In order to be able to get through something.

Shawn: For stress.

Kristina: I heard someone say, "the funnest time of my life involved cigarettes. So for me to let go of smoking means to let go of the potential for fun."

Shawn: Yes, smoking means letting go of the past, or of a person as well. I had a client who said, "I was taught to smoke by my father and he has since passed on. So I will be losing that connection."

Lawrence: There is the fitting in with a particular group.

Shawn: Yep, the social factor.

Yuval: Drinking and smoking are often connected.

Karen: And the connection to an activity also. Every morning when I used to get in my car I would light up.

Shawn: Yes there is a connection to a social activity.

Mark: Doing something for myself.

Shawn: Ah… That's the common "my friend" scenario. For people who don't have a lot of close friends, or for people who think that everyone is out to get them, cigarettes are their friends. The one reliable thing that's always there. How about the health stuff?

Mercedes: "There are worse things to die of."

Sarah: Yes I've heard that one.

Lawrence: "We are all going to die."

Shawn: Yes that's quite common. We have a friend who is in his 20s and he said, "well I'm going to be dead by my 50s so I may as well enjoy it!" Or the opposite side of this is the "it won't be me" idea.

Sarah: "Someone else may get sick but it won't be me."

Sarah: Great, so these are some ideas that the client may hold about continuing to smoke. What about some presuppositions they may be holding onto about quitting?

Kathy: Weight gain, not having as much fun.

Mark: Also people use cigarettes as a proxy for their shyness.

Sarah: Yes… Social impact.

Lawrence: Irritability, as they have no way to deal with stress.

Sarah: What about things like, "I've tried before and it didn't work."

Shawn: Client: "I have no willpower." Friend: "Really? Then give me all your money!" Client: "no way!" Friend: "so you do have willpower!" (*Laughter*)

Jess: Or "quitting is hard."

Shawn: "It's an addiction."

Jess: I can't tell you the amount people who have called up and said, "I would like to talk to you about my smoking addiction."

Shawn: So what is an addiction?

Lawrence: A physiological need?

Yuval: Something you do again and again like you have no choice.

Shawn: It's a lack of responsibility. It's putting the blame on to something else. "It's not me... I have an addiction." As we would say in NLP (Neuro Linguistic Programming), it's a nominalization.

Sarah: So whatever our personal beliefs, it's more useful for us to hold the frame that smoking is not an addiction.

Shawn: We see a lot of people who deny the responsibility for their actions, and deny their personal responsibility. We also hear them say, "people are always telling me to quit. The more they tell me to quit, the more I want to smoke." So they are passing the blame on to the person who is telling them to quit, as if it's their fault!

Kathy: What if you have a spouse who smokes and you want to quit?

Shawn: Right. It's like, "we have our shared cancer time."

Mercedes: I knew someone once who shared a long kiss with a man who then said to her, "oh I always wanted to know what it would be like to kiss an ashtray."

Sarah: Wow, that's motivation to quit!

Mercedes: Yes and right there is when she quit – and then she married him!

Lawrence: What if you have a client who has tried the patches and the gum. Is that avoiding responsibility?

Shawn: This is what I call The Challenge: "you can't fix me, everyone has tried, bring it on, give me your best shot, my problem is so good so powerful nobody can fix it, I am the greatest smoker in the world."

Lawrence: So you don't address physiological aspect of it? The idea of a physiological need, the body wanting the nicotine?

Shawn: Sure we do. We deal with the cravings, but we just haven't arrived there yet in the workshop. But physiologically speaking, it's not a powerful addiction. If you take a long plane ride, you are over the physiological addiction.

Lawrence: It's not like heroin!

Shawn: One of the reasons we say not to smoke the night before is so that they have enough time to actually get over the worst part of the addiction by the time they come through the door.

Sarah: And we might even point this out to them on the phone during the initial conversation. That along with the positive physical impact on their blood, their blood pressure, their CO_2 levels, the addiction part will be very much reduced. We want them to know that the healing has already started, that their body is already starting to become healthy.

Lawrence: And when they come back and say, "well that's not what my doctor said when he prescribed the nicotine gum."

Sarah: "And how's that working for you?" is something that I might say. They are obviously reaching out to a hypnotist because the other things have not worked and so they are looking for something new, new techniques, and new ways of approaching the issue.

Shawn: So most of the addiction is in your fingers and lips and mouth.

Kathy: It's behavioral.

Shawn: Because you know what this is don't you? (*Waving a cigarette*)

Kathy: A cancer stick?

Shawn: Yes it is a cancer stick and of course is also a penis! (*Laughing*) You've all heard of Freud right?

So in the 1920s men were the only ones who could really smoke publicly and so they were the really the only ones that cigarettes were killing. Freud's nephew Edward Bernays was an advertising guy (who happened to have invented the term 'public relations') and he was approached by one of the tobacco companies. They said, "Look. We are losing out on 50% of the market because women can't smoke and we would like to get them addicted. Profits would go through the roof, but how do we do it?"

The view at the time was that women were sacred and so would not defile themselves by smoking. The question was how to change the 'mom and apple pie' image and get the women hooked on these things. So Freud's nephew went to a Freudian psychiatrist and said, "what can we do to get the women of the country hooked on these things?"

And the psychiatrist looked at the cigarette and said, "it's a penis... Look at it... It's a penis and women have penis envy." (This is a true story, you guys think I'm making it up!) The suffragettes got the vote in 1921 and in 1929 they got all these women to march in the Easter Parade in New York City while holding and smoking cigarettes as a sign of emancipation and equality. And the rest is history!

The Intake Process

Sarah: So the client is there in your office. They paid in advance (*laughing*), and you're ready to start the session. You will have already gone into your coaching state before the session begins and I always start my sessions by doing an intake form with my client.

Now my intake form is very different for smokers than for other clients. There are some very key questions that I want answers and information about. I always want to client to fill in the first part themselves, name… address… email…etc. This is for a number of reasons. One is a nice little act of compliance, and hypnotists we know that we need to build compliance to guide your client into the "yes" mentality. So we build small acts of compliance like asking them to place their coat on the hook, asking them to sit in a certain chair, and here asking then to fill in the first section of the intake form.

I'm also looking at this point to see if they are left or right-handed. The NLPers among us will know that if a person is right-handed they are more likely to have normally organized eye accessing cues. This means that they access unconscious information with their eyes. Lets have a brief reminder. If a client looks up and to their left they are likely to be remembering an image; if they look up and to their right then they are creating or constructing an image. If their eyes move laterally to the left then they are recalling a sound; laterally to their right they are creating a sound. If the eyes glance down and to the left they are probably talking to themselves; if they look down and to their right they are accessing emotions, feelings, their sense of touch and proprioception.

A left handed person has a small chance of being organized in the opposite way. This is something that their hand preference gives me a small clue about. I will also be noting where their eyes go when I ask them, later on during the intake process, about times they recall smoking and of how they want to be in the future.

Once they've filled out the basic information then I will begin to ask them some questions, and I will fill in the form myself. There are some standard questions about being under medical supervision or taking medications. At this point it is important for us all to note that if a client is under medical supervision for any reason that they are coming to see you about it is essential that you get a medical referral from their doctor.

I will ask if they have ever been hypnotized before. I want to know what their experience was like, and I want to know if they believe that they have never been hypnotized before. It is also a wonderful opportunity at that moment to tease them a little and say, "so you think you haven't been hypnotized before eh?" And from here I can begin to explain how easy trance is and that it is a state that they go in and out of throughout their day. I will give some examples of when they have already gone into trance naturally.

For example if they go to the movies and part of them knows that they are in the movie theater and part of them is totally involved in the movie, or if they ride the subway and miss their stop because their mind has been elsewhere. These are classic examples of trance occurring naturally.

This intake form is long and will take some time and as you become more familiar with it you will find that it begins to flow very easily and changes from being a list of questions into a more natural dialogue about the client's experience. You will be getting all the information that you need from the client.

We ask standard questions like:

How long have you been smoking?
What age did you begin smoking?
How many cigarettes do you smoke a day?
Have you ever stopped smoking and if so what worked for you? (Note: not what 'hasn't' worked for them, but what 'has' worked for them. Because right there you are already building resources.)

Then we are going to want to begin to ask more specific questions about their routine:

When do you smoke? What is your routine with smoking? Where do you smoke?
What are some of the circumstantial triggers, what sets them off?

We are gaining a tremendous amount of information from the client's words and at the same time getting a tremendous amount of information from their body language and intonation. We then ask about any physical symptoms or things they may have noticed about how cigarettes are affecting them physically: Shortness of breath, coughing, etc.

So we are asking them to begin to step into some of the more negative things that may possibly be experiencing. We also ask if there is anyone else in the household who smokes. We are getting information that will give us leverage.

Shawn: Or alert us about potential problems. If the spouse smokes then it may be more difficult for them to give up especially if this person is tempting them, or actively trying to get them to smoke.

Sarah: We ask: "why did you start smoking?" and "Did you like smoking at first?" These are really important because we get information here that we will use for one of the big change patterns.

Kathy: Mmmm... No, I didn't like it!

Mark: "It made me throw up."

Shawn: And this information is gold dust for us.

Sarah: Absolute gold dust. Whether they liked smoking at first or didn't, this information is beginning to uncover some things that the client may not have been thinking about. We will then ask about the last time they smoked. We are checking up to see if they followed through on our request for them to have their last cigarette the night before. We can usually tell pretty easily if they have just smoked because we can smell it.

Then we ask, "why do you want to quit?"

Jess: When we ask, "why do you want to stop smoking?" we will get a list of reasons such as the smell (that's very common), health reasons, and the fact that they are blowing off money. One of the things I like to do is to take out a calculator and show them just how much money they are spending a week, a month and year it's usually quite a surprise. It's like putting their money in a trashcan and just lighting it up, and then breathing it in.

Sarah: Yep that is a good one! From here I will ask, "what will you be believing about yourself once you have this change?" We are beginning to move them forwards in time, to begin to imagine themselves as having already quit. Another question to do this is: "how will you be as a person when you quit?" Here we are asking about values and beliefs because this leads us to their identity. Your client is likely to classify themselves as a smoker saying, "I am a smoker." That's how they view themselves. So with a question like, "how will you be as a person?" we are giving them the opportunity to begin to change their

45

identity, to formulate a new identity without their cigarettes.

Karen: Every time that I quit I was always a smoker who wasn't smoking. When I quit four years ago, and it was with hypnosis, that identity changed. Now I do not think of myself as a smoker, I just don't smoke. And that is huge and I think that the change of identity is what kept me from ever going back.

Sarah: Yes it is huge to change someone's identity. And I think it is important to notice how the question is phrased. We are not saying, "if you quit" but we are presupposing that they will quit. We are holding the idea that they are going to be a non-smoker. There are no 'if's' here.

The next question is another very important one and one that we will again be using later in the program. "Aside from you who else is this change most important to?" Interestingly enough quite a few people will answer that it will not affect anyone else that is not important to anyone else, only to them. And yet this change is bound to impact somebody in their life.

This is another gold dust moment when their answer will provide us with the leverage necessary for the change. We will ask, "what are cigarettes doing for you now?", "What are benefits to being smoke-free?" Here we are asking, in what way will it change your life?

The Meta Pattern and The Coaching Pattern

The Meta Pattern is the fundamental structure of change. It is the foundation upon which all change work happens.

The first step of the Meta Pattern is to associate the client into the problem state. We need to see exactly how they are doing the problem. This also lights up the neurological network which represents their problem.

The second step is to disassociate the client from the problem. This places them into a more neutral place.

From here we can do the third step which is to associate the client into the resource state. Once the resource state is sufficiently big and strong we can do the final step of the Meta Pattern which is commonly known as "the collapse."

Here we are taking the resource state back to what was the problem state. If the clients' resource state is powerful and strong it will literally overwhelm the problem state and collapse it leaving a new more positive state and way of being for the client.

We give ourselves nice opportunities within the intake form to do the Meta Pattern and start to make changes for the client. By asking questions such as, "What are cigarettes is doing for you now?" or "are you noticing any physical impact on your health?" we are associating the client into the problem state. Then we will ask questions like "who will you be as a person?" in order to associate them into a resource state.

So we are very easily, naturally, and completely conversationally looping the client through this fundamental pattern of change. Now the client thinks that we are just doing the intake form so their defenses are down at this moment.

They might think that the real work, the hypnosis hasn't actually started yet, so their critical factor is down at this moment and they may be totally unaware that changes are already taking place. As hypnotists, we know that the client is actually in some form of trance, in an altered state from the moment they step into the office. We are completely aware of where we are taking them, of the changes that we are looping them through and of our intention to move them through different states. This is why we are spending a lot of time talking about the intake form. And even before they come in for a session we can do this on the phone. The hypnosis and the change work begins right from the start.

So built in to these questions are so many opportunities to begin to cycle through the Meta Pattern, and to loop it a number of times. Towards the end of the intake form we ask the client about any pastimes or hobbies they have; we also ask about how they are going to reward themselves with the money they have saved by quitting smoking.

There is so much involved in this intake form, far more than just asking standard questions and getting answers from the client. This is why it's essential to do the intake form live and in person because it is a treasure trove of information both conscious and unconscious, and a wonderful opportunity to begin the change work.

As we go over the basic questions and write down the answers for the client, at the same time we are gathering a tremendous amount of information by observing, calibrating, and noticing how the client is when they are answering. And we are looking for the unconscious responses.

Which questions make them stop and think? Which ones make them hesitate or have no answer for?

We are looking for where their eyes are going to give us a clue as to how and what kind of information they are gathering. We are collecting their unconscious gestures that match with certain states and emotions. This is why it is well worth spending enough time to go through this process as opposed to giving the client the form ahead of time for them to fill out by themselves. You are gleaning and gathering your "Gold dust" and your leverage to make this change powerful and even more effective.

Jess: One piece of "gold dust" that I will always be looking out for is how the client is organizing time, specifically their past and their future. Most people keep their past on their left or behind them and their future somewhere to their right or in front. This is one of the reasons that we observe if they are right-handed and left-handed as occasionally this orientation may be reversed if someone is left handed. Sometimes people who are left-handed may have their future on their left. This is also the case if they come from a background where the first language is read from right to left.

One way to get the sense of how they organize time is by watching where their eyes go to when they are remembering things from their past ...like their first cigarette, and where their eyes go when they are creating or imagining their future as a non-smoker. But more often than not people are organized with their past to the left and the future towards the right.

This information will come in very handy when we do a nice piece of change work called The Coaching Pattern, which is the conversational version of the Meta Pattern. While we are doing the intake we are looking for states, contexts, and triggers. We will ask them for some specific times and places that they realized they didn't like the smell/felt any negative health effects etc and will begin to associate them into the negative state. We just do this lightly enough for us to see that they are beginning to feel the negative state.

We don't want to leave them there in the negative state so we use both conscious and unconscious communication and ask "that's how you've been...how do you want to be different?" The question itself is talking to their conscious mind and at the same time as we are asking this we move our right hand down and to our right. By doing this, we are communicating with their unconscious mind and are pushing the old behavior into their past.

Remember, we are moving it into THEIR past and as we are opposite from them we have to use our right hand and gesture into what feels like our future...does that make sense? We are taking the negative state they have placed in front of them, the dislike of the smell, etc., and we are pushing it into their past with our gesture.

We then ask "how do you want to be different?" This time we move our left-hand up and to our left. For those of you who know NLP, what are we doing?

Yuval: Asking them to be creative.

Jess: Yes. Generally our created images are up and to the right so we are naturally directing the client to look up and to the right at the same time asking them, "how do you want to be different?" You are asking them unconsciously to make a picture, an image, of how they want to be as a non-smoker.

We then ask, "and when you're a non-smoker how are you being as a person?" We are asking them to associate into truly being a non-smoker. At this moment we are taking our left hand which was up in the air and moving our left hand gently towards the client. It's like we are taking the visual representation of the positive feelings associated with it and moving it into the client. So we can do the Meta Pattern cycling through within the coaching pattern both verbally and unconsciously by using gestures. We are getting two layers of communication.

We are receiving two layers of communication, the conscious and unconscious, from the client. And you can be quite dramatic with these gestures.

Sarah: And officially in the client's mind, we haven't actually started the session yet. We're still doing the intake form!

Jess: And we will be using the negative states that the client tells us about — the "that's how you been" state — later in the session. So all the reasons they want to quit provide us with really useful, important information. When we ask "how do you want to be different?" the client will be listing off all the great things that they will get for being a non-smoker. "I'll have more money," "I'll smell fresh and clean," "I'll feel good," "I'll know I'm successful," "I'll look healthier, I'll be healthier." So we get both sides of their smoking behavior and the non-smoking future for them.

Sarah: Now, we know that there are around 43 million smokers in the USA and any one of them could become a client of yours. Everyone is totally unique so therefore each session will be unique, each intake form will be unique. So having all of these skills in mind when you're doing the intake session will give you the flexibility to gather vast amounts of information and begin the change work in a very natural and covert manner.

Jess: We are giving you a structured protocol only to the extent that you are willing to play with it; even throw it out. This is what we call "the dance" where you make a move based on the move your client just made. You'll just feel it. You'll find times to use the coaching pattern that feels right.

Shawn: And the language involved in the coaching pattern is important too. We say "that's how you've BEEN" not "that's how you were" because they may still see themselves as a smoker. So "have been" allows them the opportunity to have been a smoker right up to this point. So that's where we start.

Jess: Okay, let's do an exercise. In pairs we would like you to have "coach" and "client" and go through the intake process, filling out the form, and having a go at the coaching pattern.

Sarah: Obviously you're going to have to role-play this as well, but I think you're all up for that. We'll give you five minutes each. We know that you probably won't get through the entire intake but it will give you a taster.

Sarah: So how was that everyone?

Karen: I got confused, I wasn't sure which hand to point with.

Sarah: You get a clue as to whether your client is normally organized and to where they may keep representations of their past and future by keenly observing where their eyes move to and by where they gesture when they talk about past and future events. There are questions within the intake form that specifically ask about things in the past like, "when did they have their first cigarette?" At this point notice where their eyes go. They are likely to be accessing an internal representation of the moment, and are likely accessing their past which gives us the clue as to where their past is.

Shawn: If you learn the gestures the way we taught it you will be right 90% of the time.

Jess: Even with lefties. However if you clearly see that someone is organizing their past and future in the opposite way, then yes, you would do it the opposite way to fit in with their unconscious organization of time.

Sarah: It takes a bit of getting used to, but once you have it down it's as easy as pie.

Shawn: So Karen, where is your future? (*Karen points forward*). Okay, now where is your past (*Karen points behind*). That's pretty common. It is either left and right, or behind and in front. People organize time in different ways according to the context. So let me ask, "have you ever sent a postcard from vacation?

Karen: Yes

Shawn: And would you send one next time you go on vacation?

Karen: Maybe.

Shawn: So if you were to look at those two postcards, the one that you've already sent and the one you might send in the future and they are side-by-side, where are they?

Karen: (*Indicates postcard already sent with her left hand, and the one she may send with her right hand*) And I was trying to resist!

Shawn: Lots of people are normally organized and have the past behind them and the future in front. This is especially true for people who have addictions because they can't see the consequences of what they've done in the past.

So there are all sorts of ways but for Karen, the postcard she sent in the past is here on her left, and the one that she might send in the future is on the right.

Lawrence: So was she glancing one way for the past and one way for the future?

Shawn: Yes, I said where are they when they are side-by-side? And she glanced left then right. When you get used to this stuff and you are doing the intake you automatically know if they're normally organized or not. If you can't quite do that yet just pick one way — the normally organized way, and ninety percent of the time you will be right.

Karen: So you look at the eyes?

Shawn: Yes "the eyes have it." So what you typically do with a smoker is ask, "when did you have your last cigarette? "And they may say, "Ummmm...last night." And their eyes will go up to the left and then you are done, you know their timeline. You don't have to go through "have you ever been on vacation" thing. The eye movement is likely to be very quick so you have to be ready to catch it.

Sarah: We can sometimes pick up their organization of timeline through their gestures and the sway of their body as well. People will often gesture right or left or lean right or left to indicate their past and their present. We are looking for so much more than just the verbal information, we want to know the information AND we also know that a question like "when did you have your last cigarette?" will give us the additional information about the timeline.

Shawn: See how much information we get from this intake process? Earlier we talked about possible client presuppositions. During the intake they are giving us all their presuppositions. Sometimes they are buried or implied, but they can't help it because this is their map of the world, their view of reality.

They might not say it in so many words like, "I believe that I do not have the willpower to stop" but it will be implied in what they say. You'll hear it. If you listen to the structure of their map of the world you'll hear the presuppositions that they have.

Sarah: This is why we are spending a lot of time going over the intake. Their unconscious mind is giving us so much information about how they organize time and what their beliefs are around smoking and quitting smoking. They can't help but give it to us; we need to be aware that we are asking a lot more than just the questions on the intake form.

Jess: As you were going through the intake, what type of information about the smoker did you get? What are some of the examples from our fictional smokers?

Kathy: I had an interesting situation. My smoker was not taking her medication, and wasn't being compliant in other areas of her life. So what would you do in situations like that where she is not being compliant? Would that be a roadblock to working with someone?

Jess: You would need to feel the energy behind it. It could be a compliance thing, or a pattern of behavior.

Jess: And she's not coming to see you about her habits around taking the medication.

Mercedes: I know from nursing and having to do assessments that the first 15 minutes with the patient gives you so much information. So in this fictional case the client is not complying so we would need to find ways to help her to comply. Just the very fact that the person came to the appointment tells me that she is able to comply.

Shawn: Well with all these types of things you can flip them around. Being non-compliant means that she doesn't need to follow the tobacco companies' instructions to smoke, so it can be a resource as well.

Kathy: Got it.

Jess: Maybe you can tell her to keep smoking and she won't comply with that either.

Mark: My client appreciated that smoking as an adult was part of being in a social situation.

Jess: So what was the situation?

Mark: A group of people that she wanted to be peers with. What was really interesting was that she had started smoking to fit in with the group, and now the same people had all stopped smoking — so she had become the outsider in the group. It's important for her again to fit in and be part of the group. That's where the energy and motivation came from. The other ones about health and so on didn't have the same energy or charge behind them.

Jess: And this is interesting because what you have just described is not uncommon at all. "I have all my friends at work and we go out for smoking breaks and they have to quit so now I'm left out."

Kristina: So they know what they need to do now to join in again.

Jess: Did anyone get any context, times and places specifically?

Lawrence: I did and what really struck me was that the behavior seemed to be interwoven seamlessly into the day… it was just part of their life. And it had the same weight as anything else in their routine.

Jess: When we are working with smokers we are looking for a couple of different things in terms of contexts and triggers. We are looking for environmental triggers, when smoking is just part of the routine such as "I get up and look at my alarm clock, oh it's time to smoke." There are things in the natural environment that signal to the client that it is smoking time, or not smoking time. And there are emotional triggers and contexts as well.

Part of their smoking maybe routine and another part of it is that the behavior is meeting some kind of need for them.

I often hear that smoking gives the client a reason to take a break at work when things get stressful. We really want to start breaking down the habit to specific times and places so that we have a framework of what is happening in their environment and what is happening emotionally inside that has led them in the past to this behavior.

So I often ask, when was the last time and place that you smoked? (Hopefully the answer will be "last night" since we told them to smoke their last cigarette the night before the appointment). What was happening, how did you know that at that moment last night it was time to smoke? What are you seeing, what are you feeling?

Then, we will walk through a typical day. For example last Friday, you woke up in the morning and what happened first? And as they are talking about that specific day and mentioning each cigarette that they have, they will tell you about the specific times and places that they are smoking. You'll start to get sense of their pattern and of their triggers. And it's not just one trigger — you're likely to get a series of emotional and environmental triggers that have led to them smoking.

Mercedes: My client began smoking at her first job at the age of 16, because all the other waitresses would take their break and say, "could you watch my station while I have a smoke?" So she said that she learned to smoke so that she could have a break. I asked her, what type of work is she doing now? She told me she was a producer so I said, "now you can have all the breaks you want without smoking!" And she said, "no I have to smoke." I was trying to see if I could compare what she was then to who she is now.

Sarah: There are likely to be lots of contexts and lots of triggers, so we want to find as many as we can so we can begin to work on each one.

Jess: This is also why we ask about the client's experience with their first cigarette. There is going to be something emotional tied up in that. It's not that the client sees the alarm clock and decides… Hey I'm going to smoke today. There is usually something emotional going on underneath, be it a need to fit in with the cool kids or the desire to have a break. Here we are getting the initial context as well.

Remember every behavior is motivated by a positive intention. The behavior may not be resourceful or useful, but the unconscious reasoning behind it is — throughout the process we want to begin developing strategies so that the positive intention can be met in ways that are healthy as opposed to the ways they had been dealing with it in the past.

So we are lining up as many contexts and triggers as possible. It's like how the Roman's conquered the world…one village at a time! We are using one trigger at a time. And then it becomes a domino effect.

Kristina: So when you get a trigger do you just make a mental note or do you begin to work on it?

Sarah: Yes and no. Either way it would work.

Jess: Something I like to do with environmental triggers is I will jump right into a Swish pattern right away to deal with it; other times I will make a mental note that these are the triggers that will come up as I go through the process.

Lawrence: And this is still the intake?

Jess: Yes! The client comes in, we know why they're here. Still we ask, "so what would you like to work through today?" And they say, "I am a smoker." You could ask, "so what are you smoking pork, salmon?" (*laughing*)

Because no one is a smoker. This is an identity they come in with, an idea that "I am a smoker, this is my identity, this is who I am." But no one is born a smoker. There is no baby that has been born and comes out and says, "I'm a smoker that's who I am." No! This is the behavior that they are choosing to engage in, and sometimes they may feel out of control about it.

We are here to show them that they're actually in control of it. When working with clients I really like to layer this up during the intake and the pre-talk. It is important to separate the behavior and the identity. I clearly explain that the smoking is something they have done in the past but it is not who they are. I will ask them to consider that if smoking is just a behavior, then who are they?

Sarah: As Karen said earlier, the key piece that helped her quit smoking was moving into a different identity and letting go of the supposed identity of being a smoker.

Jess: This also frames the possibility that later on, they might have one cigarette and believe that they are a smoker again. I always make a point of saying, "look if I have a cigarette sometime in the future that doesn't make me a smoker. It means I did it in my life but that's not who I am."

Because you will have clients who say that they quit for a period of time and then had one cigarette, and that one cigarette made them throw in the towel and begin smoking regularly again. So we want to give our clients a mental strategy to step back from that so if it does happen that it's okay and it doesn't make them a smoker again.

Your client is there giving you all sorts of information. They are giving your context, triggers, images and words of how they will be when they have made the change. Awesome stuff.

Meta-Programs

Aside from the information, we are looking for how they are giving it to us because the ways in which they are communicating will tell us a lot about their motivation. When NLP was being developed as a system people started to become aware that certain patterns worked for some people and didn't work for others. They wanted to know why it wasn't a "one-size-fits-all." It was discovered that we all have internal programs — called Meta-Programs that drive our behavior.

Some Meta-Programs determine the ways in which we make decisions. Others influence what motivates us and some are concerned with our self image. Within the smoking protocol there are a few key Meta-Programs that are of particular interest.

The first is a strategy for assessing their Motivation Direction called "Towards or Away." Is the client motivated by the promise of something really good, or are they motivated by wanting to stay away from something?

Are they telling us that they want to quit smoking because they want to become healthier, feel better, have more money, smell fragrant and nice? Or are they here because they don't want to smell bad anymore, they don't want to get cancer, they don't want to die, they don't want to lose all their money, etc.

This information is going to tell us where to place the emphasis for the change work. Do we place it on the upside or downside?

Sarah: And we find this out just by listening carefully when we ask the questions on the intake form. The question "why do you want to quit?" is open ended enough for them to answer in either a *towards* or an *away from* manner.

Jess: In my experience, I find the *away from* motivation is stronger for most people.

Sarah: This is such an unconscious thing that it comes through in the natural way that they phrase the answer to the question.

Jess: What we are listening for is either a "yes" to possibilities, or a "no" to possibilities.

Mark: Have you noticed any discrepancy between what people say and what their bodies will show?

Sarah: You will pick up the energy, and sometimes we need to listen for when a client may be saying what they think they should say. Are they trying to please the hypnotist? Are they saying something because they think it's the right thing to say? And with our calibration skills we can pick up on the incongruency.

Jess: Our next Meta-Program is "internal or external frame." The best way of thinking about this is to pose the question, "how do you know you have done a good job?" Is it because you just know — you have a feeling inside — or is it because it is being confirmed by the outside world?

This is about how we orient ourselves. Do we do things because we feel it inside of us, or do we do things because of the people around us? If the smoker is quitting because she knows that this is the right time, she can feel it. Or does she want to stop because her family doesn't like that behavior? Or the doctor says she has to?

What we are looking for is what is really happening in terms of their motivation — how will they know that they have succeeded? Will they know coming out of the session that they are a non-smoker because of how they feel inside or are they going to know it when they are outside, not smoking in the real world and people are commenting on their success and congratulating them?

As Sarah said you will pick up on these Meta-Programs as you go through the intake with the client. They are important to note because they will come into play later. They create leverage for us, and for the change.

Sarah: And you'll get them very naturally from your clients' unconscious responses to the wide-open questions.

Jess: The next Meta-Program is "self or other." Is it all about me, or is it about other people? In my experience, when clients come in they are motivated because of their own needs and their own desires. But occasionally I'll have a client from whom the driving force, the energy behind the change is about the love they have for others and the need to ensure that the others in their life are happy.

I had a client whose entire identity was wrapped up in her family and her need to quit was a gift that she was giving to everyone else. So a huge motivation for her to quit was the happiness and health of everyone else.

Rita: How is "internal and external" different from "self and other"? They seem to be the same.

Shawn: No, they are totally different. Let me give you an example: "I am going to take you somewhere because it is good for you." I am internally framed; I know what is good for you and I am concerned about you so I am also "other" oriented. Call me a Progressive because "I am going to help everybody in the world and I know how to do that."

Yuval: Politicians!

Shawn: Yes… So "internal/external" and "self/other" are entirely different. "Internal/external" is about judgment… Do I trust myself, or do I need someone else to tell me.

"Self/other" is about what I consider to be important in my judgment... Is it about me or is it about you?

Jess: The last Meta-Program is "Associated" or "Dissociated." Most of your smokers are going to be dissociated. If they were associated into the behavior, into the problem then they wouldn't need to come to see you. Smokers have an amazing gift to be able to dissociate like it's nobody's business. "No this isn't going to happen to me"; "Yes, I know it's bad for me but..."; "Yes I am smoking and I have no control, it's my habit, it's my addiction, it's my routine."

So in terms of Meta-Programs we need to move them from being dissociated into being associated. And we will be doing this through a very powerful pattern. If a client were associated they would have awareness of the actual behavior: "I know that this is going to kill me and 10 minutes of my life is taken each time I smoke. I obviously have a death wish."

Shawn: Well, generally a smoker will be associated into the cigarette as opposed to the consequence of the behavior. Most people are pulled to smoke. It is like, "my being is in the package of cigarettes and they are drawing me towards them." So they are associated, it's just into the cigarettes not into the consequences.

Yuval: So when you are smoking a cigarette and you are totally aware of each puff you take, are you not associated?

Shawn: Yes! You are associated into the experience. You are associated into the idea that the cigarette is your friend "Darling... You and me!" So you're not necessarily associated into yourself, you are associated into the relationship. Associated into the nicotine.

Mark: You are only associated into the energy of the cigarette.

Kathy: You can smoke mindlessly too...like chain-smoking, just smoking one cigarette after the other.

Shawn: Yes. So figuring out each individual client's Meta Programs is vital information for us — more "gold dust" that we will use to determine the direction of the session. And now I think it is time for lunch.

PROVOCATIVE WORK

Shawn: Welcome back everyone. So we've talked about presuppositions and Meta-Programs but we haven't gone into what to do with them or how to deal with them and that's what we are doing to do now. So your client, especially a smoker is likely to argue with you; they may avoid the issue, they might deny things, they may lie. Now the worst position you can be in as a hypnotist is arguing with or trying to persuade your client about something, it's not a good place for the hypnotist to be.

Not only would it take far too much time in the session, but they are likely to put you in the position where they are going to avoid responsibility: "it's nothing to do with me... It's everybody else... It's my addiction." They are going to deny that they have a problem.

So you may be faced with having to defend yourself saying. "no you are wrong... it's this", or "no... It really is your responsibility." But if you do that, it just becomes an argument.

So we're going to show you how you can deal with things like this within the clients' map of the world without getting into an argument or a confrontation. Okay. So how do you think we do that?

Kristina: We agree with them.

Shawn: We agree with them, absolutely right. This is actually the best thing that we can do is to agree with them. We can agree with them at their worst. Does anyone know what this is called as a modality?

Kristina: Pace and lead?

Shawn: That's right, it is pacing and leading, and it can be something more than that as well. It's called Provocative Therapy.

If you pace something which you generally would not want to pace it is called provocative. Not only do you pace it you exaggerate it. We pace it then we say, "let's have even more of this!" And the reason we do this is because by taking on their negative aspect, that shadow if you will, they don't have to. It externalizes it, it dissociates them from their negative because we take it all, because we agree with their most asinine statements. That's Provocative.

Sarah: There's a whole modality called Provocative Therapy which was formulated by a man called Frank Farelly. We are going to use a small piece of it.

Shawn: Yes just a tiny piece of it. So we will give you some basic ideas of how you can be provocative within the context of smoking. There are two things that have to be in place to use in order to be provocative. Anybody want to provide a suggestion?

Mark: One is good heartedness.

Shawn: Right. This has to be done in the presence of rapport. Nick Kemp, who is probably the leading proponent of Provocative at the moment says that you use Provocative Therapy like you are talking to your friend in the bar. You gently tease. If you do it outside of the context of rapport you will upset people because they will think that you are making fun of them... which you are...

Sarah: ..but with a twinkle in the eye, so they know that they are being teased and they are kind of going along with it as well. It's right on that edge.

Shawn: The second requirement is that they have to be using the issue as a block, not as a problem. So if they say, "look I have this problem I know I have it," then you can assist in dealing with the problem. But when they are arguing, or avoiding responsibility, or denying what's really going on, then they are using this thing as a block. They are not saying, "I wish I could change that stuff." They are saying "I'm going to use my own problem to defend myself against change."

Mark: So they use the issue as ammunition.

Shawn: When we coach we typically sit next to one another. We sit this way specifically so that we can face the problem together; we are a team.

When the client wants to be on the opposite side, metaphorically putting the problem between the coach and themselves, they are picking up their problem and holding it close in order to defend themselves with their problem. Rather than saying, "Hey I have a problem, can you help me fix it?" The person says, "fix me, I don't really want to do anything so just fix me… It's your job."

It's really not my job to fix the client. My job is to hold the space for them, and their job is to change in that space. So I will do everything I can to hold the space, to provide an environment for them to change, but at the end of the day it's their job to change. So I can tell them, "I don't care if you change or not, that's not my job," and that would be stating the fact.

If I want to get provocative about it I have to go to the next level which means that I have to tell them that I actually want them to smoke. I delight in their smoking, in fact I own shares in the tobacco companies, (*students laughing*), and I make a profit every time they smoke. So I'm taking whatever they say, I'm pacing it and agreeing with them. I am taking on that aspect of themselves so they can fight back against it. I'm not just taking on that aspect and agreeing; I'm taking it further than they want to go.

Lawrence: I'm not seeing it. If the client says, "fix me" and you say, "I want you to smoke"… how does that help?

Shawn: No. It's more that if they are saying, "the doctor wants me to quit but me… I don't know, I don't really want to quit… I'm here because I'm told to be here." But if they are externally framed in terms of Meta-Programs, they might come in and say something like, "I really want to quit smoking and I know that if you just put me into trance then I know I will quit." If they are completely aligned with that, then I put them into trance and I will do direct trance work. It's when they are using the problem as a block to protect it that I will use Provocative.

For example, if they say "cigarettes are my friends. "I might say "Really… These are the only friends you have in the world?… Really? With friends like that who would need enemies?" Or, "Ahhh, these are the kinds of friends who borrow your money and never give it back… I love those friends, I love helping out those friends."

That would be Provocative. You are agreeing with them and you are taking it to a level that is not acceptable to them, that is beyond their map of the world. Why? So that they have to say, "well…no… Not that far."

Let's think of a few more examples. What if your client says, "I used to smoke with my father and it is the only link I have with him now"…

Mercedes: "You'll have a closer link when you die"

Shawn: Ohhhhh Ouch! Yes you could do that, you can feel it right? We all have to find our own line as to how far we will go.

Sarah: Now you see how you have to have exquisite rapport. Because if you say something like that without being in rapport, without having that relationship established then you are asking for trouble.

Shawn: What about, "it's my addiction, there's nothing I can do about it." So they are using the addiction as a defense. It's not as though they come in and say "look I have this addiction and I really want to change it." They are saying "it's my addiction, I know you are doing your best but..." So they are using it as a shield, a deflector shield.

If they say they have an addiction and want help then I'm going to demonstrate to them that they have power over the addiction. If they want to use it as a defense against me then I'm going to take it off them. So think of it that way. If they appear to be holding their problem as a block and saying that they are powerless over it then I will agree with them and say, "yes you are powerless, you have no power...let me take that and hold it for you."

What's your star sign?

Sarah: Capricorn.

Shawn: Ah..see that makes sense, Capricorns have no chance of quitting. The only people who ever quit are the Leo's (*laughing*). Capricorns are powerless they can never quit.

You want to get to them to the stage where they are saying to themselves, "wait... hang on, it's not as bad as that." Is this making sense?

Lawrence: So would you extend this to other areas in their life?

Shawn: Yes. For example:

Client: "I have no willpower."

Coach: "I can help you, but first you have to give me all your money"..."

Client: No! I won't do it!"

Coach: "Well obviously you have some willpower. And yet, you are giving all your money to Phillip Morris... So clearly, it's not about willpower... What is it about?"

So you are taking the issue and saying, let me hold it. Not let's get rid of it, but let me hold it and let me make it bigger for you. You will do this until the client says "no that's too big."

Mark: And sometimes you say something that seems unrelated, like their star sign.

Shawn: Well it's not really unrelated, it just makes the shield bigger.

Sarah: And you are throwing in the element of ridiculousness too.

Shawn: Right. So then they have to say, "well that's ridiculous. My star sign has nothing to do with it." And then it becomes very difficult for them to defend what they said originally, because that is ridiculous too.

Lawrence: And the only thing for keeping this from being mockery is the rapport?

Sarah: Yes, exquisite rapport.

Shawn: Ultimately you want your clients to say, "let's be real about this and work on it together." If you've mocked them to the extent that they don't like you anymore then it could all be over. They've got to be joining you on some level. So if they want to argue with you, then you have taken away their ability to argue because you just agree. We stretch it so far that it won't go back to where it was.

Who here is a "Kung Fu Panda" fan? So there is a bad guy in the film called Tai Leung who is in jail and he is a snow leopard. And there is a scene in the film where the Master in charge of the Temple, who is called Oogway, is talking with his student Master Shi Fu.

70

Tai Leung has escaped from jail and Shi Fu is telling Oogway the news. He runs in and says, "Master Oogway... bad news..." And Oogway looks at him and says, "there is no bad news, there is no good news, there is only news."

Shi Fu says, "Tai Leung has escaped from jail" and Master Oogway says, "that is bad news... (*laughing*) if you believe that the panda can't save us."

People think the punch line is, "that is bad news." That's the provocative statement but then he redirects it to the real issue, which is that Master Shi Fu doesn't believe in the Kung Fu Panda; he doesn't believe in the ability of the panda to save them. Although the Master is being provocative and agreeing that indeed that is bad news... he takes it one step further to say, "it's bad news if you hold this belief, this identity."

Make sense? So this is the "yes... if" pattern. You know the client has some kind of belief or identity which is going to prevent the change. But they don't know it; they are denying it. They say it is something about how they can't quit and you say... "yes, you can't quit...if you believe that quitting is impossible."

So let's think about the "yes... if" pattern. What would you say if your client says "quitting is hard?"

Kathy: "Yes quitting is hard if you believe that you are powerless to change."

Shawn: Yes, that's great if you believe as the hypnotist that the probable lack of willpower is an issue. So you are seeking for the hidden, underlying belief, or value, or identity.

Karen: Say you knew that your client was starting their own business. You could say, "yes quitting is hard but starting your own business is a lot harder."

71

Shawn: Yes, that would be very very nice. Then they would have a problem holding on to that thought.

Rita: Would you say, "quitting is hard but not quitting is much harder."

Shawn: It depends upon their frame. This is why we are very interested in their Meta-Programs. If they have an external frame and they say "quitting is hard" and you say "yes but not quitting is harder" they are likely to agree with you. If they have an internal frame they won't. Then they may say, "no I am right and you are wrong." So it depends on the frame. You can also use a tag question, can you not? So you could say, "quitting is hard, but not quitting is harder is it not?" Because they are likely to agree with the question, "is it's not?"

Kristina: You can use the star sign too: "yes, quitting is hard if you are a Capricorn."

Shawn: That's right. They may say, "What! What !... It's not that, is nothing to do with my sign." And you would say, "so what is it to do with then?" So this is all about avoiding a confrontation, or introducing to them in an acceptable way to something which they may not have liked.

METAPHOR

Shawn: What about some other ways of dealing with the clients' presuppositions?

Mercedes: One thing you can use is metaphor.

Shawn: And what's the benefit of metaphor?

Mark: One of the benefits of metaphor is that it cuts right through all the patterns and defenses.

Shawn: How does it do that?

Mark: It talks to the unconscious mind.

Shawn: Yes. Any presuppositions that they might have can be dealt with by using metaphors. Does anyone know any "smoking" metaphors?

Kristina: Melissa Tiers shared the one about cigarettes being like a friend, but this is the kind of friend who asks you for money, and you give them some, and they are also sleeping with your girlfriend behind your back and you are still friends with them.

Shawn: Yeah. And there's the one about how you are putting poison into your drink every time you leave the room. Things like arsenic, cyanhydric acid, cadmium...the things we know are in cigarettes.

Sarah: Yes, that is a classic one. Usually with that one we are miming sprinkling all this nasty stuff into a glass and we end it by offering the "glass" to our client and asking them if they want to drink the "Kool-Aid." This adds another layer of metaphor with the Jim Jones Kool-Aid reference. That's a very powerful metaphor and we are looking for the client to "back away" from the imaginary drink. I want my client's conscious and unconscious mind to be saying "No, I don't want that...I don't want to be the kind of person who drinks the Kool-Aid either."

Shawn: Any more...now I know you know at least one more! The suffragettes?

Mercedes: Oh, yes.

Shawn: Okay, so this is the male version of the story. When you think of smoking which periods or decades do you think of?

Mark: The 40's.

Shawn: Right. The 40s and 50s, this was sort of the peak of smoking and why is that?

Kathy: War?

Shawn: During World War II they took young boys, you know 18-19 years old, put them in the Army and sent them off to fight the enemy. They were putting their lives at risk. And when these young men put their lives at risk for the government, the kindly tobacco companies cheaply supplied vast numbers of cigarettes which the government then kindly gave out to these young kids who were under enormous stress, and they got them all addicted to cigarettes. Well, those who survived. Nasty one right? You're going off to war and if you survive, we will get you hooked on cancer sticks. World War II skyrocketed the addiction. I don't know about you but I get pissed off when I hear this.

Lawrence: How are you using that metaphor to move your client forward?

Shawn: Well, I am associating them into the role of being somebody who is going off to fight for their country and as a result is made addicted. I want them to be pissed off by the story.

74

Sarah: We scatter different metaphors throughout the session. We can do this at the intake stage or towards the end of the session. Another one that I learned from Ms. Melissa Tiers is when I say, "I used to do aversion therapy, you know what that is right?" And I look questioningly at the client. They usually shake their heads no. So I explain and I will say something like, "oh it's when you think of the worst things possible that could go into a cigarette, I mean the worst things like... Vomit... Shit and dumpster juice...that's the juice that drips out the back of a dumpster, and they put all of this in a cigarette and then you bring it towards your mouth thinking of all the things... disgusting things that it contains... but I don't do that anymore I have so many better techniques to use with you today to help you quit."

Now of course while I've been saying these things my client has been doing it, imagining it, experiencing it. It's a great one to use and you are looking again to your clients' face and body language to tell you that they are so disgusted at the thought of smoking such a cigarette. This is called the aversion-to-aversion therapy. It's a powerful and effective tool, but I like to give my clients more choice about how they interact with cigarettes.

Mercedes: I used to know a doctor who would collect cigarette butts and put them into a jar of water, and a patient would sit down and say, "oh I smoke and I can't quit," and the doctor would say "have you seen my hobby?" And he would show them the jar and get them to smell it.

Shawn: Tasking is good. Get them to save each cigarette butt that they have smoked and to put them into a jar of water. The water pulls out all the disgusting stuff so you see all the crap, the brown water and the smell is disgusting.

Jess: Tasking is also great if you have a client who is not quite ready to stop at the end of the first session. You give them this task to do between now and coming to see you for the second session. Another kind of metaphor that I like to use is client success stories. This pre-frames your current client for success. By telling the success story of another client, your client will be "trying on" success, the change for themselves.

Now all the time that I am telling about this other client, how they made an amazing change, threw out their cigarettes at the end of the session and have been smoke-free for weeks, I am gesturing towards my present client. By doing this I am talking to their unconscious mind and formatting it for success.

Shawn: It's not about them, it's about someone else. That way there's no resistance, and the client can't argue about it because it's not about them. So metaphor is a wonderful way of cutting through all the resistance because it's not about them, it's about another client that you had.

Mercedes: When I was doing the intake just now with my role-playing client, I asked her when she had smoked her last cigarette. She answered that it was last night and I said, "oh that is wonderful. So you are already successful, that is really good so let's work on continuing your success."

Shawn: When you know what your client's map is, you can tell a metaphor about another client who had the same map. So you are pacing their beliefs, their identity and their experiences. The best way of telling a story about the client is to change the gender of the person. So if your client is female you would tell a story about a male client who is successful at quitting smoking and vice versa. This way it doesn't make the story about them because it is more difficult to consciously associate into somebody of the opposite gender.

Sarah: Okay time for an exercise. Look for the Meta-Programs your client may be running, and add in any metaphors or Provocative work if it is appropriate. Let's take five minutes each.

(*Students do exercise*)

Jess: How's that for you guys?

Group: Great, wonderful, fun.

Sarah: Were you able to pick up any of the Meta-Programs?

Group: Ummm...some.

Sarah: Yes it takes time. It's like you have to listen with a different ear. So we are listening to the information, the story, AND we are listening for the Meta-Programs and all the other layers of communication as well. And that's a skill that comes with practice.

Did anyone manage to slide in a sneaky metaphor? Or were you overt with metaphor... because either way is better!

Mercedes: My fake client had bronchitis, so I talked about an old man that I knew who ended up with bronchitis. I told her how he came to see me to quit smoking and how after a month or so his pulmonary functions had increased, that he was feeling better, and he even looked younger. His energy had increased to the point that he was able to start exercising again.

Lawrence: Kyle was too easy as a client! He was ready to hand me his fake cigarettes by the end of the intake form so I didn't get to tell him any metaphors.

Sarah: Awesome client! I will usually tell a metaphor or two even if I know that the client has already changed. It is a great way to consolidate the change. In that case the story about another client success would be great. You are just layering up success. So even if the client appears to have no negative presuppositions and seems to be "all systems go" for the change, I will still layer up metaphors. I am laying the ground, setting the path for the change.

Jess: You are formatting the unconscious mind for the change.

Shawn: We have a friend who used to own a parking lot and when you are making a parking lot the first thing that you do is to paint white lines on the ground so that the drivers know where to park. And that's a metaphor about a metaphor! (*Laughing*)

Kristina: So we have discussed situations where clients avoid responsibility. Let's take it in the opposite direction. Not only do they think about the responsibility, they are also proud of it. For example, when they say, "I know, it's me, it's what I do." How do you deal with that?

Sarah: I would begin by asking, "how is this a problem for you?"

Jess: They may frame it as, "yes I know that this is my behavior, this is what I have been doing." Then great! They can take responsibility to change it. If it is not a problem, then it's not a problem!

Sarah: So we have heard the telephone conversation, we have been through the intake form, we've addressed the clients' presuppositions with Provocative or with metaphor. All of this whilst being in the Coaching State. We have gathered a tremendous amount of information and even started the change work by looping through the Meta pattern and the Coaching Pattern, without the client being consciously aware of the changes taking place. We have done so much already that your client is probably thinking, "when are we going to start?" (*Laughing*).

And now, it's time for the craving busters!

'CRAVING BUSTER' TECHNIQUES

Emotional Freedom Techniques (EFT)

Who here knows EFT? Emotional Freedom Techniques?

E.F.T. is probably one of the most powerful and effective techniques that I know. It is a modality developed by Gary Craig and I will always be grateful to him for sharing this wonderful technique with the world. It is my "go to" technique if I am feeling out of sorts in any way, and I share it with every single client, no matter what they come to see me for.

Now that little bit that I just said is 100% true and it is exactly what I say to the client before I introduce this technique. This is one of these patterns or techniques that I use a big set up for. So I will say that to clients, "it is one of the most powerful techniques that I know, it is my own 'go to' technique that I use if I am feeling out of sorts, and I share it with every single client I see."

Jess: I had clients who have stopped smoking purely by using EFT.

Sarah: It is really powerful. So what am I doing by giving just these few little factoids?

Lawrence: Building up expectations?

Sarah: Yes, that's right. I'm also building their curiosity. From here I will go into my own personal metaphor about my first experience with EFT. Again, it is completely true and I'll say to my client:

"Years ago I went to see a hypnotist because I had to have sinus surgery and I was very nervous about having the surgery. During the session the hypnotist began to explain that we were going to do a very powerful technique but it looked a bit weird. As she said this, she began to tap herself on the head and face" ... (*here I am acting out what my hypnotist was doing by tapping on my own head and face. And I continue with my story*) "I must have rolled my eyes because she said, "I know it looks weird but you can give me five minutes right?"

At this moment, when I say "you can give me five minutes right?" I am indicating towards my client and noticing if they are nodding their head in agreement. If they are then I know that they are in...and I continue with my story.

"So she began to tap on herself and guided me to tap on myself all the time saying certain phrases. Later that night I said to my husband 'you are going to think that I am strange, but I am actually looking forward to the surgery tomorrow and to how much better I will feel'. The next day I went for the surgery and had no nerves at all and I put it down to this particular technique that I am going to share with you now."

So what I am doing here is building expectation, and doing a covert demonstration of the pattern as well as making sure that the client is on board despite the fact that it looks somewhat strange. From here I will go into what EFT is.

I will explain that it works with the meridians of energy that run through our body. Now sometimes these meridians become blocked and so we need to tap in order to release the block and the energy to flow freely. Have you ever drank soda through a straw and noticed a little bit of liquid get stuck in the straw? If you were to gently tap on the side of the straw then it would release... it's kind of like that. Now I don't really know how it works, but then again I don't know how my TV works and I use that everyday (*laughing*).

So here are the points where we tap. We start on the side of the hand, on what is known as "the karate chop" point. If you imagine doing a karate chop then it is that exact place on the side of the hand where we begin. We tap gently with the fingertips and it doesn't matter which hand you tap with.

The next point is on the top of the head and I usually use the flat of my hand. From here we tap on the brow bone close to the bridge of the nose, then on the corner of the eye socket near the temple, then under the eye of the bony part.

From here we tap under the nose, in the little dimple under the bottom lip, in the center of the chest, on the sternum and last under the arm on the bra-line or for the guys in line with the nipple.

After tapping under the arm we return to the top of the head and begin another round. So those are the points. We also add in certain phrases. When doing this with your client, the hypnotist will say a phrase and ask the client to repeat it.

Tapping Points

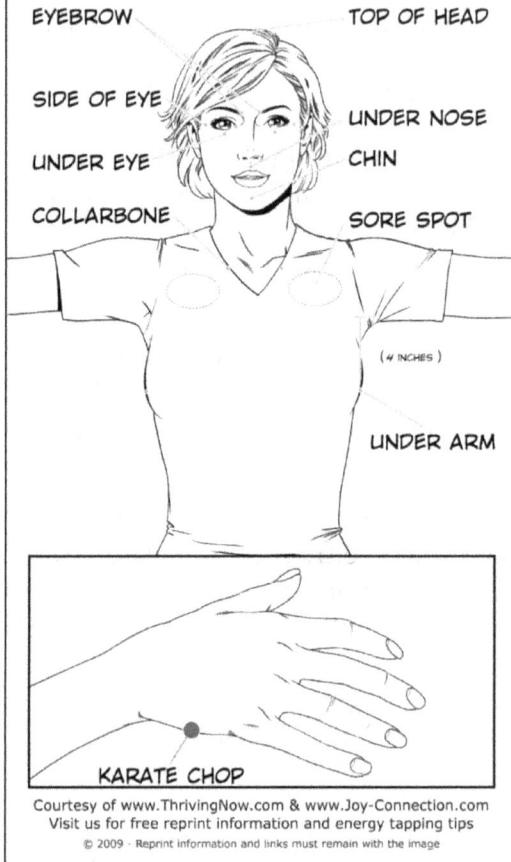

EYEBROW — TOP OF HEAD

SIDE OF EYE — UNDER NOSE

UNDER EYE — CHIN

COLLARBONE — SORE SPOT

(4 INCHES)

UNDER ARM

KARATE CHOP

This technique is very intuitive. If I say a sentence and it doesn't quite fit the client's experience, I always ask my client to feel free to change the words. If something pops into your mind while you are doing EFT then be aware that your unconscious mind has brought it up for a reason and either tap on it right away or make a note of it and tap on it later.

OK..lets do this as a group. I want you all to think of a small issue or problem, everyone got one? Good. Now on a scale of 0 to 10 with 0 being the least and 10 being the most, I want you to rate how you are feeling. What number did you get?

Group: 10...9...7...5...5...3

Sarah: OK. Now because we are in a group it is impossible for me to name the exact feeling for each and every one of you. So what I will do is to say "this feeling" and you can substitute the exact word that you are feeling... Got it? OK. Now repeat after me,

"Even though I have this feeling..." (*students repeat*) "I still deeply and completely love and accept myself."

We do this three times.

"Even though I have this feeling," (*students repeat*) "I still deeply and completely love and accept myself." "Even though I have this feeling" (*students repeat*) "I still deeply and completely love and accept myself."

Now tapping the top of your head ...

"this feeling", the brow bone ..."this feeling", the corner of your eye..."this feeling", under the eye..."this feeling", under the nose..."this feeling", in that dimple under your lip..."this feeling", on the sternum..."this feeling", and under the arm..."this feeling."

Now repeat this sequence by yourselves two or three more times. Okay. Now continue tapping the points and repeat after me:

"It's time to let it go," (*students repeat*) "I release it" (*students repeat*), "feeling it reduce"(*students repeat*) "letting it leave"(*students repeat*)

Now repeat this sequence by yourselves two or three more times. Great... now let's say:

"And in its place I choose to feel... (*What do you want to feel? Add the positive emotion that you want to feel right now*) Calm and amazing!

Keep tapping and repeating how you want to feel. Then we tap on the inside of the wrist to end the sequence "and the crowd goes wild! Woo Hoo!!."

Now take a nice big breath in and out and check in with the feeling. Notice how it's different now. What is your number now?

Group: 4......3....2...2...3...Gone

Sarah: Isn't that something! It truly is for me the most powerful technique that I know. Yes I know it looks weird but it works. It is one of the most effective things particularly for cravings which is why we want our client coming in not having had a cigarette for hours and craving one. We use EFT to demonstrate how easy it is to eliminate that craving. It is one of those moments when the client goes "wow."

Karen: I love that look on their face when they have the "wow" moment. They look at you like "what did you just do to me?"

Lawrence: Does it matter which side we tap on?

Sarah: No, you can start on one side and change half way through particularly if your hands get tired. Some people like to tap with both hands — either way is better!

I will then usually run through the protocol with them, because this is an amazing tool that I want them to use at home and anywhere outside of the office. This is one of the things I love about EFT. It is not something they have to come into the office in order to experience. I want them to be using this, so I usually go through the points and the phrases for the conscious mind. It's like there are four phases.

1. The set up: "Even though I am feeling X, I deeply and completely love and accept myself." We say this three times. I also explained that they can change the words "love and accept myself" to something like "I am a great person." I do this because sometimes people find it difficult to say those words. When we are doing this in the office, I watch them very carefully when I say "love and accept" because they may have some hesitancy, or emotion come up around this and we can change it immediately. This is also more information from me as the change worker, and maybe something that we need to address.

2. Here we get in touch with the negative emotion and while we tap a few times around we say something like "this craving." When it feels right we move on to step 3.

3. Here we let go of the negative emotion and say something like "it's time to let it go" or "allowing it to leave" and "feeling it reduce." When it feels right we move to step 4.

4. I believe that if we have let go of something, this leaves a space for something good to replace it. So here I will say something like "and I choose to feel calm." I love the empowered feeling of saying "I choose." Those are the four main steps and I always end the whole thing by tapping on the wrist, taking a breath in and out, and checking in with the emotion.

Jess: Along with using it for cravings EFT is great for other emotions as well. Sometimes you will have a client who has a lot of emotions tied up with having to seek help to quit. Somehow they feel they have failed, or they had a weakness because they had to see somebody to help them. Those are not particularly resourceful states for stopping smoking. So we tap on them and clear them out right at the beginning.

Karen And it's powerful to give voice to anything that comes up.

Shawn: Absolutely that's important.

Sarah: Right, if something comes up and the client thinks that whatever has come up is directly connected with the issue, we will tap on it there and then. If they are tapping on a cigarette craving and all of a sudden a memory comes up or something that just doesn't seem to fit, I will ask them to consider if it is connected in any way. The unconscious mind has brought it up for a reason. If it doesn't seem directly connected then I will ask the client to note it down and to tap on it later.

Jess: What's very nice about this also, particularly with cravings, is that it gives the hands something to do. We are replacing one behavior with something far more resourceful for them.

Shawn: "Even though I'll have nothing to do with my hands…"

Sarah: So it's another wonderful way to address their presuppositions, cravings, and any limiting beliefs about change. I've even tapped on "even though I don't believe this EFT will work."

All right, so that was a quick introduction to EFT. There's a lot more to EFT and lots of information available online.

Jess: EFT is completely and absolutely awesome, and believe it or not there are more things that you can do to teach clients to take control of their behavior. I had a client not too long ago come in and we started with EFT and she said, "wait wait wait I know what this is, this is EFT, and I have to say that I am not a huge fan." What do you think I did? That's right, something different! Because there are always more tools.

The Backwards Spin

Our brains encode sensory information in different ways. The primary modalities are visual, kinesthetic and auditory, and within each are sub-modalities with distinct qualities (color, light, movement, speed, direction.) When we have an emotion there will be certain sub-modalities tied to that experience, whether it is conscious or unconscious. When we start changing the sub-modalities of a feeling, the feeling itself changes.

So let's play. Everybody gets a feeling, one that is less-than-resourceful. Pick something small and get in touch with the negative feeling associated with it. Everyone have one?

Now focus on that feeling and notice where it is located in your body whether it is a physical feeling or emotion. Notice where it starts, where it moves to next, where it goes to after that. Notice the direction that it is moving in. How does it cycle back down to the original place it started? Begin to trace the emotion of it. Is it moving fast or slow? And when you are ready, I would like you to imagine that you can take that feeling and pull it out in front of you. Have a sense of it being in the space in front of you, separate from you and turn it the opposite way. Make it go in reverse... That's it. And now slow it down to a speed that's more comfortable. And when you have a sense of that, pull that new feeling inside of you and add a color... A comfortable color... Maybe a relaxing color... Maybe a calming color.... Maybe you'd like to make it a brighter or softer color. Perhaps you'd like to add some sounds, it could be a comforting sound or maybe a song, something that increases your sense of ease. And with that you can come fully back into the here and now, into this room. So what happened? What did you notice?

Karen: The movement of my feeling was just up and out, so when I took it out and reversed the motion, it just imploded.

Jess: And after it imploded what happened? How did you feel?

Karen: I felt fine.

Jess: Anyone else?

Mark: I had a feeling of discomfort that started in my back and moved to my shoulders. I moved it out and the color green popped into my mind and I didn't even spin it. I just enjoyed the feeling that this new energy felt right.

Jess What I usually like to do is to ask my clients to show me the direction that the feeling is moving in. With smokers, and particularly with cravings, they will be running a loop. Some people have the feeling and it moves up and then outside of themselves and then it is gone. So when we find the direction it is moving in by moving it outside the body and reversing it and changing the speed, the opposite message to the person's neurology says, "fire in the other way." It becomes very difficult for them to maintain the craving because you're flipping it around. So how would you like to have another experience of this?

Karen: I've done this a few times with kids.

Shawn: They shouldn't be smoking! (*Laughing*).

Karen: (*Laughing*)…in regards to anxiety and the emotion they are feeling, and sometimes there is not a movement. They tell me it is just there like a block or a stone.

Shawn: Let me give you the key to using this pattern. The key is in the pre-frame or setup. If you ask the person about a feeling and ask "is there movement?" There is a very very good chance that they will say no, probably a 50-50 chance. If you pre-frame it you are likely to get movement almost every time, depending on the pre-frame. Actually, the one I like is slightly different from the backward spin. I say:

> *"After all, what is an emotion?... Some people say your emotions are the wash-of chemicals that come down from your brain to your body to let your body know how to organize itself. So if you feel afraid, or see something that is scary, the information comes in through your eyes into your brain and your brain sends a chemical wash down into your body, so that your body knows that it should speed up the heart rate, increase the breathing, and send the blood to the vital organs and arms and legs. So it's that chemical wash down from the brain to the body. But what you actually feel, on the other hand, is the body saying "I am ready" — so the heart begins to speed up and sends a signal up to the brain. So on the one hand we can say emotions move down from the brain into the body. On the other hand we can say that the emotion is the signal that the body sends back up to the brain. One view of emotions is that they come down from the brain to the body, the other view is that it comes up from the body into the brain. So here's the question, which way is it for you? As you get in touch with some emotion now, just notice the direction. Does it move down from the brain to the body, or is it one of those that moves up from the body into the brain?"*

Yuval: Are you talking about the fear emotions?

Shawn: It could be any emotion even positive ones. For how many people does it go down? How many people does it go up? The direction depends on how you frame it. So if you frame it as a spin then the client will be looking for a spin. If you frame it as an up or down, then it will be an up or down. You have to do a powerful frame — you have to convince them and their unconscious mind that what you are describing is correct.

Sarah: You have to draw the lines in the parking lot!

Shawn: That's right, you have to paint the lines in the parking lot so they know. If you do that you will almost always get them to give you a movement. The reason I like the up and down one is that it has a more uses. If an emotion comes down it tends to be a "down" emotion — a low-energy one, a settling emotion like peace.

The more up things like excitement and joy tend to move upwards, that's just the way things go and it corresponds as well with the breath. The exhale is more of the downward sense and the inhale seems to fit with the up emotions. But if you do a sufficiently powerful pre-frame you'll tend to get the answer that you want. Does that help?

Yuval: Yes thanks.

Sarah: The pre-frame that I will use if I'm going to do the backwards spin is that there are two different ways of how to feel emotion. We have all had the experience of being in the movies and watching a scary film. And you watch the kids going into the scary house and say to yourself, "No… Don't go in." And then the kids go down scary stairs into the basement and you say to yourself, "No… Don't go down!" And just as they are stepping into the basement something JUMPS out...

Group: OHHH....(*laughing*)

Sarah: (*laughing*)… And that's what I do. I tell my clients a story so I can make them jump and feel that an emotion moves dramatically up and then out of the body and is completely gone.

I then go on to explain other types of emotion. The ones that just seem to continue, to linger, but are harder to get rid of because they just seem to be there. While I am explaining this I will be moving my hand in a circle near my stomach. I am showing them the spin. So I am setting up the understanding and expectation of finding the spin of their emotion. I am painting the lines for the unconscious mind. I will then get them in touch with their craving and ask them if it is a feeling that just quickly leaves, or is it a feeling that seems to continue. It is very likely to be a feeling that lingers and continues.

Once we have established that I ask where the feeling starts, and then where it moves to. I'll then ask them what direction it moves in to get back to its starting place in order to continue to cycle. I'm getting them to trace it with their hand. I found that the client is much more likely to be able to find the spin and stay in touch with it if they are moving their hand at the same time. It also helps me to be able to move my hand in exactly the same way as they are so I can track where they are in the process.

Shawn: And even if they find that there is not a spin, you can help them find the color, or a weight, or a size or shape. There will be some sub-modality that you can play with and turn it into the opposite.

Sarah: So be prepared for anything.

Jess: What ever the qualities are of the unresourceful state, we flip it. Sound, movement, color. When I do my pre-frame for this, I will explain something about how emotions are chemical reactions within the body and they don't stay necessarily in the same location. We are giving them a roadmap of what to look for. And anything the client gives you is correct. Any of the sub-modalities of the experience of the craving can be used.

When I did my NLP Practitioner Certification and we learned the backwards spin, there was someone in the group who described the negative feeling as a rock that was pulsating, so we changed the speed. They said it was pulsating in and out, so we changed it to be pulsating out and in. And they got a change. So it's all about just using whatever the experience is and flipping it so that their neurology can have the experience of doing it in the opposite way.

So with that, let's do an exercise. In pairs, one person be the hypnotist the other the client, go through the backward spin or the up-and-down. Ask your client to find a less than positive emotion, locate it in the body, find the movement and the submodalities around it, put it outside, change the direction, speed, size, pull it back inside, add color and pleasant sounds and notice how the experience changes. Any questions?

Kristina: Do you add color and sounds when it's inside or outside?

Jess: Yes! Either way is better! Try it out and find out what works better.

Sarah: Laughter is another great thing to put in there too, and I also love to put in some sparkles. Calibrate to your client they will let you know what works!

OK let's take 5 mins per person and go have fun with the backward spin.

Sarah: Welcome back. How was that everyone?

Yuval: A good positive feeling!

Mark: I found a nice resource state within the movement; so my client found the stillness.

Sarah: Right. This is such a lovely pattern to play with. You never know what your client's experience will be so I say, try everything!

Calibration is key. I have some clients who have not wanted to pull the feeling back inside. Some will clearly say no, and others will hesitate. In these cases we have come up with creative ways to allow the feeling to dissipate, disappear, explode etc. I will ask clients to "experiment" with the shape of the spin.

I always start by asking them to spin it the opposite way because by doing so we are implying for them to feel the opposite way. From here I ask my clients to experiment with the shape, size, and speed until they find what feels really good for them.

The classic pattern is for them to put it back in... that was Richard Bandler's classic pattern in Neuro Hypnotic Repatterning™." But if that is not what works for the client then we have to become more creative. It's our job as hypnotists to calibrate what is working for the client. Sometimes the client is very compliant and will bring the feeling back in and you will see from their body language and facial gestures that they don't like it so much. If this is the case ask them to take it back out again and do something different with it.

Rita: Could you give them the choice?

Sarah: Not usually. I usually suggest that they bring it back in, calibrate their response, and go from there.

Shawn: There are at least two benefits to bringing it back in. One is a reintegration of the part, so they are voluntarily accepting to bring that part back inside of themselves. The second thing is that if we get rid of something we like to replace it with something else — because if we leave a void there is a good chance that it will come back.

Generally I wouldn't give them a flat out choice because a lot of people would say, "no I don't want it." So I would say to bring it back in and then calibrate to their response.

Lawrence: So could you say, "now that you have changed the flow and the speed, bring it back in and see how you feel about it?"

Shawn: Yes that's exactly what we would do. Ask them to bring it back in and say, "notice how it's different now."

Sarah: So for a very simple pattern: find the spin... bring it outside... spin it the opposite way... pull it back in. There's a lot of subtlety to it.

It fits perfectly into the Meta Pattern because you have shown them that they have control over the sensation which they may not have realized before. By moving it in the opposite direction we are layering up that they have control and suggesting to the unconscious mind to find the opposite feeling.

Jess: And this creates a real magic moment for the client. This and the EFT are incredibly powerful. It is such a breakthrough moment when the client realizes that their craving has been completely transformed. They are taking control and responsibility because now they have these two patterns; they don't have the excuse for going for a cigarette. They now have strategies for handling the behavior as well as the feeling.

REVIEW

Jess: Let's take a moment to review. We've talked about the initial phone conversation where we are listening for clients' energy and congruence, and asking questions like "why do you want to quit?" And "why now?"

Sarah: We are finding out if they are absolutely ready, completely committed to and fully aligned with making this change.

Mark: We are listening for hesitations and congruence.

Sarah: Yes, and we are asking if they are changing for themselves or for somebody else.

Jess: Right, so you've had the phone call and your new client has come in for their first session. What did they do the night before?

Group: Had their last cigarette.

Yuval: They've been smoking all night!! (*laughter*)

Jess: So they come in and they are a new non-smoker and they are sitting in front of you ready to continue the change. What happens next?

Kathy: The intake?

Jess: Yes. During the intake what type of questions will we be asking?

Kathy: "How long have you been smoking? When do you smoke? Where do you smoke? Have you ever stopped?"

Sarah: So we are looking for context, triggers. What else apart from the basic answers are we looking out for, observing, and calibrating?

Lawrence: The Meta-Programs.

Mark: Their map of the world.

Sarah: Yes, we are looking for their Meta-Programs, their map of the world, their presuppositions and perceptions. During the intake process what else can we do?

Mark: Calibrate to their congruency.

Jess: Yes we are looking for congruency, for the motivation, all of that. There is a tremendous amount of information that we are gleaning other than just the words they are saying.

Sarah: We are looking for leverage, why they want to stop smoking, who else this change will most effect.

Mark: We are looking to do the Meta Pattern.

Sarah: Yes, and the Coaching Pattern. This is why we spent such a long time going over the intake form because there is so much information that we can gather during this process. Now I usually find that the intake process moves into being a natural conversation, and the questions are not always asked in exactly the same order that they appear on the form. It is fine to use the form more as a guide for you to jog your memory and remind you of the sorts of questions to be asking. What else can we do?

Kathy: Metaphors.

Sarah: Yes, if I don't get a few metaphors in during the more formal intake, then I will definitely do them immediately afterwards. Things like the aversion-to-aversion, and the "best friend/Kool-Aid" metaphor. You can also be Provocative during the intake too. And throughout all of this what are we, as hypnotists, doing?

Karen: Seeing the client as someone who has already quit, and being in the coaching state.

Sarah: Right, all the way through right from the very start, even before the client comes in we go into the coaching state and maintain it throughout the session. Haven't we done a lot of things! And we are only at the intake form. So from here we move into doing EFT on the cravings. And remember this is only a protocol to the extent that you can let go and be flexible with it.

Mark: Do you do EFT on the triggers?

Sarah: Yes, and particularly on the cravings and presuppositions. Remember we have asked our client to smoke their last cigarette quite some time before they come in so they are likely to have a craving. We want to show them how powerful EFT is and how easy it is to change. We can also use the backwards spin as a craving buster.

Jess: Through the intake we get a sense of the contexts and triggers that may lead to the client smoking and there's often an emotional state linked into it, sometimes it's automatic, and a lot of times the client will tell you that they smoke when they feel a certain way for example if they feel stressed or anxious. If the triggers are leading to an emotional state such as stress or anxiety then we will use EFT for that too. We want to show the client that EFT and the backwards spin are not just for cravings but can be used to help change negative emotions and unresourceful states too. So we are already building a skill set, not just to bust through the cravings but also to start managing the things that they were using the cigarettes to manage in the past.

Lawrence: Would you present it to the client in that way? In that you are empowering them?

Jess: Yes.

Sarah: Yes.

Shawn: Yes.

Sarah: Wow, an emphatic "yes" from the three of us!

HYPNOTIC PRE-TALK AND INDUCTION

Sarah: Now if it is the first time that the client has ever been hypnotized, this is where I would do my big pre-talk for hypnosis. What kinds of things are in your pre-talk?

Mark: "All hypnosis is self hypnosis."

Mercedes: " We do it all the time"

Karen: The movie metaphor.... "even though you know you are in the movie theater, if it is a good film you get sucked in."

Kathy: The trance that happens when you go into the elevator, or when you are driving.

Sarah: Yes, examples of trance happening naturally and easily. Showing the client that they had already experienced hypnosis in their everyday lives. That they have already experienced this and are masterful at going into hypnosis. I also explain what trance might feel like for them. The kind of relaxed feeling you get when you just wake up and can't quite be bothered to get up yet.

Now we know that the client has been in hypnosis right from the start. But clients usually think that they are getting to the real juicy stuff now! Do you think we have already started the change work?

Group: Oh yeah!

Sarah: Big time... absolutely.

Lawrence: Do you reveal to the client that you have actually been doing hypnosis from the moment that they walked into the room?

Sarah: To be honest, it depends. I usually allow them to enjoy thinking that the hypnosis is something that happens in the soft cushy chair. Because we appear to just be talking and sometimes doing some thought games and experiments, their defenses and filters are down.

Jess: If I have a client who, either consciously or unconsciously, expresses a little apprehension about formal hypnosis part of the session, then I will say "well look, did you realize that when you were doing the backwards spin or the tapping you were actually in hypnosis?" And they say "really...oh ok." So at some point it can be useful, and it is always a calibration.

Sarah: So it is at this point that we will do our hypnosis pre-talk, and then we will go into our Craving Busters, EFT, or the Backwards Spin. All of these are big convincers of the power of the unconscious mind. So it would be at this moment that we would do a hypnotic induction...

Jess: In terms of inductions for smokers, the one I like to do is a variation of Igor Ledochowski's "Non-Awareness Set." This will be familiar to any of you who have taken our Conversational Hypnosis Professional Hypnotherapy Certification...or CHPH. This induction asks the client to get in touch with any sensations or physical experiences that are in their body, and that they are not consciously aware of. So for example, feeling which hand is warmer than the other, which hand is heavier than the other. Bringing into conscious awareness the unconscious experiences.

We don't have a tremendous amount of time to go into the whole "Non-Awareness Set" so the short and sweet version that I will share with you is this: ascertain which hand they smoke with then ask them to relax in the chair and to focus on their hands and begin to notice which hand is lighter. If they say that their "smoking hand" is lighter then I will say something like:

> *Isn't it amazing that your right hand (or left), that in the past was doing that less-resourceful behavior is now going to help you create the change....*

If they say that their 'non-smoking hand' is lighter then I will say:

> *...so your left (or right) hand is lighter... that must mean that your right (or left) hand is feeling heavier...isn't it incredible that the hand that was creating the problem before is completely still, heavy and unable to move... I wonder what's happening now?*

So within the induction I like to create this beautiful metaphor of the smoking hand either being completely inactive and stopping the problem, or being the catalyst for change.

PERCEPTUAL POSITIONS

Sarah: To finish up today, Jess is going to lead us into some of the steps of the next pattern that we are going to learn tomorrow.

Jess:

What I'd like you to do is to take a moment to put your feet flat on the floor, and look at Sarah and me... just have a sense of how it feels to be sitting in your body...seeing through your eyes...hearing through your ears...you can feel the weight off your body supported by the chair... you can see Sarah and me at the front. Now, I'd like you to imagine that you could send your awareness into either Sarah or into me...so you could see through my eyes looking back at you...you could hear through my ears the sound of my voice, looking back at you... How it feels to be sitting up here in this chair, looking back to you.

Now you could then shift your awareness up to some pleasant comfortable point in this room so you can see both yourself and the rest of the class, the other students, Shawn, Sarah and myself, and then you can float into one of us, looking back at you again. Notice how it changes. Now of course, you could once again float into that comfortable place in the room, where you can see yourself and everyone else, and know that you are part of a class, and this class is in this building, on the ninth floor of 545 Eighth Avenue in Manhattan, the Manhattan in New York state, on the East Coast of the US, on the planet Earth, in the solar system, and the Milky Way galaxy. And then of course, you can bring your awareness back to being in the solar system, on the planet, on the East Coast of the US, on a tiny island in New York State, on Eighth Avenue in Manhattan, in

545 on the ninth floor in this classroom, and completely in yourself. And you can come all the way back, completely, now... Feeling refreshed, relaxed, alert, and awesome! What was that like for you guys?

Kathy: Trancy.

Karen: I got nothing.

Jess: OK... what was that like, going from being in yourself to being in Sarah or me? What was that like?

Lawrence: Didn't stay there long.

Kathy: Interesting.

Karen: I just couldn't get there.

Sarah: Yeah..that's pretty common..it's Ok.

Jess: Did you find it easier going out of yourself, and seeing the whole room, the 'fly on the wall' position?

Karen: Not sure.

Sarah: Ok, lets have another go. So just imagine being a fly on the wall, seeing yourself...and your other classmates, and Shawn, Jess and myself as though you were just an observer. And then just float back into yourself completely joining and reintegrating. How was that?

Karen: I have a really hard time visualizing, I mean, there are times when I will get little flashes but I am much more empathic, I get feelings and when I am trying to see things I get really frustrated with myself because I can't see it.

Shawn: So when you try to see things you get a feeling?

Karen: If I'm really trying then I get frustrated, but if I let go I can get feelings from other people.

Jess: What color is your front door?

Karen: Ummm...it's glass.

Jess: It's glass, and about how high up off the ground is the doorknob? Just an estimate.

Karen: Ummmm…from the ground or from the step?

Jess: Either way.

Karen: Ummmm… from the ground it's about 6 1/2 feet.

Jess: Okay, so walk inside your house or your apartment…

Karen: Yeah and I've done all of these exercises and what I see is very very faint…

Jess: That's fine.

Karen: And I really have to think about what the things are. Like in my house, I've lived there for 13 year so it's really familiar but going up to the corner of this… you know… I just...

Sarah: And having just a very faint image is what a lot of people will experience. But the more you do it, who knows how much that will develop and grow for you? I know if I am reading a novel, it's not as though I am seeing an actual movie of what's going on, I'm just getting little faint images… So something is happening.

Karen: Yeah.

Sarah: It may be that the images are going by so fast that the conscious mind has difficulty catching them.

Karen: Yeah… it's grey.

Jess: Do you daydream at all?

Karen: Yes, I daydream a lot.

Jess: What you experience, that is your way.

Karen: It's a feeling.

Jess: Then that's fine.

Shawn: And this pattern is all about feelings, it's just that for us poor visual types we have to see it before we can feel it. So you will be straight in...

Jess: Yes, you will skip the middleman!

Sarah: You're ahead of the curve!

Mark: Even in the Meta-Programs there are people who organize by feelings and relationships.

Sarah: How many of you could transfer easily from your self straight into either Jess or me?... Okay, some of you could. How many of you found it easier to go into the 'fly on the wall' position and float into Jess or me from that position?

Kathy: That was easier.

Sarah: Yes, a lot of people find it easier to go to the "fly on the wall" first before floating into another person's experience. It's easier for some to have that steppingstone.

Jess: So what we'd like you to do is to get into pairs and just lead your partner through this experience of being in first position (*being them*), then maybe being in second position... (*them drifting into you*)...then try the "fly on the wall" position, that's called third position, then back to second position, and then back into themselves.

Sarah: And we don't want to go all the way out to the Milky Way and the galaxy! Please make sure you put them back where you found them at the end! (*Laughing*).

This is a quick exercise. Two minutes each.

Sarah: Alright everybody, so how was that? How was that for you Karen?

Karen: Well I decided I'm not going to force myself into seeing something because I am just going to frustrate myself, so I decided to go with emotion and see what I feel.

104

Sarah: And see what you feel... I like that!

Karen: So when I was seeing things from Mercedes point of view I just had this feeling of sort of being straightforward and saying it like it is with a wry sense of humor, and then when I floated up it was just a total feeling of non-judgmentalness and just observation.

Sarah: Perfect.

Karen: So there were just different feelings.

Sarah: And how do you feel about the experience?

Karen: It was very interesting and very powerful, and reminded me that I can get a lot even if I don't see things. I don't have to see things.

Sarah: And that is so useful for us as a class to understand because not every single client will be able to see the pictures. So being able to get them in touch with a feeling is absolutely perfect.

Shawn: The only reason we ask people to visualize things is to get them into a certain feeling or a state, so you are way ahead.

Karen: Is interesting because I want to see it, and I just get frustrated.

Shawn: My advice is to not even go there.

Karen: But when I am trying to problem solve...

Shawn: Just feel your way, just let the pictures go, don't bother with them, they are not worth while.

Karen: I like this exercise but how do we use it?

Sarah: We are just beginning by practicing some of the building blocks, the tools that we will put together into a pattern tomorrow... just giving you a tiny little taste.

Jess: Building the skills for a completely brand-new pattern... it's coming... and this is the first step, being able to guide your client into different experiences and locations through that process.

Mark: It's all about location, location, location!

Sarah: *And as you look back to look forward to tomorrow and all the things that you have already learned since you came in here this morning... That's right... You can begin to congratulate yourself on having learned so many things already, things that might be familiar to you, that maybe you have now got even more insight on, maybe things that were completely brand-new to you. You have opened your eyes to moving into new possibilities, inside and out...*

Jess: *...you have... set the scene, going from the phone call to the intake, listening for Meta-Programs... Self, other, towards or away, internal or external, associated or dissociated, getting contexts, triggers... The backwards spin...*

Sarah: *...associating people into states, dissociating from a state, associating into resources...that's right... and collapsing the two, such a tremendous amount of information... Gold dust... You've been able to glean for yourself... And for your client...*

Jess: *...you've gone through the process of stacking the deck in your client's favor, all of the changes...*

Sarah: *...talking to their unconscious mind... Painting the lines in the parking lot of your clients unconscious mind...*

Jess: *...up until this point... Unconscious to them, change is occurring... On the deepest level...*

Sarah: *...And I wonder just how many lines have been drawn in your unconscious ... in these last few hours... And as you just drop inside, to begin to contemplate... That's right... Just how much you've learned unconsciously...*

Jess: *...knowing how good you are, as masterful change workers...learning...*

Sarah: *...growing...in new ways... To behave...*

Jess: *...and understanding on a new deeper level...*

Sarah: *... That you have... Inside yourself... as you drop even further...*

Jess: *... Resources your client has...confidence...integrity...*

Sarah... *Your own unconscious mind... That's right... To fully access everything on an unconscious level...*

Jess: *...seeing them as already changing...now...*

Sarah: *...you can rest assured...that the things you have been learning...*

Jess: *...and feeling peace, security...*

Sarah: *...will continue...and I've heard that songbirds learn to sing in their sleep...*

Jess: *...It's true... I know the man who knows the woman who did the research...*

Sarah: *... They take the new songbirds, and place them in with a master songbird... who sings... and sings...all the songs...and then at night time...they attach monitors to the new songbirds and record exactly all the activity that going on...while the songbirds sleep and dream...*

Jess: *...sleeping and learning...*

Sarah: *...and they find that they are practicing... in your sleep...*

Jess: *... Mastering... All the songs...*

Sarah: *...putting things together...mastering this new information...*

Jess: *...learning new unconscious ways...*

Sarah: *...of becoming even more of who you are...*

Jess: …to harmonize this new information…

Sarah: … So songbirds truly do learn to sing …that's right…in their sleep…and I know that very soon you'll go home and have your evening and that at some point tonight…

Jess: …that's right…

Sarah: …you'll go to bed…and when you go to bed…you'll sleep and when you sleep…you'll dream…now some of you may have exciting dreams…

Jess: …and some of you may have boring, mundane dreams…

Sarah: … Some of you may have Technicolor dreams…

Jess: … some of you may have black and white dreams…

Sarah: …some of you may have dreams with a cast of thousands…

Jess: …or just a few…of you …may think that you have had no dreams at all…

Sarah: …and let that be a sign of the changes taking place…

Sarah and Jess: …on the deepest unconscious level.

Sarah: …so you can wake up now…bright eyed and bushy brained…ready for Saturday night in New York City! The best city in the world!

Jess: …next to Philly!

Group: (*Laughing*)

Sarah: So thanks for a great day everyone… See you tomorrow.

Day 2

Sarah: Good morning everyone. As we always do we are going to start with an open frame, which is a time for questions, comments, observations, thoughts, musings.

Yuval: Yesterday when Shawn talked about smoking and responsibility, how do you create the conversation with the client? I think for many smokers those two things are not connected.

Sarah: What would you do?

Yuval: I don't know. As soon as you use the word "responsibility" and "smoking" they didn't match. Smoking is a risk and the complete opposite of responsibility.

Sarah: We place it within the frame that smoking is a choice. No one is born a smoker. You can be as open as this: "were you born a smoker? No. So at some point you made the choice to smoke so that is a responsibility that you have taken on board for yourself." They have responsibility for that choice and they need to be in a position of recognizing that before they can begin the process of change.

Shawn: I think we need to be clear about what we mean by responsibility. So if somebody goes, "I'm smoking, I am irresponsible." Then they are taking responsibility for the fact that they are smoking. So what we were talking about yesterday was somebody who was saying, "it's not my fault, it's the responsibility of something that's not me." This would be the cigarettes or people who tell the person to stop smoking. That's the difference. The reframe could be, "okay it's caused by this thing outside of yourself what could you do to impact that interaction?" You don't need to say, "oh no it is your responsibility." All you need to do is to say, "well it may be the responsibility of this thing outside of yourself which is perfectly true. It's the responsibility of Philip Morris... They put things in the cigarettes to get you hooked, it is certainly their fault, but you have power in the relationship as well."

So it's not to deny the responsibility of those around the smoker. It is about empowering the person.

Yuval: So what I am hearing is that you do not blame them.

Shawn: No. I blame them if they are at the next table in a restaurant smoking, not if they have come in wanting to quit.

Lawrence: In the therapeutic setting you are divorcing responsibility from any kind of value judgment about which way the client has chosen to exercise that choice.

Shawn: Well, if I were to make a judgment I would say, "everyone in the world is entirely responsible for their choices." That's my view, the Gnostic view. This is not the case with a client however. They are absolutely right if they go, "It's my mother, my father, my friends at school, Phillip Morris, my biochemistry, my DNA." All of these things are true to some extent.

Lawrence: I was thinking more in terms of, "I take responsibility for whether or not I smoke." Separate from, "smoking is good, smoking is bad." I mean judging the behavior separately from judging the responsibility for the behavior.

Shawn: I judge smoking to be bad for me. Right, so I could expand that, smoking is bad for me therefore it is bad for you. I can't take responsibility for everyone else in the world. Well we could do but it's better not to (*laughing*).

Lawrence: But you choose not to.

110

Sarah: I think that is an important distinction for us to keep our judgment, what we think is right or wrong, out of that interaction. It is not for us to say what is good or bad for the client unless they are very externally framed. They may need to be told what is good or bad.

Shawn: For example, I will do the sniffing test. If they walk into my office and they had just smoked I will sniff the air and I will make a face. You could say I'm making a judgment but actually I'm just sending them the unconscious message that there is an olfactory downside to smoking. Is that a judgment? You could say it is, and I am doing it on purpose.

Sarah: This comes down to the idea that we are not the smoking police. It is not our responsibility to change everyone in the world.

Mark, you had a question?

Mark: Yes. With reference to personal responsibility, there was a whole theme yesterday around blame and nominalization of a problem, there seems like there is an opportunity to blame someone else. It can be like a smoker comes to you with the expectation that you will fix them.

Sarah: You will get clients like that especially those who are externally framed. If you remember Nina's client who just wanted to be told to stop.

This is why in our release form we have a statement that says the client takes responsibility for their change. Not everyone is that externally framed. Most need a bit more of a process in order to quit. I can understand the client who comes and says, "Just fix me!" They want to come into the office and go to sleep for an hour in the chair while you sprinkle fairy dust and they wake up completely fixed.

Shawn: If someone comes in for a generative change then the worst thing you can do is to fix them. That is exactly what they do not need but if they come in because they want to stop smoking and they are externally framed you can do a directive piece of change work, creating the behavioral change they want. They leave not smoking, improving their health, and saving money — but that does not necessarily mean they are improving as a person. They stop smoking but that is not necessarily a generative change.

Sarah: Certainly in my earlier years of doing this, if the session did not go exactly as I had wanted and perhaps they didn't get the big change, I would take it so personally. It would be like I didn't do the right thing — I couldn't get them to change. I decided I could not carry that responsibility anymore; it's too much. I cannot have that responsibility for every single one of my clients. As long as I know that I've done everything that I can do I have to let go of the rest. The responsibility for change is not yours — it belongs to the client.

Jess: I will say to my clients, "I will use everything in my skill set to help you create this change." There is an underlying communication that I will do my best so you better do your best. We have the responsibility as change workers to do just that, to use our skills to the best of our abilities. However, we are not responsible for the change. It is the client who is making the change. You could have a client come in who has spent the last 20 years perfecting the art of chain-smoking. They are going to have to be the one to take the first step out of that to create the change. We make the atmosphere. We hold the space. We set the players on the stage, we create the set — but it is the client who has to go through with the acting of the play.

Any other thoughts, questions, musings?

Rita: Do you find that having the clients sign a waiver that they take responsibility to make the change makes a difference in their mind?

Jess: Yes, absolutely.

Sarah: If I am feeling a little more provocative and I have a client who is like, "make me change! Just do it! Make me go to sleep and do hypnosis stuff on me," I put this in their hand. (*Sarah holds up a genie lamp*) I say take this and rub it. They are like, "what?....Oh I get it!"

Jess: I do something very similar with my clients. I say, "look I don't have a magic wand. I wish I did because if I had a magic wand I would wave it and say, "change!" And the change would happen. I would be a millionaire and you wouldn't be in my office right now because I would be on a yacht somewhere." So interjecting humor and playfulness to break that frame of, "fix me," can be a powerful tool.

There are other times, like Shawn said, where the client is so externally framed that they need someone to say, "stop that." In that case, sure, in the trance you can use very direct strategies in your change work.

Rita: Don't you find that most people are externally framed?

Shawn: Generally it is true that most people who come for this work are externally framed. Some people come because they believe in the power of their own mind and they want to be taught how to use it. So it is mixed — but I would say that most people who come for coaching are externally framed.

Mark: Are you saying that some people who come to see you act as if they are externally framed when they are actually internally framed?

Shawn: I will say this: that if you do this long enough you will get any combination of people walking into your office. So it is actually a good exercise to think about what kind of people might come and see you, and then what kind of work would you do with that kind of person. It is a type of mental gymnastics. You could imagine the responses they would give you and how you would respond in turn.

Sarah: If there are no other questions I would like to just take a moment to thank George for the awesome tweet he sent us last night. It was a picture of the cigarette and it lists the benefits of not smoking over a period that stretches from twenty minutes to fifteen years.

Shawn: So after twenty minutes the heart rate and blood pressure drop back to normal levels. After twelve hours level of carbon monoxide drops to normal. In two weeks the circulation and lung functioning improve. After one year the risk of getting coronary disease is half as high as that of a smoker. After fifteen years the risk of heart disease is equivalent to a non-smoker.

Yuval: It takes fifteen years for the body to return to normal?

Shawn: Yes and after ten years your risk of cancer is half of that of a smoker.

Sarah: I particularly like that after twelve hours the carbon monoxide has leveled out — because when you have a client who smoked their last cigarette the night before, they have already achieved that and their body is rebalancing itself. That is powerful.

Any other questions or is our open frame closed? Ok great Let's move on.

Jess: Today we are starting our adventure into the big change patterns for smoking cessation. Today is going to be all about time, the ways clients use time, and the ways in which they can transform time to change their smoking habit.

We spoke yesterday about seeing your client when they walk in as already being a non-smoker. They may not have that picture as clearly in their mind yet but the whole idea here is we are moving the client inch by inch, step-by-step from their former self as a smoker to stepping into their identity as a non-smoker. This is ultimately a part of who they are anyway because no one is born a smoker. They are stepping away from the behaviors into a fuller experience of who they are.

For the purposes of learning we will be role-playing stop smoking clients. We want to ensure that as non-smokers you remain that way! We would like for you to create a completely fictional smoker. Our suggestion is that if you are a female choose a male client, and if you are a male to female client.

Put nothing of yourself into this character. This should be completely fictional. At the bottom of the sheet we also ask you to identify the Meta-Programs you have observed.

Karen: Can you quickly go over the Meta-Programs?

Sarah: If they answer the question, "why do you want to quit?" by saying they don't want to get sick and they don't want to get cancer, then they are more 'away'. As opposed to someone who answers that question by saying they want to be healthy. It's all in the phrasing.

Rita: What if they want both?

Sarah: The question then becomes which side has more energy.

Shawn: It is a scale. No one is completely a "toward" person or completely an "away" person. Everybody is on the scale. They either lean a little bit more toward or a little bit more away. Or they could be a lot toward or a lot away but no one is completely one or the other. Everybody is going to be a bit of both and of course it is contextual as well.

Sarah: All right. Everyone has one character and it's not a totally fictional character like a Klingon or something like that, right? We want this to be as normal as possible. We just want you to have these profiles ready for the exercises will be doing later today.

PERCEPTUAL POSSIBILITIES PATTERN

Jess: What I would like for each of you to do is think about someone who is very special to you. It could be someone you care deeply about, a family member, a friend, someone you are very close with and trust. This is going to be someone with whom you have a very strong relationship.

Does everybody have someone in mind?

> *Good, now close your eyes for a moment. Get yourself comfortable. Just take a few moments to center yourself feeling the chair underneath you. When you are comfortable enough I'd like for you to imagine that this person is in front of you. However you imagine things — whether by seeing or by feeling — you can sense how this person is standing, the expression on their face, perhaps even the rate at which they are breathing. And as you see them there you can begin to feel your connection to that person. You can feel all of those wonderful emotions that link you to that person. That's it. And really feel that.*
>
> *I don't know if for you these feelings represent friendship, companionship, or something else. Whatever those feelings are, you know that this person in front of you is important, special. And when you're ready, open your eyes and reorient to the room around you.*

Would anybody like to share their experiences?

Kathy: It felt good.

Jess: It felt good, and did you begin to get the sense of connection with that person?

Kathy: Oh yeah.

Jess: What we would like for you to do next is to get into pairs and do the exact same exercise. One person will be the hypnotist and the other the client. Really focus on building the state of connection that your client has with that person that they are imagining. You may want to ask who this person is and use that information to build the state — or if the person does not want to share, then you can do it in a more general way like I just did here. You want your client to experience the fullest positive emotional link to their relationship with that other person. Any questions?

It is very straightforward. This is a quick exercise, only two minutes each.

(*students do exercise*)

Everyone back and enjoyed that? Fantastic!

> *Now take a moment again to make yourself comfortable and close your eyes. You can feel your breathing easy and smooth. You may have a sense of where you are sitting, resting comfortably on the chair. Maybe you can notice a pleasant relaxation begin somewhere and spread throughout your body.*
>
> *As you do that you can imagine that person who is so important to you standing in front of you. Have an awareness of the clothes he or she is wearing, the expression on their face. Perhaps you can even see their breathing. As that happens begin to feel the connection you have with this person. They mean so much to you, how do you know? Notice how you feel being in their presence. Feel that bond that brings you both together.*
>
> *When you are ready, drift out of yourself so that you can see both you and that other person. You can now drift into that other person so that you can see through their eyes, hear through their ears, feel how it feels to be them. You can be aware of their thoughts, beliefs and who they*

118

are as a person. You may even look over to that you standing there and you can begin to notice how you are standing, the expression on your face, and maybe even the breathing. Feel the connection that this person has for you beginning to develop. Allow it to grow, feeling just how special you are to them and how much you mean to them in their life.

When you have had a full sense of that, drift back out of that person so you can see you and you can see them. Now drift back into yourself. Allow that person to fade and come all the way back to this room in New York City.

Welcome back. How was that? How was the experience of moving from first position out to third position and then down into second, associating into your loved one?

Mark: Too short!

Jess: Too short!

Lawrence: It was a bit disconcerting.

Jess: What did you find disconcerting about it?

Lawrence: You know, I am with this person every day and imagining them in this way almost had a vibration to it. It was disturbing in a good way.

Sarah: Disturbing in a good way!

Lawrence: Surprising.

Kristina: I got all emotional with this exercise. Something in this makes me want to cry. It's a shift in perspective and it's very powerful. I am longing to see that person now.

Jess: This is a very powerful experience. It is not often we think about what it's like to be in the shoes of those we care about.

Sarah: It was so lovely to watch everyone when Jess was leading the exercise. When she was leading you into the first moments of seeing that other person, first everyone gets all settled in, then I begin to see (*Sarah models smile and other pleasant physiological shifts that occurred in the class.*) It happened with everyone. It literally went across the room. It was lovely.

Jess: Anyone else?

Karen: It really does help you to get a perspective from the other person and to really experience what they are experiencing. There was a real conflict within a person in that I was able to feel their love for me — but there was this feeling like almost being pinned to a wall. I am unable to express this fear that was there of that emotion. It was really, really interesting.

Jess: To have that shift in perspective is a very intense experience. As Kristina mentioned a minute ago, we often take these relationships for granted. It is very rare to actually sit down and really think about our relationships on such a deep level. To see and experience how the other person experiences us can be a big shift.

Karen: Cognitively I know this person went through some bad experiences in his past, but now I also can really get a sense of what his emotions must be like. It has really given me insight into why he is as guarded as he is. I had a physical sensation like almost being shrink-wrapped in the chair in that it was like, "okay wow, now I can really begin to understand why he acts like he does."

Jess: Perspective is everything.

Karen: Yes.

Jess: And because you had this powerful experience it means that when you use the pattern with your clients you will truly understand from the inside out just what a powerful emotional shift this can be.

Anybody else?

Mark: I noticed that this was a very tender and sensitive experience. I wasn't expecting it to be and I am surprised at just how sensitive it was.

Jess: Yes it absolutely is. Although just doing this one part of the pattern could do a great deal of good, keep in mind these are the building blocks. There is another wonderfully enjoyable portion to this.

I would like for everyone to think about, remember, or imagine some point in your life when you achieved something fantastic. It could be something like when you first learned to ride a bike. It could be when you decided to come to the stop smoking workshop and became so masterful that you are saving lives left and right. It could be going through school and graduating. Make it a meaningful experience where you went through a process of learning, growing, and accomplishing. It could be a memory from the past or it could be a future memory. Either way is better.

Does everybody have something in mind you'd like to work with?

Great, now again close your eyes for a moment, settling back in. Fractionation is a wonderful thing. You can notice where you're sitting, relaxation and comfort in your arms and legs. And when you're ready you can invite into your mental space that person who is special to you. You can feel the connection you have with them as you notice their posture, their expression, their energy, feeling all of those good feelings you have for them. That's it.

Now drift up out of yourself so you can look down and see both you and that other special person. Only as

121

quickly as you are ready you can drift down into them, and become aware of that person looking back at you. That's it. Feeling that connection they have for that you over there. You can become intensely aware of the feelings this person experiences for you. Perhaps it is love, trust, friendship, or maybe that feeling does not even have a label.

You can feel good knowing that both you and that person are about to share a very special experience together. From this position, as this important person, I would like for you to begin to watch yourself go through that process of accomplishing, achieving something wonderful. It is almost like you're watching a movie of you learning, growing, achieving something wonderful. And maybe start to have a sense of the emotions that the person feels while watching someone they love achieve something so very important to them. Maybe it's a sense of happiness, feeling of pride, or maybe it's amazement. That's it. And really have a sense of all of those emotions, the joy that that person has watching you accomplish something spectacular. That's it.

When you get to the end of that, having achieved that amazing thing while in this position, go and congratulate yourself. "Good job that is fantastic. I am so proud of you."

When you're ready you can float out of that person so you can see them and you can see you having achieved that goal. Now drift down back into yourself. I think it is absolutely wonderful that a person shared this experience so why not thank them for sharing this learning process with you, sharing a few moments of accomplishment. That's it.

And when you're ready you can open your eyes and reorient to the here and now.

Kristina: I had an interesting experience.

Jess: What happened?

Kristina: I couldn't connect the fact that I was proud of myself from the perspective of that other person. I don't think it was a big deal for that person.

Jess: Did anyone else have a similar experience?

In your case it may have been that the person you chose for this experience did not have a strong enough emotional charge for you. If we were working one-on-one I would spend a lot of time with you really building up the experience of connection between you and that person.

When you have established a very strong connection, or an attachment, it is impossible for that other person to not be moved by your experience. Remember, the heart of this is not a speculation about what they might feel, it is what your unconscious mind is feeling. That other person inside of your mind is you!

Anyone else?

Kathy: I just felt immense joy to be able to share the experience with this person.

Jess: Yes. Did you get a sense of the type of feelings this person had watching you achieve something awesome? What type of emotions?

Kathy: Pride, mostly pride and awe.

Jess: I really like that one, awe. Now in pairs you have 3 to 4 minutes each to do this exercise, have fun. Once more, here are the steps:

Step 1 Establish the connection with the person.

Step 2 Next have your client drift out of themselves' and into the other person. Establish the connection that other person has for the client.

Step 3 Have the client watch themselves achieving something wonderful. Really enjoy building up the states for your client.

Step 4 When this process is complete, have the other person congratulate the client. Then they can drift back into themselves and thank the special person for sharing this experience.

(*Students do exercise*)

Jess: All right guys let's bring it back around. How was that? How was it as a hypnotist helping the client navigate positions?

Mercedes: As I was establishing the connection, I could see a shift in the client. And as I was building up the connection between the client and her imagined person I could see changes in the client's breathing, facial muscles, and color.

Sarah: You mean you are using your calibration skills?

Mercedes: Yes.

Jess: Yes, this is a powerful experience for the client. You will notice subtle and not-so-subtle shifts in their physiology.

Did anyone find it challenging to keep your communication straight when talking to the client while they are another person watching themselves?

Group: Yes.

Jess: Would you like a very easy way to get around that?

Group: Yes!

Jess: Find out the name of the person your client has a connection with and then when they are in the position of that person call them by that name. So, I'm going to associate into Shawn and when I do Sarah will call me Shawn as I look back at Jess over there. Once the client is in the position of the other person, you use that other person's name.

Any other thoughts?

Kathy: I think this exercise is very fascinating because often we do things and we don't value them. We have become used to them and think that they are not that special, or that they are no big deal. To look at it through someone else's eyes, to feel the depth of emotion that the other person experiences is very eye-opening. It is very affirming.

Jess: It is a very powerful thing. It is almost like they are experiencing that accomplishment for the first time.

Anyone else?

Karen: I just love watching the client as the experience dances across their face.

One thing that popped into my mind as I was experiencing this and learning it is that I could very easily take this to the school I work at and do this with the kids. I get a lot of kids who just can't get outside of themselves to get the perspective of another person. They could practice this first with a loved one to get the sense of it then try it with others. This is a great way to help them get outside of themselves to see a different perspective on their relationships with their peers.

Jess: That is wonderful. It makes me very happy to hear your thought process going in this direction. You really should take a moment to be proud of the fact that you are taking this exercise, a building block, and are able to expand it into a beneficial process for your students. That is really fantastic.

Anyone else like to share?

Mark: I did not take a person with whom I had a clear positive relationship. I chose someone with whom I have mixed experiences, some very good and some not so good. That came out very much in the interaction. Because of that I think it is useful to point out the importance of choosing someone whom you have strong positive relationship with.

Kristina: I felt the same way. I think what would be good is to emphasize that the person you choose needs to love you.

Jess: All relationships have their ups and downs. All relationships have positive and negative experiences. This is life. The key here is to choose someone with whom your positive experiences outweigh your negative ones. When working with a client, this becomes even more important. We will talk more about this once we get to the pattern.

Kristina: I think if I would have picked someone I don't know it would have been more powerful. Someone like Julia Roberts. I've only had good experiences with her. (*laughing*).

Jess: Well, a person the client does not know will likely not have the same emotional power as someone who is a part of the client's life.

Remember too, these are only training wheels. This is not the complete pattern yet, but we are getting there.

Yesterday we spoke about Meta-Programs and how smokers have a big problem with associating into the consequences of that behavior. We also talked about leverage and how incredibly important leverage is for change. It's not enough that the client comes in and says, "Yeah I want to quit smoking." We are looking for the emotion, the state behind it. If a client comes in and the emotion is not quite there yet we need to begin by building leverage. One of the quickest ways of doing that is by making them really confront what happens when they smoke. We need to create an environment where the client can really step into all the possibilities of achieving their goal of being a non-smoker.

It's like if you think about having a fork in the road and the client could walk down one path where they stay a smoker, having all sorts of terrible things happen. Then they could walk down the other path as a non-smoker experiencing health, vitality, and all of the really great outcomes that they would like for themselves.

It can be very difficult for a client to visualize or even conceptualize on a deep level either of those possibilities. Remember they are very skilled at dissociating from outcomes. So we need a way to introduce these possibilities that is more indirect than, "imagine this, this, and this." We want to start building states so that we can leverage the change. We want to use their amazing ability of dissociation to actually associate them into two possible futures.

To show this we are going to do a demonstration. Sarah will be our pretend smoker. This is going to be a cognitive demo. This can be a highly emotional pattern so we are going to invite Sarah to only role play it and not dip into any experiences that are anything other than pleasant.

For this we need to then give Sarah a character to play. Let's take a few moments to put together a brief sketch of the smoker Sarah will be playing.

Is Sarah's character going to be male or female?

Group: Male.

Jess: Male, good. What should his name be?

Mark: Jethro.

Jess: Jethro is good. How old is he?

Group: 60.

Jess: Why does he want to stop smoking?

Mark: He has cardiac problems.

Kristina: He is tired of the smell.

Mark: If he stops he will save money.

Jess: Anything else on the negative side, things he doesn't want?

Kristina: He doesn't want cancer and a few of his friends have had it.

Jess: Good, what else on the positive side?

Kathy: He wants to be fit, to have energy.

Lawrence: He wants to live longer.

Mark: He wants to have a peaceful house.

Jess: Good, anything else on the negative side?

Mark: Fear.

Jess: Fear of what?

Sarah: Death.

Jess: Okay our sketch is almost complete, is there anything else on the positive side?

Kathy: He wants to set a good example for his grandchildren.

Jess: I think this is a good sketch. Is he a toward or away person?

Group: Away.

Jess: Is he internally or externally framed?

Mark: Externally.

Jess: Is he self or other?

Lawrence: Self.

Jess: Since he is a smoker he is associated into the behavior and dissociated from the consequences.

How will Jethro be as a person after he as made this change?

Yuval: Free.

Jess: Free, I like that.

All right Sarah so you know this is just a role-play and I will be taking small breaks to make comments about the structure of this pattern. Is that okay with you?

Sarah: Yes.

Jess: And your unconscious mind throughout this demonstration can keep you safe and comfortable knowing that this is solely for the purpose of teaching others how to be powerful forces for good in the world.

Sarah: Yes, thank you.

Jess: What would you like to work through today?

Jethro: Well I want to quit smoking.

Jess: Why do you want to quit smoking?

Jethro: I have some health problems and it's taking its toll on my health. I just want to get healthy.

Jess: Okay. And when this is no longer an issue and you are no longer a smoker how will you be as a person?

Jethro: I'll be free.

Jess: When you are free what are all of the great things that will come from that?

Jethro: Well for one thing my wife will be happy and I'll be more fit and healthy. I will get to enjoy a longer life with her and my grandkids.

Jess: That's fantastic! So aside from you who else in your life is this change most important to?

Jethro: No one, this is about me.

Jess: It is only about you? There is no one else important in your life for whom this change would be meaningful? There is no one who would be thrilled or happy that you have made this change?

Jethro: There actually is someone.

Jess: Are you sure?

Jethro: Oh yes!

Jess: Who is that?

Jethro: It's my wife, Elsie.

Jess (*to Group*): We are just getting some general intake information here, like we covered yesterday. If this were an actual intake then it would be far more refined and a bit longer. In a normal session, the pattern that we are about to do, generally follows the formal trance induction, deepener, and metaphors for change. For our purposes today we will not actually do the trance induction we will simply go through the structure of this pattern.

Jess:

Okay Jethro, in your mind I would like for you to imagine Elsie there front of you. Notice the expression on her face, what she is wearing, her posture. As you do that begin to get a sense of the connection you have to her, the feeling. Maybe it is love, friendship, trust, companionship, whatever emotion connects you to her now. Notice where you feel that emotion the most and allow it to grow as you see Elsie there.

(*To Group*) So here we are beginning to build the sensory experience for the client. This is just a way of deepening experience before you begin to layer up the emotional connection between Jethro and Elsie. This seems all familiar, right?

Group: Yes.

Jess:

All right Elsie is there in front of you. I would like for you to begin to drift up out of yourself as an awareness. So you can look down and see you there and Elsie there. And when you're ready float down into Elsie. You can have a sense of what it's like to see through her eyes, hear through her ears, and feel how it feels to be Elsie. Maybe you can notice the difference in height. Or perhaps the sound of your voice that is different. As you do that Elsie, notice Jethro, how he looks and how he is standing.

Begin to feel that connection you have with Jethro. As you do that you can begin to really sense that connection you have to Jethro. Perhaps you are aware of a certain feeling or emotion, something special as you look at him in only the way a wife can look at her husband. Allow that connection to grow in strength.

(*To Group*): Now we are beginning to layer up the sensory experiences from the point of view of Elsie. Did you notice

131

the shift? The client is no longer Jethro, he is now Elsie looking back at Jethro.

We are now beginning to take advantage of the client's natural ability to dissociate. What they were doing before was to dissociate from the effects that smoking has on themselves. Now we are inviting them to dissociate from themselves completely. They already have a strong belief that smoking will not harm them so why not use that to create the change.

> *Okay Elsie you know that Jethro would like to make a very important change and I would like for you to share an experience with him to help him make that change. Now some parts of this experience may be a little difficult. However, you know that anything in life worth achieving takes a little bit of work, some effort. The rest of this experience is going to be absolutely wonderful.*

Are you happy to continue this process?

Elsie: Yes.

(*To Group*) What I am doing here is pre-framing the experience. I want the client's unconscious mind to be completely on board with the process. I am also communicating indirectly that they may experience some difficult emotions and that this is perfectly okay. I want to reassure them that whatever happens, they are perfectly okay. Those emotions will fit into a larger process.

> *Now I'd like for you to watch Jethro as he has a decision to make. This decision comes with certain consequences and outcomes. Your only job is to watch him experience the decision he is making.*
>
> *The first option he has is to go through life continuing the habit of smoking. As he continues down this path,*

what's the first consequence he experiences if he continues smoking?

Elsie: He is coughing.

Jess: He is coughing. He is there coughing, uncomfortable. How does it feel to see him feeling like that?

Elsie: It makes me sad. I don't like seeing him like that.

Jess: It does make you sad, very sad. Jethro is there coughing. What is the next consequence he encounters continuing down that path?

Elsie: It's harder for him to walk around or climb stairs.

Jess: It's hard for him to walk around and climb the stairs. What is it that you are noticing about it being hard for him to climb the stairs?

Elsie: He is struggling and is out of breath. It looks like his heart is beating super fast.

Jess: His heart is beating superfast. How does it feel to see that?

Elsie: It's very sad.

Jess: It is very sad, take a moment to really be with that feeling.

(To Sarah And The Group): Let's take a time out here. You may have noticed that I spent time repeating back the exact words that Sarah was giving me. This is important because consciously it may sound a bit annoying, but to the client's unconscious, which is the part of them working right now, it builds the state. It paces where the client is and allows us to continue to build up their emotional experience.

Keep in mind that we are building Elsie's state, not Jethro's. We are not asking the client what is it like for them to have the experience. We are asking them what is it like for that loved one. It's a completely different set of emotional experiences for the client.

(To Elsie) so what is the next consequence for Jethro?

Elsie: He is visiting doctors.

Jess: And what is happening?

Elsie: He is having an electrocardiogram.

Jess: He is with the doctor having an electrocardiogram and how do you feel seeing that?

Elsie: Really scared!

Jess: You're feeling really scared. Really pay attention to that feeling. Be with it.

(To Sarah And Group) Let's take another timeout here. When you are with the client you may spend some more time really amplifying these negative states. Because I am working with Sarah as a demo, I do not really want to build the states in her. When you are with a client however it is useful for them to have the experience of these less than pleasant states. Think of this as a reality check for them. Their action in smoking has very real consequences not just for them but also for those around them. The quicker they fully understand this at the unconscious level the easier the change becomes.

(To Elsie): I would like for you to fast-forward to the next serious consequence in Jethro's life.

Elsie: He is dying.

Jess: And what is it you are seeing that lets you know he is dying?

Elsie: He is lying in the hospital.

Jess: How does it feel to see him lying there?

Elsie: It's devastating.

Jess: Devastating, stay with that for a moment.

(*To Sarah*) Come all the way back.

(*To Group*) We are taking a moment to break state here for Sarah. While doing the actual pattern you will keep the client in that negative state for a few moments. When they get to the death scene you may want to walk them through the funeral. Do not linger too long here, just enough to let the client really dip into those powerful emotions.

> *Now there is wonderful news because there is a new and fantastic path that Jethro gets to take. Jethro has come here today to make this change, to stop, to become a non-smoker. It's like returning to a fork in the road, back to the decision point. Since Jethro has come here today, I know that he is going to take this other path and become a healthy non-smoker. So what is the first wonderful outcome he gets to experience as a non-smoker?*

Elsie: Ah his skin looks a different shade. It's a healthy color, no longer gray.

Jess: A healthy color to his skin, and what is it like to see that healthy color?

Elsie: It's like the old Jethro.

Jess: The old Jethro, how wonderful! What's the feeling that you are experiencing?

Elsie: I'm pleased.

Jess: You are pleased. Notice just where in your body you are feeling that pleased feeling, having the old Jethro back. As he continues what is the next wonderful outcome?

Elsie: We are walking together; we are going on a long walk. I don't know where but it's on a hill somewhere.

Jess: You are both walking and it's a long walk. I'm curious what is the expression on Jethro's face?

Elsie: He's smiling! He hasn't looked like this in years, I am so happy.

Jess: You are happy. Why not turn that up, you can make that feeling even stronger and enjoy resting in that, that happiness, having the old Jethro back, having a walk in the hills. And even after that what is the next wonderful outcome?

Elsie: Ha, he's playing football. He's playing with our grandson.

Jess: He's playing football with your grandson, how incredibly amazing. How does he look?

Elsie: Oh he's happy!

Jess: As you watch them play football, what are you thinking?

Elsie: I'm just thrilled to see them playing together.

Jess: I wonder, could you turn that thrilled feeling up and make it even stronger? That's it. What is the next amazing outcome?

Elsie: Jethro's birthday.

Jess: Jethro's birthday, and how old is he?

Elsie: He is turning 70.

Jess: 70! Where's the birthday at?

Elsie: I don't know where it is but there is a big ass cake! Jethro is happy.

Jess: How many people are there?

Elsie: The whole family.

Jess: Wonderful, how does that feel?

Elsie: It feels awesome!

Jess: It feels awesome! Really enjoy that awesome feeling of knowing that Jethro has accomplished this and has created such a lovely life.

Is there any other powerful, wonderful outcome that comes to mind right now?

Elsie: It's happiness that is spreading all the way through.

Jess: Its happiness that is spreading all the way through, and does it have a color?

Elsie: No it actually doesn't, it's clear. It's just a feeling.

Jess: Wonderful. What I would like for you to do now is to see Jethro there and congratulate him for making this amazing change... That's it.

(*To Group*) During this phase we really take time to build up the positive state and share in your client's joy, happiness, or what ever else they may be feeling. Reflect that state back to them in your own state and tonality.

If you remember from earlier Jethro had conscious positive reasons for quitting. At this phase those reasons may be experienced on a deeper level. Or, the unconscious mind may generate new positive outcomes that the client had not considered before. When this happens it is even better because it shows that the unconscious mind is fully invested in the change. During this process you may want to sprinkle in the information the client gave you consciously, or you may prefer to let their unconscious mind do it all. Use your calibration skills.

> *Now when you are ready you can drift as an awareness out of Elsie and back into you, Jethro. Bringing with you that happiness. So drift out of Elsie now so that you can see both Elsie and Jethro. Float back in to a transformed Jethro.*
>
> *You know, Elsie just shared a really wonderful experience with you. Take a moment to thank her. That's*

it. Since you are so close and have this connection why not hug her. Bring her into you so it's like she melts into you, becoming a part of you. There you go.

(*To Group*) At the end of the process the client congratulates himself for having made the change while he is in the position of a loved one. We then guide him back into third position and finally first. Jethro/the client then thanks the other person for sharing in the experience. What he is actually doing is thanking his unconscious mind for making this change. Thanking the unconscious mind with a very powerful practice.

Finally, because Jethro and Elsie (*client and imagined loved one*) are the same person, it is important to integrate them back into one complete person. We like to do it through a hug, having the other person melt into the client, becoming one. There are a number of other ways you can do this, but this is an easy way.

(*To Sarah*) Welcome back, how are you?

Sarah: I am well thank you.

Jess: Any questions?

Lawrence: Have you ever had a situation where a client does not have a second person?

Jess: In our experience there is always someone else. It may take a little bit of time to pinpoint that person but they are there. If we did have a client who had absolutely no one what we may do is have them associate into themselves as a child some point before they smoked. Honestly though, we haven't come across this.

Sarah: Sometimes they will first say no one, "this is all about me." If you explore that with them you will uncover someone.

Jess: Something to keep in mind with this pattern is that sometimes you will get a couple who are both quitting smoking. One person may choose the other person as being the most important person. If this is the case we need to move that loved one into the future so that they are a non-smoker before the client. We do this for a couple of reasons. First, it increases the leverage. If the partner is still a smoker in the client's mind then the energy will not be as strong as it would be if the partner was a non-smoker. The second part of this is that at the end of the process we are reintegrating the client and we do not want to reintegrate a smoker back into the client.

Something else to watch out for too is if someone chooses a smoker who has no desire to quit. The odds of this are quite low but be aware if it does happen. There are a couple of ways to handle this. The first is to find out why the change in the client's life is important to that person but not their own change. You may be able to leverage the reasoning. For example if a mother feels like she can't quit but wants the son to then you will want to explore why. It may be that she doesn't want him to go through the same health difficulties as her. This could be very strong leverage. What you may want to do in this case is to highlight those issues when the client is associated into mom.

You will also want to build up the idea of the mom quitting as the son goes through the process. This is because when it is time for integration we want both parts of the client congruent. If the client has changed but integrates that smoking part back into him then it sends the wrong message. It doesn't matter if the mother is still smoking in the outside world. The unconscious mind will get the metaphor.

If you choose to do it this way then you will also want to add in suggestions after this pattern about the client being all right with the fact that important people in his life smoke and he has made a different decision. We don't need the client going out and ruining relationships because he has taken it on himself to be the smoking police.

The much easier option is to simply guide the client to choose someone else.

Like I mentioned a moment ago, the odds of this happening are quite low. I know we haven't come across it. If you do, just be aware that you have options.

Lawrence: Do you ever have a client pull themselves out of the trance state as you're going through the process of layering up the dire consequences?

Jess: It is not outside of the realm of possibilities, but I haven't encountered it.

Kristina: Do they cry?

Jess: Yes. Actually it is fairly common. And in this context it is good; it is a resource.

Sarah: When this happens it is very useful for us as hypnotists. When working with the client you will layer up the negative states far more and all the time you are 'holding the space' for them to experience this within a safe place. Jess was very careful here not to do that because it is a demo. You want them to feel the negative impact of continuing smoking and some of those may be quite nasty. That is going to be a big part of the powerful leverage you are creating.

It really is powerful. Both the negative and positive states become a tremendous resource for the client.

Jess: What makes this whole pattern so powerful is that it is all about building states in such a way that the client has the fullest experience.

When I first began seeing smokers I did the traditional "Fork in the Road," pattern. This is where the client imagines a crossroad and then imagines going down each path (the one that leads towards an inevitably painful demise, and the one that leads to healing). The client directly experiences both of these options, as themselves.

I found that this was not always useful. They would pop out of the experience and say something like, "yes but that won't happen to me."But when you have them step into someone else and watch themselves, the set of emotions is completely different. They are experiencing the consequences from the point of view of someone who is most important to them in their life.

We have all had the experience of the death of a loved one. We also have experienced the joy of someone special to us accomplishing something fantastic. These are the emotions that the client is tapping into. These emotions are not, "what if's", they are experiences they have already had in different contexts.

When we work with the negative path we like to facilitate three or four negative experiences, and the last scene should be the moment of death — but we will not directly suggest it. Instead we will question them about what they think the smoking will do to that person walking down that path. Clients tend to generate that spontaneously once they get closer to the end of the smoking road.

On the positive side we like to do more outcomes. Generally we will do somewhere between five and seven outcomes. At this point we really want to build up a strong state when the client is coming out of this pattern.

Sarah: We call them consequences and outcomes. Even the language you use is important because it continues to reinforce the negative and then the positive.

Rita: Would you suggest that they imagine being on a respirator or something like that?

Sarah: You are more likely to ask them what is happening. This allows their unconscious to bring up the consequences and events in a way that is more immediate to them.

Jess: Keep in mind as well they are not imagining themselves being on a respirator. They are imagining being someone else watching their loved one (the client) have the experience.

Shawn: Here is the point. People will dissociate from the negative consequences of the behaviors. It's a natural defense; it's automatic. So what this pattern does is it allows them to dissociate from the consequences to them and associate into the consequences of someone else. I think it is a brilliant pattern.

Sarah: Even when they are associated into the other person, a part of them is still having the direct experience of the consequences and the outcomes.

Shawn: In many ways it is much harder to watch someone else suffer.

Mercedes: It absolutely is.

Shawn: That's why whenever there is a dirty job around the house I have Sarah do it. It's much more difficult to watch someone else (*laughing*).

Sarah: Thank you so much.

Jess: I think we should now break down the pattern so that you have all of the steps. First I would like to thank Sarah for being our brave volunteer. And Sarah, I'd like to thank your unconscious mind for playing along.

Mark: Have you ever had someone say that the other person didn't melt back into them at the end the pattern?

Jess: No. At the end of the process you need to integrate them. I do not like to leave my client's with multiple parts lying around my office. It's just weird.

Sarah: Even though they are imagining being that other person they are still themselves.

Jess: We have also spent a lot of time building up the positive nature of the relationship. Who doesn't enjoy a hug from someone they love? Once you have the hug you're more than halfway to integration.

Mark: So in this demo was Elsie the giver of the hug or the recipient?

Jess and Sarah: Yes!

Jess: Now I know you are wondering what to call this pattern and I want to reassure you it has a name. I thought of it last week.

This is the Perceptual Possibilities Pattern or P^3.

Does anyone remember step one?

Kristina: Create a connection with the special person and float up.

Jess: Good.

Step 1: Create a special connection and associate in.

Sarah: Remember to take some time to build this person up in the client's mind so that they connect on the emotional level with them. This is like what we did this morning followed by floating up into third and then down into second position. It is not simply a matter of "see the person and float into them." We need to guide them.

Mark: Sometimes it's easier to step into the person instead of floating.

Sarah: Yes, they can float, drift, step into the other person. You get to play with this.

Jess: Be creative. You may find that some wording works better with some clients then others.

Step 2: Experience the world from another's perspective.

Next you have the client notice what it's like to be that other person, remembering to build up the experience. We may do this first through sensory and then through emotional experiences. The client needs to experience the connection the other person has with them. The connection that the client has with that person may not have the same type of feeling as the connection the other person has with them.

Now we are ready to begin the journey. As I mentioned before, it is useful to pre-frame this experience either at this point or during the pre-talk. The specific frame that I use is to remind the client that anything worth accomplishing takes work.

Step 3: Watch loved one go down through the negative consequences.

Next we begin going through the negative consequences. These are usually three or four. We are looking here for the client to access a big emotional state. When you ask the client, "how do you feel seeing that?" they may give very minimal answers. They may say something like, "that feels bad," or, "it feels not good." Regardless of what they are saying we are calibrating for what is actually happening in their physiology. While the answers may not be expressive you will see the changes in their breathing, their facial expressions, their tension, and other indicators of the unpleasant state. We are building the strongest emotional state possible to link to the smoking.

Step 4: Break State.

After you have built up the state the client will need a break state in order to go down the pleasant path. A very simple way of doing this is to negate the negative path as a possible option. You could say something like, "that was just one possibility; you are here today making a change in choosing a different way of being." This is an interesting way to break state because not only does it allow them to take a step back, you are also giving a very direct suggestion to the client. You can also think of this as the client returning to a point of decision, back to the fork in the road. We move them out of the emotional space to give them time to level out whatever emotions they were experiencing.

Step 5: Watch your loved one go along the route of positive outcomes.

Now it is time for all of the positive outcomes, everything wonderful they will experience as a non-smoker. In the demo we had things like: smelling good, having energy, good health, saving money, playing with grandkids, and his 70th birthday. You really build up this, making it stronger, bigger, and more powerful.

Remember as a hypnotist you have to go first. You have to access the states you want for your client because then they become sub communicated to the client's unconscious. Simply put, get excited and feel happy for their success.

Rita: Do you suggest it to the client or does the client generate these outcomes?

Jess: Throughout this entire process we are allowing the client to generate both the negatives and the positives. We encourage them by asking things like, "what's the next positive outcome, what's the next step, what happens next." The entire time we are echoing back the client's responses and injecting even more emotion into it.

Sarah: Instead of saying, "what's the first one? Great. What's the next one? Great." we want to inject feeling into it. You may say, "what's that feeling? Happiness, great! Where do you feel that?.... does is have a color?.... can you turn it up, make it stronger?" Each time they come to an event that's positive we build that state making it stronger, more intense, and more powerful.

Shawn: We are also using their anchors. If you remember, "big ass birthday cake," that popped. For the client it was a hot word.

Jess: On both the negative and positive sides you'll see the physiological shifts. Through the verbalization they are reaffirming the experience through yet another sensory channel. They have in the visual, what they are seeing, they have it in the kinesthetic, what they are feeling, and now they have it also in the auditory.

Lawrence: When they are describing various scenes in the positive outcomes do you engage them with direct questions about the scenes to elicit a greater emotional response? For example, I'm thinking about the, "big ass birthday cake." Would you ask how many candles?

Shawn: You would ask first if there were candles on the cake. You don't want to assume that they are automatically there. You don't want them to say, "there are no candles."

Step 6: Congratulate loved one for making this positive change.

Now that we have built up the positive outcomes we take a moment to allow the client to congratulate himself. While the client is in second position, he as that other person congratulates his future self for having made the change. This is a type of indirect future pace. This also allows the client to reaffirm the fact he is a non-smoker. Because he is doing it from second position his conscious mind will not argue against the fact that he is a non-smoker.

Step 7: Reintegration

Once it is complete, now it's time to drift out of second position and back into third. The client can see the other person and themselves. The client then moves into first position, Jethro becomes Jethro again. The client then thanks the other person for sharing this experience with them.

Now it's time to integrate the client into one, complete, whole person. Client takes that part, the other person, and makes her a part of him. Jethro hugs Elsie and the two become unified.

Mark: Do you visually mark the space for the different positions?

Jess: If their eyes were open we may visually anchor the different positions but typically by this point the clients eyes have closed.

Sarah: I purposefully kept my eyes open during this demo because I didn't want to go too far into this experience.

Jess: With Sarah I used gestures to push the negative experience into her past because I didn't want her to linger in an unneeded emotional experience.

Mark: Let me ask you, Sarah, at the end when he floated back into Jethro did he still have a sense of Elsie?

Sarah: Strangely enough, I did. I could sense her there in front of me.

Mark: So the assumption is that the other person is still present?

Jess: Yes. After Elsie congratulates Jethro he drifts back into himself. Elsie is still there because we haven't suggested otherwise. That means we have to take the time to reintegrate that part of the client.

Any questions?

Kristina: How do you transition through the break state?

Jess: I will do something as simple as suggesting that you're here, now, to make a change. It's like you're standing at a fork in the road, going down the road of accomplishing this goal, and really feeling how amazing it is to achieve this. You very literally think about it, standing where you can either go left or right. You want to return the client to the point of making the decision to go down the positive path.

Any other questions?

Lawrence: I am just amazed at how powerful it was to witness that. I was tearing up as you were going to the positive outcomes. I was right there with Elsie. Has it ever not worked for you in one session?

Jess: This is a part of the larger protocol. This step may be all that is needed for the client to achieve the goal, but I like to do other things because the client will have very real things in life that have sustained this habit including anchors, beliefs, and elements of their identity.

We want to stack the deck in the client's favor, so this stop smoking protocol has a number of different layers to create tremendous leverage. And we want to continue that by empowering a client through their own skills and resources to maintain this new smoke-free lifestyle.

Within the protocol this is the first pattern I do during the overt trance. This lays the foundation and drives the client's motivation through the session. After this we look at things such as the first time they smoked, which is very important to the smoking cessation process, as well as contextual triggers.

Karen: So you do the intake in trance?

Sarah: No the intake is done before the formal trance. Remember, they will be cycling in and out of trance during the intake. If we go back to the list we were developing yesterday we would have done all of these things. We would have addressed their concerns about quitting, and we also would've taught them the craving busters. If it was their first time into hypnosis we would have done the pre-talk maybe some convincers and then a formal induction. If they were used to hypnosis and they had been in hypnosis with us before we would have simply done an induction and then into this pattern.

Rita: What do you say to them after this pattern? Do you say congratulations you are a non-smoker?

Jess: Not yet, there is a lot more we do with the client. This is just a step on the path. This is building the leverage to move the client towards the big change.

Lawrence: Have you ever had someone who is so dissociated that even when in second position — even in the presence of their loved one — still says, "no that won't happen"?

Jess: We have never seen that with the client. It is not outside the realm of possibilities but if it happens it is rare. Remember that our assumption is that the person the client has named has a big investment in the client making the change.

Shawn: It's important that you see the affect when you initially ask them about the other person. You want them to choose someone with whom there is a connection. There is also the client's recognition that this person wants them to change. The loved one understands the consequences of the client's actions. The loved one would not be invested in the change if they didn't understand those consequences.

Jess: Once I had a client who I knew was a mother. When I asked her to name who, aside from her, was the change most important to, she said "no one, only me." So I asked her if she was sure, and she said yes.

After a few moments she said, well maybe a friend. But there was no emotional charge in it. I finally asked her, what about her kids. To that, she responded, "oh my God," as her jaw dropped her eyes widened. I knew instantly: there we have it.

Mark: Do they have to be alive?

Jess: It is very rare, but sometimes a client may choose someone who is deceased. What is important is the emotional connection. So it could work quite nicely depending on how you as the hypnotist framed it.

Shawn: It will work well if the person who is deceased had a connection with the client smoking during their life. For example, a powerful resource would be a client who used to smoke with their father who has now passed.

Karen: I will be seeing a client in the near future for smoking. I know that they don't have a significant other, so is a parent a good choice?

Sarah: Sure or it could be a brother or sister, an uncle, a friend, a grandmother.

Jess: You may be surprised that when you ask this question, more often than not people will come up with someone on the first go-around. There have been times where I would expect the person to be a girlfriend or someone like that and it turned out to be an uncle or cousin. The emotional connection is what tells us we have the right person.

Shawn: There is an old Zen story. A man went to go see the famous Zen master who was a painter and asked him to paint a picture of happiness. A week later the master presents the painting and it says, "grandfather dies, father dies, son dies." The guy is confused and wants to know how is this happiness. The master says, "well if it doesn't take place in that order then you have a problem." The idea that that parent is going to outlive the child can be a horrible proposition.

Mark: You never know what will be an asset for our life.

Jess: This is very true. I had a couple of people who did not have a great dynamic with their parents. That's okay we found someone else, a friend.

I use this pattern very frequently and the odds of someone not finding a person are extremely low.

Mark: What are the actual words you use to achieve this?

Jess: I simply ask, "aside from you who else in your life is this change most important to?"

Sarah: This is why it is right there on the intake form.

Sarah: So let's role-play one client, and one hypnotist. However, when you get to the part of going down the negative path, we'd like you to completely come out of the role play and have a very cognitive discussion with your partner. This is so you don't inadvertently help someone to go to a place that is not such a great state to be in. Does that make sense?

So associate your partner in and do everything except to go down the unpleasant path. At that point tell your partner to come back, using their real name, and spend some time talking about it.

Lawrence: You do not want us to do a full induction.

Sarah: No absolutely not.

Jess: Feel free to build up the positive states though at the end.

(*Students do exercise*)

Jess: How was that guys?

Mercedes: Wonderful.

Jess: And this is only a role-play. Imagine how much more powerful this is in trance.

Lawrence: What type of induction do you use with this?

Jess: I prefer to use the non-awareness induction which I learned from Igor Ledochowski.

Sarah: I love the induction Jess uses, of which hand is going into trance first. This has a wonderful presupposition that trance will be happening.

Jess: I will look for a difference in sensation such as warmth, lightness, or anything else the client may mention as their experience. I will then tie that in with their smoking hand. I will suggest to the client how amazing it is that the hand that in the past caused them so much trouble is now creating the solution. If it is the other hand I will point out to the client how incredible it is that the hand that used to cause the problem now is completely motionless, still, cool while the other hand begins the process of creating change.

Shawn: That's like cheating isn't it, it's like a win-win.

Sarah: Why yes it is!

Shawn: For me as the subject the one thing I noticed is that there were very definite sub modality shifts.

Jess: What were the shifts you noticed?

Shawn: The smoking path was dark while the nonsmoking path was brighter, larger, and more spaced out. It felt almost like a Visual Squash. Both sets of emotions became one.

Mercedes: It is nice to see so much from NLP comes into play, and see how you really can move things around.

Sarah: Really, this is the structure or scaffolding. It's your job to bring the rest. So have fun using the structure in a way that gives you freedom to explore more ways of doing this.

Jess: We've spent some time looking at future possibilities, and you know that this is only one half of the client's timeline. There is an immense amount of resources from the clients past as well.

The pattern we will be going through this afternoon is about how to use the past to create a change for the client that happens not just at the level of behavior, but very quickly generalizes up to the level of identity. It's called the Smoking Destroyer Pattern

THE SMOKING DESTROYER PATTERN

Jess: The pattern we are going to share with you now is called the Smoking Destroyer and it utilizes another familiar pattern to the NLPers in the group...the VK Dissociation. Remember...the "Movie Theatre" Pattern?

Group: Oh yeah.

Student: I don't know that but it sounds intriguing!

Jess: That's right, it does, doesn't it! Lets have an experience of this ourselves before we go through the steps so you know what it feels like from the inside .We will do this in small bite-sized pieces so we can explain as we go along and so your conscious mind has something to hang on to.

Shawn:

What we would like you to do is to sit back and relax. While you are relaxing there in your chair imagine that you are in a comfortable movie theater. You can see the screen down in front. It is one of those theaters, perhaps where they play those old black-and-white movies, the ones that nobody wants to watch anymore. This movie you are about to watch is going to be some event that maybe wasn't the way you would have liked it to be. In a moment I am going to turn out the lights and lower the house lights and you'll see the first scene of the movie. That first scene will be sometime just before the event took place. The movie is going to play through to the final scene, which is going to be a scene from after it is over. Everything is good again. Your ready? Okay, we're going to lower the house lights so you can see the opening scene. The movie begins and you can make it a black and white, grainy film as it plays through to the final scene. Then we raise the house lights again.

154

We are going to do this a few more times but we are going to make a few editorial changes.

Now lets begin to play around and have fun. I've pressed the wrong button on the projector and it's going to run backwards. You can see the movie running backwards. All the way until it's the opening scene. This time I'm going to change the focus on the lens so it just a little blurry, okay. It's going to get a little bit blurry. See the openings getting blurred. You can still just about make out what it is. Are there any other sub modalities would like us to use? Would you like to make the screen very small?

Jess: Yes let's make it small.

Shawn: *Okay, we are going to move the projector close to the screen so the picture starts to get very, very small. Do you see the screen there?*

The house lights come back up. As you think about the whole event how is it changed now?

Kathy: It's different, there is less emotion.

Shawn: Right, it does change the feelings around it. Anyone else?

Mark: For me I feel more detached.

Shawn: More detached.

Karen: What do you do with someone who doesn't see things?

Shawn: The only reason we ever look at pictures is to get in touch with feelings. It's absolutely true. There is no reason for anyone to see pictures in the work we do except to get in touch with feelings. It's we who have to see the picture first to get in touch with the feelings who you should feel sorry for!

Okay, so this is of course a classical technique in NLP, the Movie Technique or V-K dissociation. We typically run the movie, safe scene to safe scene, and we begin to change the qualities of the movie or sub-modalities in terms of NLP. We change the color of the movie to black and white. We move it forwards and backwards, clear to blurred, those types of things.

Any questions on the technique? We are just giving you a building block here.

Kristina: I am very visual normally but I found that it wasn't until the third time through that I saw it on the wall. Before then I was watching it in my head.

Shawn: You were watching it in your head, that's the best place. Here is a piece of advice, don't watch it in Mark's head! It will be crowded it in there. (*laughing*)

Lawrence: What type of events are you putting up on the screen?

Shawn: Normally in NLP they are negative events, and we will talk about how to use this with smokers in a moment.

Jess: We are going to do a quick exercise in pairs. Spend two minutes each just playing with the sub-modalities of a movie. It might be the same movie as you saw up here or it might be another small event that you would like to dissociate or detach from in terms of your feelings.

As the hypnotist you might want to make the movie smaller, darker, less clear. Just notice how that experience changes the state. Any questions?

Rita: Is it important to know what the movie is about?

Shawn: No, not at this stage. Your client should know though.

Jess: Later when we move this into the smoking session then it is more important to know what it is about, not for now though.

Kathy: After you watch it backwards do you keep watching it backwards?

Shawn: Either way. Forwards, backwards, color, black and white — the more you change it from a reality type movie that is 3D, wrap around with surround sound, the less associated to the feelings the person will be. Smaller, less associated. Black and white, less associated, dimmer less associated, in general. If you can't see the picture at all then you are not very associated. That is exactly where you want to be.

Jess: All right, 2 minutes each and we'll add another layer.

(*Students do exercise*)

Jess: How was that?

Kathy: What do you do with someone who doesn't see images ?(*referencing her partner*)

Jess: What did you do?

Lawrence: I changed the emotional content.

Jess: Great can you give an example?

Lawrence: "And we're going to go through it again and the emotion will be there but this time on top of it all you are going to feel silly."

Jess: Wow, very nice! And how was that for you?

Karen: It was really good and it helped me not only to experience it but now when I meet another person such as myself I will know how to work with them.

Shawn: As you go through the next few steps it's going to be easier and easier for you... and more difficult for these poor "visualies."

Jess: Are you ready for the next step?

Shawn: You have all had experience of the movie and feelings changing. For the next step we are going to play it through again. This time you're going to invite your younger self, the one who is even younger than the 'you' who went through this experience, to come and join you in the theater. And you are going to coach your much younger self to have new resources and skills and different behaviors.

You can give the much younger you all the benefits of the knowledge you have now. Maybe teach them EFT or some other technique you know. How many of you would have liked to have the skills and resources you have now when you were younger? It would have changed things a lot right? Now you have the opportunity to do that. Once you have coached them you will both watch the movie together.

You can use the same movie or a different one, either is ok. Makes sense?

Karen: That would make sense if you could remember what the movie was about that you were working with.

Shawn: Excellent, pick a new movie. It's funny how that happens isn't it. You change the sub-modalities and you lose track of what it is about.

Okay so the steps are going to be: create the opening scene, invite your younger self in. You're now going to coach them, giving them resources, learnings, and wisdom that you have now that would've helped them in the scene.

So invite yourself in whatever way makes sense to you. Lets do this together as a group first so you can all experience it.

Beginning scene in the movie theatre, invite the younger you in. I wonder what resources, teachings, and wisdom you can give to them. Coach the younger you (the one who is sitting next to you) before the movie starts....give them tools like EFT or the Backwards Spin. Now when you are ready you can watch the film together noticing how it has changed.

When you are ready come back to the room. How was that for the kinesthetics in the room?

Mercedes: I remember being little and not wanting to wear gloves. It upset me so much that they wanted to put gloves on me. The adult me was able to make the situation okay so that the younger me could react differently.

Jess: Isn't that interesting. You were able to change your relationship with that memory through coaching the younger you. Did anyone else have this experience?

Kristina: Yeah, I did. At first the younger me was on my left but I pulled her onto my lap.

Shawn: Nice I like that. That is lovely.

Kristina: We were finally able to watch the movie and things changed.

Yuval: As soon as I talked to the young me, the drama of the movie disappeared.

Shawn: The nice thing about this pattern is that it gets around the internally framed piece. You're coaching yourself and for the internally framed this makes perfect sense.

Jess: Are you ready for another exercise? Do the same thing in pairs. It could be the same partner you worked with already, or if you want to change that's cool too. Go through the whole process adding on this last piece. Have your client bring your younger self in and coach them.

Finally, watch the movie together. That's it and then come back. Okay? Two minutes a piece.

(*students do exercise*)

Jess: How was that guys?

Group: Good.

Jess: Is everyone getting a sense of the ways in which you can coach and resource the younger self?

Lawrence: We each got the sense that just the act of having the conversation changed the whole issue.

Shawn: Right.

Yuval: This is still dissociated right?

Shawn: Right at this point it is. In the next step we are going to begin to associate the client into the new scene.

Mark: This creates a completely new state.

Shawn: Yes.

Kristina: It was interesting. I told myself that this event was going to happen in a moment but everything is okay. Once that was said everything was good.

Shawn: All right we're going to the next step.

So far we have the movie, the younger you and the coaching you. Now I'm going to invite the younger you to float into the movie and experience it from the inside out. But this time the movie has the new resources...as if like magic...and goes through the event with the new resources and skills(*Film sounds*)

House lights up. How was that?

Mark: Astonishing. It was like "yes, you are doing it!" It has that kind of feel.

Shawn: Awesome.

Any questions, anyone want to share anything else?

Kristina: This is a double dissociation. You have to watch yourself watch yourself.

Shawn: It kind of is, yes. It gives a person the chance to begin to feel the new emotions in film. They are partly associated with the younger self. It is the beginning of the association.

This pattern puts the client in the position of personal responsibility. They may not want to be responsible for themselves but now they are responsible for someone with less power than themselves.

Mark: This is really powerful stuff.

Shawn: Okay we have one more step. This is after the coaching part and after the moment when the younger you has floated into the movie and experienced it with new resources.

Rewind to the opening scene of the movie. You are going to ask the current you to associate into that movie and experience the new movie. You got it?

This time we will play the movie all the way through to the present. Throughout your entire life, you can think about all of the changes that you will be experiencing as a result of this small change. (*Film sound affects*)

House lights up. How was that?

Jess: Yes, anyone want to share?

Mercedes: There is some change happening here.

Shawn: And this is only a demo.

Kathy: It is amazing how this changes your perspective from the age you were at the event all the way to now.

Mark: It changes your life.

161

Jess: One little change can go a very long way. It is like the idea of the butterfly flapping its wings on the other end of the world creating a change in the weather pattern on this side of the world.

Shawn: It is one little change spread over an entire lifetime.

Jess: So I know you are wondering, "how on earth do I use this with a smoker?" It is a good thing you're here because we are about to show you. Before we do, just out of interest, what kind of age is typical for a smoker to have smoked their first cigarette?

Group: 14, 12, teenage years.

Jess: Yes very often it is teenage years…not always … but very often.

Now, let me ask you this. How many of you, when you were a teenager, really wanted to be told what to do by someone older?

Yuval: No way, I thought I knew it all!

Jess: Right, and how many of you would have wanted to take advise from someone much younger?

Yuval: From a little kid…no I can't see that working well.

Jess: Exactly, so it is typical that the movie the client makes of themselves having their first cigarette will show them sometime during their teenage years.

This is one reason that we invite a much younger them into the theatre and coach them. Not the teenager because they wouldn't listen, but a younger self.

This also means that if we coach the 7, 8, 9, 10 year old, they have 4 or 5 years to practice these new resources before they even reach the point of having their first cigarette. They are in a much different place and ready to make a much different choice.

Mark: How does that work?

Jess: Well when you ask the 7 or 8 year old to float into the movie they magically grow up to that age. The unconscious mind does this beautifully for us as the concept of time is much more fluid.

Smokers have all sorts of emotional triggers and attachments especially to the first time they had a cigarette. Generally someone does not wake up one day when they are a teenager and say, "you know what, I'm going to go buy a pack of cigarettes and smoke them. The initial drive for the smoking behavior is usually in the social dynamic. This can include being cool or being included in the group, and within their world that is super important.

Although they have grown up and they have matured there is still a bit of the desire to fit in driving the behavior on a deeper level. We want to start breaking the connections with the initial smoking experience and start giving the client resources so that the underlying dynamic that led them to take the very first cigarette is neutralized. This way they will have a lot more resources going forward.

You'll recognize many of these steps. During the intake we asked some important questions about the client's first smoking experience. We wanted to know details such as how old they were when they had their first cigarette, did they enjoy that cigarette, what was going on, and who were they with. We want to know what happened the very first time they decided to smoke.

Step 1:

The first step is to orient the client into the movie theater and watch the movie of their first smoking experience. The movie begins a few moments before they make the decision to take that first cigarette and ends when they had finished the cigarette. The first time through the client watches it in a dissociated position. This means they see themselves on the screen.

Once they have completed this, we have some interesting choices to make because they either enjoyed the first cigarette or they hated it.

a) If they liked it, change the sub modalities of the movie — this is the typical VK dissociation. Guide the client to make the picture darker, further away, changing the speed, rewinding it, fast forwarding it, changing the quality of the sound.

or

b) if they hated it, associate them into it and get them to go through the experience of smoking their first cigarette so that they relive how nasty it was while holding a cigarette. As they are doing this we place the cigarette in their hands. We are creating an anchor between that bad feeling and the cigarette they are holding.

Lawrence: An actual cigarette?

Jess: Yes.

Lawrence: These are the cigarettes they brought in?

Jess: Yes it is important to use their cigarettes, their brand because they have all the associations with them.

Step 2:

Bring them back to sitting in the movie theater and do a soft Break State. We need this because we want the client to be feeling as resourceful as is possible. If they are still feeling uneasy from the smoking experience we want to give their neurology the opportunity to reset. We want to keep this within the context of the movie theater so you may just want to ask the client about what their favorite snacks are at the movies.

Step 3:

Invite a much younger self (5- 10 years old) to come into the movie theatre and adult coach child and give them lots of resources, tools, and skills.

We are aiming for a bit younger than the age they were when they had that first cigarette — between five and ten years old. We want them to give the child vast amounts of resources, which the child can spend many years practicing before the moment of the first cigarette.

The younger them enters the movie theater and we have the coaching process between the adult and the child. The coaching might include teaching the younger child to manage stress or other emotional difficulties using the Backward Spin or EFT

During this coaching session you as the hypnotist are going to be coaching the adult in ways to coach the child. This includes a very important lesson on how to say no and feel confident and secure in doing so. You may coach the adult to say something similar to:

"There is going to be a moment in the near future when someone offers you cigarettes but I know you are such an amazing kid that you can really enjoy saying no to them. And as you grow up you can use all of these resources, the skills, these abilities to feel good, to increase relaxation and health."

The words are not as important as the intention behind them is. The adult client is giving the child resources for life. Keep in mind that you as the hypnotist is not the one who is coaching the child. It is the adult's responsibility to the teach their own younger self.

Think of how powerful this can be. Their success is now completely in their own hands.

Karen: So if you started smoking at 12, the younger you who sits beside you in the movie theater is younger than 12 right?

Shawn: So here's the thing, if you started to smoke at about 12, 13, 14, who wants to coach a teenager? Really? They don't really want to listen to anyone older!

Karen: Yes they can be obnoxious.

Kathy: They can be tough.

Shawn: They don't listen to advice, they don't take direction, they'd mouth off to you (*laughing*). But if you get a kid who is going to listen to you...

Mark: Right, that makes sense. In terms of working with the younger you, it's important to go younger and talk to the much younger child.

Jess: That's it exactly.

Step 4:

Adult and younger child watch the movie together and watch themselves saying "no" to the first cigarette. They see themselves using the resources, tools, strategies and techniques taught to them as they go through life.

That younger them on the screen is going to continue to age and grow through the years, having multiple opportunities to say no. We can highlight life events that we know in the past would have triggered them to smoke — such as a break at work. Each time the movie shows one of these events the client gets to watch themselves saying no. Not only do they say no over and over and over again they also implement the strategies that that the child was taught by the adult. The adult gets to watch younger them manage stress, increase confidence, and find healthy ways of fitting in until the movie ends and the client is at the present age.

Karen: So when the child and adult watched the movie, it is a different movie?

Shawn: Yes the movie will be different. They will be saying, "not me Mr. Nicotine."

Step 5:

The younger child floats into the movie and becomes the age of the teenager, who makes a new choice about not smoking. Adult watches the new movie.

Now it is time to begin to associate the client in. The younger them, the child is going to float into the movie. So that seven-year-old is going to float inside of the teenager on the screen. They become the age of the teenager...or whatever age they were when they smoked their first cigarette. We do not need to worry about suggestions of aging because the unconscious mind will understand the process. In trance logic the client has spent the years in between the coaching and the first offer of smoking, practicing and mastering the skills taught to him or her.

The client now watches the new movie alone. The learnings and messages from the new movie are being reinforced as this is happening. During this process we speak with the client and really build up the positive state associated with saying no.

"So what is it like to see yourself up there saying no, feeling good and growing in confidence?"

"Oh it feels fantastic!"

"That's right it does feel fantastic."

Lawrence: So just to make things really clear, when the child associates into the movie, sometime between the movie theater and associating into the movie they age to the appropriate age of the teenager?

Sarah: Yes.

Jess: It's time distortion, so the suggestion is that they grow up to the teenage self with the new resources and skills so they are able to make a new, better healthier decision. Got it?

Step 6:

Adult floats into the movie and becomes the teenager and gets to fully experience being more resourceful and confident in saying "no." Grow all the way up to the age the client is now.

After we have really built up that positive state it is time to associate the adult into the movie. They start from the experience of the younger them saying "no" to that first cigarette and getting to say "no" a number of other times throughout life. We then age the person all the way to their current age.

What is very nice about this process is that it helps the client to create the change on the level of identity. The most common response after this pattern is that the client feels like cigarettes are foreign to them. The cigarettes are no longer a part of who they are.

Would you guys like a demo?

Group: Yes please.

Jess: Okay. Shawn, will you role-play so the students can have a sense of how this pattern works?

Shawn: Sure.

Jess: Shawn would you like to use a different name for the demo or your own?

Shawn: My own name is fine.

Jess: Now Shawn, because you have a totally awesome unconscious mind, you understand that this is just a demo and completely fictional.

All right Shawn do you remember the first time you smoked?

Shawn: Yes.

Jess: How old were you?

Shawn: I was eight.

Jess: Eight, and when you had that cigarette what is happening?

Shawn: I am behind the shed at school.

Jess: Are you alone or with other people?

Shawn: I am there with other people.

Jess: How many, do you know?

Shawn: Three.

Jess: Three, are they friends?

Shawn: Yes they are friends.

Jess: What is happening, what is the context?

Shawn: I am sneaking behind the bike shed at school to smoke.

Jess: And did you enjoy that first cigarette?

Shawn: No.

Jess: No you really didn't. And you know that you have tremendous resources now as an adult that the younger you could have used.

Shawn: Yes.

Jess: Great.

> *What I would like for you to do is to find yourself in an old movie theater. It could be one of those theaters with comfortable chairs and maybe old ornate artwork on the walls. You can see in front of you a screen. In a moment on that screen a movie is going to play, and it's going to be of the very first cigarette you had. It can begin right before you made the decision smoke and end after you finished that cigarette. You can see the expression on your face as you have that nasty cigarette can you not.*

Shawn: Yes.

> *Now in a moment I would like for you to float into that movie so you can really remember what it was like to have that first cigarette. As you do I would like you to hold the cigarette. (Shawn holds a cigarette in his fingers). When you're ready just float up and drift into the movie screen so you can be inside of the film. You're there having that first cigarette you can notice how nasty it is and how awful it tastes, the stench, notice how it makes you feel. And now when you're ready you can float back out.*

> *Now that you are there back in the theater I'm curious what is your favorite snack? Some people like popcorn and a soda, others candy, still others like hot dogs. What is yours?*

Shawn: I like popcorn.

Jess: Yes, me too.

> *Now I know that there is a younger you, a child with so many hopes and dreams for the future. And you know*

how it is when a six or seven-year-old thinks about all of the possibilities waiting for them. They cannot help but be filled with a wonderful anticipation for the things that will be coming.

So I would like for you to invite that young you of six or maybe seven years old into the movie theater. You have so many resources and skills that can make a world of difference for that little boy there.

You can invite that six or seven-year-old Shawn into the movie theater to sit next to you. I would like for you to have a conversation with him. You may find that you would like to share some ways in which he can enjoy maybe being a little naughty aside from that old behavior. There are many ways in which little boys can get into playful trouble until the day comes for them to grow up. When that happens they change.

As you do that maybe you would like to give him other resources, ways of managing stress and ways of feeling confident. Most importantly you can teach him how to say no, how to say no to cigarette. Let me put it this way. How incredibly naughty it would be for him to say no to that first cigarette. He could say no to that cigarette and really enjoy saying no countless times.

Now I'd like the two of you to watch that movie and see how it has changed. You, Shawn, are up there saying no to the boys behind the shed. As you both watch that, the younger you is growing through the years with all of the resources and knowledge and saying no to any and all cigarettes, going through high school, university. Look at him saying no and feeling amazing, maybe even a little naughty. Go all the way to the present day.

You may find that you want to take a moment and just thank the little Shawn sitting over there and maybe share a special message with him. Kids enjoy hearing wonderfully pleasant things from those they look up to and admire. This is especially true if it's coming from older, cooler kids.

When you're ready the young Shawn can float up into the screen and into the new movie... That's it.. Really enjoy watching him say no to that cigarette. How does it feel to see that Shawn up there saying no?

Shawn: It feels really good.

Jess: That's right it does feel really good. You get to watch him grow up through the years using these resources and saying no. Each time he says no your enjoyment can double. Those good feelings, confidence, happiness can multiply.

Watch him as he says no again. How does that feel?

Shawn: It feels amazing.

Jess:

It really does feel amazing. So why not watch him do it again! And allow those good feelings to grow.

When you're ready you can drift up into that movie screen and become one with that eight-year-old you. You can now experience this from the inside and out. You get to say no and maybe even feel a bit naughty about it at times. You can do it again, and again, and again with all of those resources and confidence. Really enjoy realizing you are an incredibly resourceful person and a non-smoker.

That movie can play all the way to the end, to the present day. When that has happened you can allow that scene to fade and your eyes to open. You can completely reorient to the outside world here and now.

Welcome back!

Shawn: Thank you.

Jess: Thank you. This is the pattern. Any questions?

Lawrence: Before you sent little Shawn into the movie it seemed like you had him walk-through events without being in the film yet.

Jess: Yes present-day Shawn and little Shawn first watch the new film together.

Lawrence: Okay they are watching it again.

Jess: We are giving the client a number of opportunities to practice the new behaviors before they associate in.

Are there any other questions?

Yuval: If I did not like the first cigarette why would I do it again?

Shawn: Exactly.

Sarah: We really build up the negative state associated with smoking that first cigarette. Plus it is usually easier for someone to recall their first cigarette rather than when it became something good or nice for them.

Shawn: If they don't like it, then we do not change the sub modalities. We are creating a negative anchor with the physical sensation of holding a cigarette.

Jess: But really, this pattern is not about liking or disliking the experience. It is about re-orienting the client to the memories of smoking. They are creating a new relationship to the old behavior, a relationship in which they choose not to engage in the behavior.

Something else to consider is that smokers often carry the belief that if they have one cigarette they are automatically a smoker. This is why some people who have a cigarette after quitting go right back to smoking a pack a day. If the client has his belief that smoking one cigarette makes them a smoker then we need to go back as early as possible preferably to that first cigarette and change the identity being built.

Shawn: If you change the first one then the next cigarette in the chain becomes the first one, and the one after that becomes the first one. There is a type of domino effect.

Kathy: And if the person doesn't remember that first cigarette?

Jess: This is about changing their identity and if we do that it needs to begin at the first moment where identity begins to shift, the moment of the first cigarette. However, if the client doesn't remember their first cigarette you could work with another smoking moment early on. That is fine.

Memories are metaphors. It doesn't matter if the client gives an instance that was not the first cigarette in reality as long as they believe that it was. You may also find that a client may not consciously remember the first cigarette, but while in trance that memory pops up.

Kathy: What if they remember the first cigarette but cannot remember if they liked it or not?

Shawn: Then we would change the sub modalities. They probably enjoy the cigarettes now, they are smoking after all, we do not want them superimposing that liking onto the memory. If you change the sub modalities in one you are changing the sub-modalities of the rest.

Mercedes: So if they say they don't remember, we take them to an early instance of smoking?

Jess: Yes. This is all metaphor. When I work with a client I have no clue if that first cigarette that they mention is actually the first cigarette. In their mind this is a representation of an early moment where they made a decision to smoke and that's what is important.

Shawn: You can suggest to the client's unconscious mind that they can allow a memory of an early cigarette to emerge to help them create this change. If they don't

174

remember whether they liked it or not we assume they liked it — and do the sub modalities change.

Lawrence: When the adult coaches the child, are we suggesting the type of resources the adult should teach the child? Or are you only suggesting resources that you have taught the client like EFT and the backward spin?

Jess: Keep in mind that this was only a demo so I kept it very general. When we are actually working with the client we will use the resources we've built during the session as well as resources and skills that we know they already have.

During the intake you will learn an awful lot about your clients and will begin to get a sense of where their talents, abilities, and skills lie. You introduce those into the conversation and feed back any positive information they have given to you throughout the session. And, you invite them to add their own things into it.

After all, they may have resources that they were not even aware of until the session; or they may have skills that they didn't necessarily talk about with you. Invite them to bring those to the table as well.

Shawn: There is one thing which you know they have: they have made the decision to stop smoking. This is the opposite of what the child had. If the client is particularly unresourceful you can do the pattern and lead it back to where they are now.

When you're doing this type of re-imprinting pattern even the tiniest resource can be looped several times so that it becomes a big resource for the child. The child will be better for it. It becomes an iterative spiral.

Lawrence: So if the client does not have many resources you would run through that cycle multiple times?

Shawn: Yes. When you loop it through you will find that the client will get into a huge state. I did a demo with someone… it wasn't for quitting smoking but something else. They had a very difficult time finding any resources. They were not in a very nice place.

However, once we found one tiny thing it began to change. Even though it seems like a very, very small resource we know we are in a good place because all we have to do is loop it around. Each time we ask the client to watch the movie they become more and more resourceful.

Does that make sense?

Group: Yes.

Jess: It's interesting because when clients come out of this pattern they often feel as if they were never smokers to begin with. Smoking is something that is other to them. It is outside of them.

Jess: Would you like another demo?

Group: Yes…please

Jess: OK. Sarah, would you like to role-play for us?

Sarah: Sure.

Jess: All right Sarah are you ready?

Sarah: Yes.

Jess: Okay, lets do a bit of set up before we begin. What will be the name of your fictional character?

Sarah: Bernie.

Jess: How old is Bernie presently and how old was he when he had his first cigarette?

Sarah: He's now 27 and he had his first cigarette when he was 14.

Jess: What was the context of that cigarette?

176

Sarah: He was in the bathroom at school.

Jess: Is he alone or with other people?

Sarah: He is with other people.

Jess: Did he enjoy it or no?

Sarah: Definitely not.

Jess:

> All right Bernie I would like for you to imagine that you are in a movie theater and you can see a screen in front of you. I would like for you to go ahead and watch the movie of that very first cigarette. You are 14 years old, in the bathroom, and you didn't like it very much did you?

Bernie: No.

Jess: And what was it that you didn't like the most about it?

Bernie: Oh, the taste.

Jess: That terrible taste. Now watch that scene play to the end after that cigarette is finished.

Bernie: He doesn't even make it to the end of that cigarette.

Jess:

> Okay, what I would like for you to do now is to imagine that you can drift up into that movie and as you do that here is the cigarette to hold. You are there having that first cigarette in the bathroom at school with those other boys. You can really taste that awful cigarette as you smoke it. Maybe you are even feeling a little sick. It is so terrible that you cannot even finish it.
>
> Now, drift out of that scene back into the theater back to you sitting in that comfortable chair.

177

Do you like popcorn at the movies?

Bernie: No I don't really like popcorn.

Jess: What do you like at the movie theater?

Bernie: I like a big soda!

Jess: Don't tell Mayor Bloomberg!

Bernie: (*laughs*)

Jess:

> *So now what I would like for you to do is to invite a younger Bernie, even younger than the Bernie who had the first cigarette to the theater. Maybe he is about six or seven years old.*
>
> *What are some things you think young Bernie would need to know to make that event different? What would he need to know to say no to that cigarette?*

Bernie: He would need personal strength, confidence, and trust in himself.

Jess:

> *So in the comfort of your own mind have that conversation with him. Teach him about trust, strength, and confidence. Give that knowledge to him in any way that is appropriate and he will understand. Perhaps you would like to remind him of times in his past he felt that way or maybe you simply take that feeling, that ability and gift it to him.*
>
> *Once you have completed that it is time for you and young Bernie watch that movie play only this time it will have changed. People get to watch 14-year-old Bernie saying no to that cigarette. So when you're ready allow that new movie to begin. Young Bernie can say no, having all of that confidence, inner strength, trusting in himself. The interesting thing is this new movie does not stop after that event because there will be many more*

opportunities throughout Bernie's life where he gets to express that confidence and enjoy having a sense of trust that continues to grow inside of him by saying no again and again. Really feel that confidence build with each opportunity to say no to that cigarette.

Now take a moment to thank young Bernie sitting there next to you for having shared this experience. You may even want to give him a special message, something between just you and him. It may be about all of the wonderful experiences waiting ahead for him.

When he is ready you can drift up into that screen so that the Bernie who was six or seven now becomes that 14-year-old saying no. Again you can let that play and really enjoy the experience of watching you say no while growing in confidence, strength, and trust in who you are. What is that like to watch that now?

Bernie: It's like, "Yes I'm doing it!"

Jess:

That's right you are doing it! Really allow that feeling to grow. Each time Bernie says no, you get to feel more and more amazing. Maybe you even have a sense of pride. There may be even something that he needs to say to those boys in the bathroom and he can do that as well.

Bernie: Yes.

Jess:

That's right. Bernie can grow up through the years saying no again and again and again to every cigarette. That film can go all the way until Bernie is 27 years old, smoke free, confident, trusting in your own inner strength.

When you are ready you can allow that movie to start from the beginning again and this time you can float into it and really experience from the inside out what it is like to get to say no at 14 and then through the years. So drift into that movie now. That's right, saying no and really feeling that strength develop as your confidence grows, trusting in your own inner strength to guide your way. You grow up through high school, university, into your twenties and all the way to today. That's it.

Now allow that scene to fade and you can find yourself back in this room feeling what it is like to be sitting where you are. That's it. And when you have completely integrated this experience your eyes can open and you can feel awake, alert, and fantastic!

Great Job!

(*To Group*) Does that make that a little clearer?

Group: Yes!

Sarah: Merce you have a question.

Mercedes: I am not sure about the process. Once the younger Bernie is in the theater how does the movie change?

Jess: Okay. We have the younger Bernie in the theater and the current Bernie coaches him. They both now watch the movie of 14-year-old Bernie saying no. The film cannot be the same because Bernie has now changed.

Sarah: I gave the younger Bernie all of the resources so the 14 year old on the screen cannot be the same because he has had 7 years between the talk in the theater and that event on the screen. That is plenty of time to practice confidence, strength, and trust.

Jess: He spent the years between 6 or 7 and 14 practicing those skills.

Sarah: Because he has had all of this time to practice there was no question that at 14 years old he was going to say no.

Lawrence: The first time older and younger Bernie watched the film on the screen younger Bernie is the same age as the Bernie in the film?

Jess: No he is the seven-year-old.

Lawrence: He is always younger then the Bernie on the screen?

Jess: Yes. In trance you can have a person jump all over in their time line and it will make sense to them. Trance logic is very different from conscious logic.

Shawn: Here's the thing. The Bernie who is being coached does not actually have to be younger than the one on the screen. However if you have a client who started smoking at the age of 25 you don't have as much leverage. The more time between the younger self being coached and the first cigarette, the better. It creates more leverage.

Jess: The other thing to consider is that this was a very general demo. When you're working with the client you will have more information around the context of the first cigarette. This will let you know which direction to go in when you're coaching the adult. They may need other resources aside from just saying no. We are changing the client's relationship to that event in their memory.

Mark: What does the coach say to the client in order to get the new movie to play instead of the old one?

Jess: "In a moment a new movie is going to play. This is a special one for both of you to enjoy. In this film you get to enjoy watching you say no and have all of the resources you need to continue enjoying life as a non smoker."

Shawn: What you have to bear in mind is that the difference between being with the younger you watching the movie and being by yourself with the younger you associated to the movie is zero. Either way you're watching the movie and what you will typically get is a sub-modality shift.

Jess: The only reason why we do it in this way is to give the client a number of reference experiences of saying no.

Alright, would you guys like to have a go at this? So in pairs, role-play. We'll give you 15 minutes each.

(*Students do exercise*)

Jess: All right guys come on back. How was that? Did you begin to get a sense of dissociating, associating, dissociating, playing with the movie, playing with the personal history, playing with the submodalities? Changing an entire lifetime of smoking. Helping a young person at 13, 14, 15 when they were making a decision when they had a choice. Before, they made one choice, now they have made a totally different one and it has generalized out, completely changing who they are.

Karen: I found it interesting that we are role-playing and I was still able to come up with all the stuff that this "guy" was telling his younger self, not really things that I would have thought up as myself. How powerful would it be with somebody who is really using their own experiences, their own life!

Jess: And just think, when someone is in trance their experiences are magnified and their emotions are magnified. It becomes far easier to do the association and dissociation pieces because they are right there with you.

Shawn: It's really nothing to do with smoking. It's much more to do with giving the younger self resources when it comes to decision-making, self-confidence, self image those kinds of things. And remember we are not coaching the 14-year-old... We are asking a much younger self to come sit with us in the movie theater, around six or seven years old, and the client is coaching them.

Jess: So adult client gives much younger self all the resources, and then unconsciously, when they float into the movie, they become lets say 14 years old, ...they grow up fast as they float into the movie (laughing), they are now in the scene... 14 years old... With a number of years of experience in how to deal with things.

The unconscious implication is that because all three are actually the client (the adult, the teenager about to smoke, and the much younger child) the resources have been generated. We as the hypnotist imply that things have changed when we say, "now watch the movie and notice how it is different" or "watch them saying no," or "what other skills would be useful in this scene?"

Karen: When I was role-playing the client, my older self was coaching my younger self and we were at the point where the younger self had resourced the teenager. We were watching the new movie, and the teenager self was telling the other boys in the movie not to smoke; he was teaching them the skills.

Shawn: So you have re-resource the imaginary friends of your imaginary client (*laughing*)

Jess: So maybe you will get phone calls from these imaginary friends telling you that they have quit smoking and they don't know why! (*laughing*).

Any other comments before we move on?

Yuval: I noticed with this type of re-imprinting work that people will have strong emotions.

Shawn: People can have strong emotions and that is fine. Keep in mind that there is a big difference between strong emotions and something like an abreaction. The tears of a strong emotion can be a very good thing for the client. We want the client to experience emotions. This is how change happens. Change comes from emotion. This is the fuel of change. If someone isn't emotional about something then they will not get the change.

Sarah: And we are not talking about floods of tears necessarily here. We are looking for an emotion being expressed.

Shawn: You are not specifically trying to get them to feel a negative emotion. That is why this pattern is dissociated. If they are watching it they will feel a little bit of emotion but because they are not in the movie they will not be fully associated into the emotion.

Jess: Think of this like a traditional re-imprinting in NLP. That event is happening somewhere else and I am safe here. The only association before the end of the pattern is found in the associating into the negative kinesthetic reaction to the cigarette. The rest is dissociated until we have built up a positive resource.

Kristina: When you are associating a client into the first smoking event do you really build up a sick feeling with the cigarette?

Jess: I want the client to have an intense experience of that memory. I don't want them to get sick or anything like that. Think of this as a revivification. If they didn't like their first cigarette and yet are smoking now, they probably haven't really been remembering that first time. If they were then they wouldn't be smoking.

Any other questions?

Lawrence: I am trying to put this pattern within the context of the entire session. Would this be after the Perceptual Possibilities Pattern?

Jess: You can think of these patterns as being specifically within the context of time. P_3 is about the future and the smoking destroyer is about the past.

Shawn: The Smoking Destroyer Pattern strips away the client's identity as a smoker. For the P$_3$ we need and use that identity in a contrasting way — so we have to do the P$_3$ pattern first, before we use the Smoking Destroyer to strip away the identity.

So we have two big patterns covered so far. We worked with the client's future and we worked with the client's past, leaving them in the present — which is a gift as Master Oogway in "Kung Fu Panda" would say.

The Protocol So Far

1. Initial phone call

2. Intake process noting Meta-Programs, Client pre-suppositions, time line organization, who else this change will effect, gathering leverage for the change

3. Provocative and metaphors

4. Craving Busters - E.F.T. and the Backwards Spin

5. Hypnosis Pre-talk and convincers (if it is the client's first time in trance)

6. Induction

7. Perceptual Possibilities Pattern

8. Smoking Destroyer

And all of this is done while in the Coaching State and while "Holding the Space"

Mercedes: I have to say this is a very comprehensive system. As a nurse I am always looking for real tools I can use in the outside world. So often we go to trainings where we walk away with no practical tools. This course is excellent and really delivers. With all of the training we have in NLP and CHPH I can really see the value here.

This is truly a tool that I can use out in the real world. Thank you.

Jess: Well thank you Mercedes we have worked really hard to put this together and we know it works.

We have changed timelines, we have changed identity and there are other things that we can do to continue this process. You'll learn ways of neutralizing environmental triggers so that the old automatic programs that the client was running before won't to be triggered anymore. We have ways of creating resources so that in the future they have a recovery strategy and ways to use deep trance phenomena to stabilize the change.

Jess: *So now...just take a moment to make yourself comfortable because trance is such a wonderful way to integrate everything you have accomplished this weekend, and I want to thank each and every one of you, with each of the best of both of you, or the best parts of each of you for sharing this weekend with us...we have accomplished so many amazing things and as you consider those and all of the things you have to maybe you can become aware of the comfortable feeling somewhere inside, may be comfort in your shoulders, or the legs or the neck or the mind wherever that comfort is for you and how ever you experience it you can rest your focus on that...*

Sarah: *... and as you rest... your awareness... begins to grow on just how comfortable you are, relaxed you are and on how good you are feeling now...*

Jess: *... if it's your breathing... relaxing through you now... and I do know that you get to find out... and really enjoy knowing... that you have an unconscious mind that can allow you to change minds, change experiences, change states with ease and comfort. Some of you may know stories about Milton Erickson, the world famous hypnotist from the 20th century. He used to live all the way down in the American Southwest, and back then he probably didn't fly to get to Arizona, he drove down through the US, changing states one at a time... and when client would come*

186

into his office and the first thing that Erickson would do was to come into trance... and when he's in trance... he very slowly looks up and he knows the client, right here in front of him is changing, because all we are is changing on the deepest unconscious levels...

Sarah: *... all we are is changing... all you are...is changing..all.. you are changing...*

Jess: *... with ease and comfort...*

Sarah: *... and Erickson knew this, holding on to the picture, the image, of your client is having changed already... seen as complete, whole... already changed... continuing the process of changing... as you are now...*

Jess: *... changing with ease...*

Sarah: *... learning...*

Jess: *... growing...*

Sarah: *... effortlessly...*

Jess: *... comfortably...*

Sarah: *... having fun...*

Jess: *... in ways that may surprise you...*

Sarah: *... flying on the wings of possibilities...*

Jess: *... a bright new future...*

Sarah: *... and finding ways of being even more of who you are...*

Jess: *... as a change worker and as an amazing human being...*

Sarah: *... practicing and allowing you ideas to truly sync in... deeply into your unconscious mind..*

Jess: *... changing and growing... process is happening...*

Sarah: *... and children learn easy and quickly changing all...the time...*

Jess: *...and I've heard it said that songbirds learn to sing in their sleep.*

Sarah: *... it's true... I know the man who met the woman who did the research.*

Jess: *... they take the young songbirds and put them in with the master songbird...*

Sarah: *... and the young songbirds listen and enjoy the songs that the master songbird is singing.*

Jess: *... and then at night, when the little songbirds go to sleep, and tuck their little heads under their wings, the researchers monitor the little song brainwaves and they notice that the same areas are lighting up in their brain as they do when they are first learning.*

Sarah: *... and I know tonight, at some point you will go home, enjoy your evening, and at some point you will go to bed...*

Jess: *... and when you go to bed, you will sleep... and when you sleep... you'll dream...*

Sarah: *... now some of you will have exciting dreams...*

Jess: *...and some of you will have boring mundane dreams...*

Sarah: *... some of you will have technical dreams...*

Jess: *...or black and white dreams...*

Sarah: *... some of you will have dreams with casts of thousands...*

Jess: *... or just a few... of you... will think that you have had no dreams at all...*

Sarah: *... and let that be a sign of the changes occurring on...*

Jess and Sarah: *... the deepest, unconscious level...*

Sarah: *... So you can wake up now...bright eyed and bushy brained...ready for Sunday night.*

Jess: Great job this weekend everyone thank you so much.

Day 3

Jess: So, let's begin with an open frame. Did anyone have any experiences since last week? Does anyone have any questions? Anything you'd like to share?

Karen: I did the "floating into another person" bit with one of the fifth-graders I work with. We were working on setting a goal for her to complete by the end of the school year. I was thinking about an academic goal, but she said, "you know, I've been really mean to my grandma and I want to be nice to her."

So I did the exercise with her, and I was watching her face and you could see there was lots of stuff going on and she was able to come up with ideas as to what she could do to make things better.

Shawn: So she floated into her grandma? Wow. You have changed that kid's life.

Karen: Yeah, I think I might have, a bit.

Shawn: You might have "a bit" transformed that kid's life!

Karen: Yeah it was neat!

Shawn: 30 years from now she'll say, "You know, there was this teacher at school, and she did this thing and it transformed my life!"

Karen: And we talked about that afterwards. If you're upset about something and you want to get the perspective of the other person, do this. It will help you to see how that other person is seeing things and feeling things — kids don't always have that perspective.

Jess: And teaching her that pattern at this age ensures that she's going to be doing it in other situations. Any other comments? Stories? Successes?

Mercedes: I tried the techniques with some people and really saw the change. And what I like so much about it is that we got real tools. It wasn't just cutesy, you have something to walk away with.

I was working with somebody who is in charge of nursing assessment, and I told her about how we were breaking things down in the phone interview and the intake, and she said, "have you thought about speaking to other student nurses and sharing this?"

Jess: I have a couple interesting experiences this week. On Thursday I had a client who came in to stop smoking, and in terms of Meta-Programs she was probably the most "toward" person I have ever met. When we started to talk about the reasons that she wanted to stop smoking, everything she said was "I want to feel healthy, I want to have more money, I want my fiancé to be proud of me."

It never even occurred to her to say, "I don't want to get sick, I don't want to waste money and I don't want to smell bad." As she began to talk about the positive, she began to cry. So when I did the Perceptual Possibilities pattern, I only took her through two or three of the negative steps and then did six or seven on the positive side.

Because when you have the person's Meta-Programs you can start to take any of these patterns tweak them, tailoring them to match the client's resources. Being incredibly "toward" can build immense leverage in a very positive direction.

The other thing was that we had arranged for a smoker to come in tomorrow so that we could do a demonstration of the protocol. I spoke with a woman on Thursday morning, and I was asking her, "Why do you want to quit?" Her first response was, "I'm a hypnotist so if I want to work with smokers I guess I shouldn't be a smoker." Would you have taken her on as a client?

Mercedes: Who does she want to do this for?

Jess: I asked her "Do you really want to quit?" And she sighed and said, "I'm not 100% sure." What do you guys think, would you guys take her on if she's not sure she wants to quit?

Lawrence: I would take her on for a session to clarify whether or not she wants to quit.

Mercedes: Perhaps she wants the acknowledgment and praise of her teacher.

Jess: There was a very strong external frame. There was also no energy behind the quitting. When you have a client and you ask them if they really want to quit, and they say they're not sure, there are two things you can do. You can have one session to explore the issue — I might've done that if she was a private client and not a demo subject. Or, I could say, call me back when you're ready to quit.

Something to bear in mind is that although we do want high success rates and we want people who are motivated, we are not the smoking police. If somebody doesn't want to quit at some level we need to honor that. But if they're not committed, if there's a part of them that still doesn't want the change, it is important to respect that.

Unfortunately now we don't have a demo for tomorrow! But it was an interesting conversation I thought it would be interesting to share.

Shawn: Perhaps her issue is at the level of identity. She wants to take on the identity of being a hypnotist, but she has a behavior which clashes with that, at least as far as she is concerned. This is called a confusion of logical levels.

191

She has a behavior which is not lined up with the identity that she wants.

Sarah: We are not saying that because you are a hypnotist you shouldn't be a smoker. I'm sure there are lots of hypnotists out there who smoke and who are fully aligned with their role as a hypnotist, and help other people to quit.

Lawrence: Could you address that by having her reassess the behaviors which go with that identity?

Shawn: Leaving aside whether or not she wants to quit and assuming she wants the identity of the hypnotist and she wants to continue smoking, you could expand her identity so that it's big enough to include the behavior of smoking.

My guess is that if you did that successfully, she would quit anyway because by stepping into that new identity she would realize she didn't need the smoking anymore.

Mark: I've worked with a lot of people like that and the Provocative approach works very well. Standing up for the existing behavior and matching it, yields tremendous results.

Shawn: Yes. Check out the videos of Fritz Perls who worked in the 50s and 60s and was a chain smoker. He would smoke while his clients were there and in fact there's a story that he once made a client hold out their hand and he used it as an ashtray. I don't know if that's true, but you will see videos of him in session and he is always smoking a cigarette. He's got a thick accent, and a quite aggressive attitude toward his clients, and I would've said to this woman, "you could be just like Fritz Perls! This famous therapist!" And maybe she would decide to be another type of hypnotist! That would be a provocative way of going.

Mercedes: Sometimes people get caught up with the idea that they have to be perfect before they can help somebody else.

Kathy: This is a huge problem for health coaches, who think they can't work with other people because they haven't totally fixed themselves, and it holds them back from doing the great work they could be doing.

Shawn: There is a story about a mother who brought her child to see Gandhi because the child ate a lot of sugary food, and she thought it was bad for him. And Gandhi said, "I can help him, but bring him back in two weeks."

The mother says, "why in two weeks, why not now?" And Gandhi says," just bring him back in two weeks." So in two weeks the mother brings the son back, and Gandhi speaks to the son and persuades him to stop eating sugar. The mother is very grateful and she says, "I don't understand, why did you make me wait two weeks?" And Gandhi says, "two weeks ago, I was eating a lot of sugar myself."

Jess: So even if we are not Gandhi, we can still help people to achieve their goals. So let's get moving into the second half of the protocol.

Today we are going to be exploring a couple of different patterns. The first one is a pattern Shawn developed called the Tiger pattern. After that, we will move into what to do when the client has secondary gain issues.

Secondary gain means when there is something else driving the behavior, some advantage or an "upside" that the client may or may not be consciously aware of. The client is smoking because smoking fulfills something else important in their life, and if they give up smoking, that need is not met.

We address the secondary gain because ultimately that is what is propelling the behavior. Yes, a small part of it is the habit, the mindlessness, but ultimately what is driving the behavior is the benefit which the client is getting out of it.

With the patterns that we were doing last week, we were working at the level of identity, and were were creating enormous amounts of leverage for change. But we haven't completely addressed what is underlying the behavior, but we are doing today!

Shawn: (*Unwraps a pack of cigarettes*)

Kathy: Did you have to buy those?

Shawn: We don't have to buy them, our clients leave us packs of them. Look how nicely it's wrapped — it's like the present! Aren't the cigarette companies nice!

Mercedes: I know people who leave them in the refrigerator to keep them fresh. Then they don't get stale, they don't get old.

Shawn: Right, because then they wouldn't be very nice! (*Laughter*) Stale is the least of their issues!

THE TIGER PATTERN

Shawn: The Tiger pattern, on its face, is very very simple. But really it's very very complex and rich, so we are going to spend a little bit of time on it. In this pattern we use the action of holding the cigarette and bringing it closer to the mouth and then away from the mouth. The normal way people smoke.

Before we get to the details of the pattern, we are going to take you back to the primeval swamp. Imagine that your ancient ancestor is in the swamp looking for food, and that they see a saber tooth tiger. (Hence the name of the pattern.) What is the one piece of information they need to know over and above everything else?

Mark: Does he see me?

Shawn: Yes, something like that...

Mercedes: Get out of the way.

Shawn: That's not information, that's a behavior. What is the piece of information which they want?

Yuval: The distance between them?

Shawn: Something like the distance...

Karen: Is he coming towards them?

Shawn: Bingo! Is this saber tooth coming toward me or moving away from me? Is the distance between us getting bigger or smaller? Because even if there is a distance between you and the saber tooth, if the saber tooth is coming towards you then you still have a problem. If the distance between you and the saber tooth is smaller, but the saber tooth is walking away you're probably in better shape. He didn't see you, or he isn't hungry. So what's important is, 'is the tiger coming towards me or is the tiger moving away from me?' And this is a fundamental piece of information, this is the fundamental way that we sort information.

Tomorrow we'll talk about the Swish Pattern which also is about moving pictures away and then moving them closer. You'll find that the sub-modalities which most impact us are size, distance, and brightness. This is because size and brightness are proxies for distance, in general the bigger something is and the brighter something is the closer it is, something gets bigger when it's closer, and smaller when it's further away. Same with brightness.

The Tiger pattern deals with whether something is moving towards us, or whether it's moving away.

There is a fascinating fact about compulsions. In my experience, when somebody has a compulsion it seems to be that the person's attention is *inside* the object of compulsion. They are pulled towards it because their attention goes inside it.

For example, we once did a demo with a muffin. We had the lady sitting in the chair and the muffin sitting on the table. We got the lady to put her attention on the space *in between* herself and the muffin, then to bring her attention back inside herself, and then to put her attention inside the muffin, and then to put her attention inside another object.

The time when she felt the most compulsion to eat a muffin was when she put her attention inside it.

Karen: Can you clarify what you mean by putting your attention inside something?

Shawn: Sure.

> *As you sit there, feeling your body in the chair, take a look at this nice bottle of water. Now put your attention on the space in between yourself and the water... Notice the relative spatial awareness between you and the*

water, where you are in relation to the water and where the water is in relation to you... The space in between... Now take your attention and bring it inside yourself, inside your body. You're still seeing the water but with your attention inside yourself... Now put your attention inside the water...

Put your attention back into the space in between, and I'm going to ask you to lift up one of your hands and direct the palm of your hand towards the water, almost like you were touching the bottle even though you can't reach it. So you're making a connection with the water, even though you can't touch it... Now put your attention on the space in between yourself and the water... Bring your attention back inside yourself, back inside your body... Bring your attention back into the space in between you and the water... And put your attention inside the water...(Student laughs).

Karen: Yes, when my intention is inside it, I want to grab it!

Shawn: So when a smoker wants a cigarette, they are not pushed towards it by desire. In general their attention goes inside it and they are pulled towards it, unconsciously.. And that's the second point.

The third point I want to introduce in terms of the pattern is something called the foreground-background switch. Essentially, it says that if you are paying attention to something, such as a cigarette, then by definition you are not paying attention to everything else. So the cigarette is in the foreground of your attention, and everything else is in the background of your attention.

Everything else in the universe! (Well, I guess you could be paying attention to your matches.) But your attention has gone down to one thing and everything else goes into the background. If you were paying attention to everything else, that cigarette would be so minuscule and unimportant it won't capture your attention at all. It would be just one thing out of everything in New York, or everything in the US, or everything in the world or the universe.

So those are the basic principles. The idea of closeness and whether something is moving closer or further away; the idea of your attention going inside the cigarette and pulling the smoker closer; and the idea of foreground and background. These three ideas are fundamentally hardwired into us and into our relationship with the object of our attention.

The Tiger pattern assumes that you have the negative and positive anchors set for the smoker. The negative anchors are around the bad things that will happen if they continue to smoke; the positive anchors around all the good things that will happen when they are a non-smoker.

If you are not getting a visceral reaction during the pattern, it means you have not got the anchor set correctly and that means you do not have the leverage to help them change.

We had a student in our NLP Master practitioner class, and she said, "I have been doing the Tiger pattern and it hasn't been working." I said, "tell me more about that, how has it not been working?"

The Tiger pattern is essentially getting the client to bring the cigarette closer to their mouth and then watching for their negative reaction. The student said, "I get them to hold the cigarette, and get them to move it closer to their mouth, but there's not a negative reaction."

I said, "that's impossible if you've done the first part of the pattern. Why? Because when you are working with a smoker, and you have them in your office with their cigarettes, they have to find the cigarettes disgusting or negative in some way. If they don't, then they are not going to quit."

So as you are doing this pattern and they are bringing the cigarette closer to their mouth, you are firing off the anchors which you have already set for the negative state. And if you have set those anchors right, then they have to go into the negative state. It's not about the cigarette, it's about you firing off the negative anchors.

So the great thing about this pattern is that it shows you whether or not you've done what you need to do to get leverage over the client. If you have, then the pattern is automatic. If the pattern is not working, then you have not done what you need to do in order to get leverage. Does that make sense?

Mercedes: So when they are craving, they are focused on the cigarette?

Shawn: When they are in a craving, they are most likely focused *inside* the cigarette. So in the pattern we are going to use a number of things. What is this called, hypnotically speaking? (*Holds a cigarette between his fingers*)

Group: Catalepsy.

Shawn: Quite right, it is catalepsy. If somebody smokes they are in catalepsy, which means that the unconscious mind has taken control of a part of their body, in this case their hand. If they are smoking, they don't want to consciously track where the cigarette is. If they did that, at some stage they would forget and they would burn somebody.

So there is a part of the mind whose intention is to make sure they don't accidentally burn their friends. (*Waving cigarette*)..."Oh, I'm sorry!"

And another part of their unconscious attention is inside the cigarette, pulling them in. And because they are unconsciously paying attention to the inside of the cigarette, they are unconsciously not paying attention to everything else. And this is the basis of the pattern.

So on the face of it we are simply associating this gesture (*moves hand closer to mouth*) with the negative, and this (*moves hand away from mouth*) with the positive, but as hypnotists you need to be aware that there is a lot more going on than meets the eye.

And just to give an experience of this, we will do a demonstration for group. So what I would like you all to do is to think of some behavior that you have behavioral control over. It could be what you eat...anything you're concerned about in your future which you have behavioral control over now.

Mark: Nail biting?

Shawn: Sure it could be nail biting, drinking too much coffee, eating too many chips, whatever you do or don't do. Has everybody got something...? Or are you all perfect...?

Student: How about exercising?

Shawn: Great, that's a great one!

> *So what I would like you to do is to think of the adverse effects of your behavior — the adverse effects of not exercising, or eating too many donuts, or whatever it is that you picked. It could be something you see on your body like putting on weight, something you feel inside yourself like not being able to breathe properly, perhaps a reaction that other people have to you, or some combination of those things...*
>
> *And as you think about that part, allow a symbol to form in your mind. It could be a picture of that thing, all purely symbolic, perhaps a picture of yourself in the*

future if you don't do the exercise, or continue to eat the jelly doughnuts...

Have you all got something? Some symbol or image?

What I would like to do now is to hold out your hand, right or left, and see that picture that image that symbol on the palm of your hand. Do you have that...? So you're seeing the symbol on the palm of your hand...

And I would like you to begin to put the negative experiences — whether that's a feeling, a lack of energy, a response that people are giving to you, whatever that might be — put those negative experiences inside the symbol. Put them inside the symbol, so that they are inside.

And then I would like you to allow that hand to move up towards your face only as fast as you can double the intensity of those negative feelings with each inch that it moves...

Moving it towards your face only as fast as you can double the negative feelings. Allow it to move closer inch by inch... Each inch doubling the negative feelings... The negative feelings... The negative responses you're getting from the people around you... Now just allow the hand to return to where it was.

And as you look at the symbol now I'd like you to begin to pay attention to, aside from a symbol, what's everything else that's not that. What's everything else that is not that, everything in the world, everything in your life, that's not that. Everything that is not that symbol. And I would like you to move your hand away, inch by inch, only as quickly as you notice that for each inch it moves away there's more space between you and the symbol... And therefore everything else is able to fill that space up, everything that's not the symbol can come into your life and through that space. Everything else

201

you want to be can come into that space and fill up that space.

Now allow your hand to move back toward your face, and for each inch it moves toward your face double those negative feelings. The negative feelings associated with that behavior, or lack of behavior, the negative feelings double. The negative feelings you have, the negative responses of the people around you, doubling with each inch as it moves towards your face.

And now allow your hand to move away, and with each inch it moves away, everything else, everything else you want in your life, can move in to fill that space in-between. Each inch it moves away there is more space for everything else to come in, everything else that is not that...

Now shake that symbol off your hands (*demonstrates*) and come back into the room.

How was that?

Mark: Wow.

Shawn: That's a wow from Mark. Did everybody get something...? And this is the basis of the pattern, and we do this with cigarettes and it looks like it's very simple, but there's a lot going on under the surface. It looks like we're simply doing a sliding anchor with a cigarette, but actually there's a lot more going on with the pattern.

Lawrence: When you're running your client through this, are you seeing changes in their affect? Changes in their posture?

Shawn: You have to be seeing that. When the smoker comes to see you when you asked them "why do you want to quit?" and they say, "Well, for my health I guess, (*shrugging shoulders*) and maybe...errrm... I don't want my clothes to smell," then that's not it. You have no leverage if that's what they tell you.

Anyone can tell you that they want to quit smoking because of health or the smell, or whatever. If there is no affect in why they want to quit, then there is no leverage. We are asking them why they WANT to quit, not why they think they should. "Want" is a state of desire.

So before you start this exercise you have to be in the position where you can ask them, "As you consider the health effects of cigarettes…" and you see them going to a negative state, you see a negative affect. This pattern then becomes a slam-dunk because you say, "I want you to move the cigarette towards your mouth only as quickly as you can consider the health effects of cigarettes…"

So you know before you start that you will get the negative affect, the negative state, the negative reaction. Don't do this pattern if you don't have the anchors set!

Lawrence: So the anchoring is the things that we've done prior to doing this exercise?

Shawn: Yes, you're starting to set the anchors when you're doing the intake. On the intake form when you asked them why they want to stop smoking and they talk about the negative health effects, you have to see them going into the state. If you don't, then you might as well give them a piece of paper listing the reasons people stopped smoking and asked them to check-off the ones that apply to them! Check check check.

This is all about leverage, this is all about having the emotional palette they will need to quit. Positive and negative.

Jess: When I do this pattern, I like to do it after I've done the Perceptual Possibilities. After you've done the Perceptual Possibilities you will have very strong positive and negative anchors set. The likelihood that they would want to bring the cigarettes to their mouth after that is very slim.

Karen: So if we do the Perceptual Possibilities pattern we would have the anchors set — but you're saying that even if we haven't done that pattern we would have anchors from the intake for why they want to quit?

Shawn: I am saying that if you don't have the emotions associated with why they want to quit, then both you and your client are in bad shape! At some stage in the process you have to hook them into the negatives of smoking, and the positives of not smoking. You can't fail with this pattern if you have the anchors set. When you're doing the pattern, it's nothing about the cigarette, it's the anchors that you're using. And then moving the cigarette closer, fires the anchors off that you already have.

What does that do, in terms of anchoring?

Group: Collapsing them?... Adding to them?... Making them more conscious?... Moving away?

Shawn: You're transferring the anchors onto the cigarette.

Karen: The cigarette becomes the anchor! Moving closer for the negatives, and further away for the positives.

Shawn: Right! Think of Pavlov's dogs, they ring the bell and the dog salivates. This has nothing to do with the bell, is has to do with the food. They ring the bell and feed the dog, and the dog salivates. They ring the bell and feed the dog, and the dog salivates. Finally they ring the bell and the dog salivates. Originally it was the food that was the anchor for the salivation, but then they transferred the anchor onto the bell.

You have to set your negative anchors with the clients during the intake, or during the Perceptual Possibilities pattern, and you transfer those onto the cigarette. The cigarette becomes a sliding anchor for the negative state and the positive state.

Sarah: This is also a great convincer for the client. This is probably the first time in years that they have had this reaction to cigarettes and so they think "something must be different now!" It's a very powerful pattern.

Shawn: And think about where they have to put their attention to want to smoke. They have to put it inside the cigarette so that's where you put all the negatives. If they pop their attention inside the cigarette, they realize they don't want to be in there because it's disgusting. Get this away from me!

Yuval: So if all you're doing is giving them words, then the pattern may not work, but if they have the feelings...

Shawn: Right. Once more make sure you have the anchors set before you do the pattern. When you have the anchors set and they start to move the cigarettes towards their mouth they're going to think "Oh God, I feel really bad!" So they will think there has been this magical change. What they don't realize is that you have set the anchors.

Karen: I haven't done my NLP training, so anchoring is harder for me to grasp. So let's say the client hasn't been exercising enough because they get tired. Would I be talking about that with them as their hand is coming closer?

Shawn: You are young right (*laughter*)... You're not old! So if you don't workout on a regular basis, you might say something like:

> At this point in your life you have a choice of two directions. You know that if you continue to work out, continue to keep yourself strong, keep your joints strong, keep your muscles strong, stay flexible, keep your heart and lungs in good shape, stretch, keep your bones

205

strong, then as you get older these are the sorts of things that will pay real benefits and real dividends. And we have all seen the people who are climbing mountains and running in marathons and we think 'how do they do that?' Well the fact is they reached a certain point in their life and they made a decision that they were going to take care of themselves. And that decision allowed them to have decades of high quality healthy active life.

There are other people who make a different lifestyle choice, and at some point it becomes too late for them. They've made a lifestyle choice and they are not working out, not stretching, not maintaining their strength, not taking care of their heart and their lungs. Instead they're sitting in front of the TV, they're eating junk food, they're not taking exercise, and not making the effort to walk a few blocks every day to walk upstairs rather than taking the elevator. And over time it begins to show on their body both outside and inside.

And other people might see them and rather than thinking, "wow, this person is 70 or 80 and is climbing a mountain" they might say, "This person who's 55 and looks like their 80!' So these are the choices we have in our lives especially as we reach these watershed years.

So as you think about the options which you have, which we both have, of saying "screw it, I don't have the time and I don't have the energy, I am going to sit in front of the TV and eat junk food, I'm going to take cabs everywhere, I'm not going to walk it's too much effort." And you know where that leads.

So as you hold out that hand now, and you consider that as a possibility, that option or being a couch potato, unhealthy, and where that leads to... That's right!... And now you're feeling that... As you consider that as a possibility I don't want that hand to move towards your face any faster than you can double those feelings. And I know that's not a path that you are going to take but it's possible, you could if you chose to. So I don't want that hand to move towards your face any faster than you can double what that would be like, to be a couch potato, unhealthy... There you go, this is anchoring! (Laughter)...

Any faster than you can double those negative feelings, and negative consequences, what it will be like at the age of 55, to have had five years of no exercise, your joints becoming stiff and locking up, your muscles and sinews wasting away inside (Laughter)...

But now there is another option (student's hand immediately begins to move away from her face, which takes on a look of relief - class laughs)... *Which is everything except that, everything that is not that, everything aside from that. And as that hand begins to move away from you, it begins to create space for all those other possibilities to come in. Now I don't know what those possibilities are for you, as that hand moves away, whether that's the possibility of exercising or how you look when you do, or how your muscles will feel when they are loose and lean and strong and flexible, when you're able to run easily for the bus. Or whether it's just a picture of you at the age of 85 climbing a mountain and having everyone else say "wow, how did she do that" and you know that it's because every day you're making good choices, and every inch that hand moves away it opens up space for you to have those options...*

That's right, and now you can shake that off your hand. That is anchoring, and when you are with a client you can talk about the implications of their choices, and when you see something happen you know that's it, that's the anchor.

Rita: Do you do a break state?

Shawn: You do a break state, but if you're in the middle of an exercise you don't necessarily want to do a big break state because it will also break trance. So a simple way of doing a break state is to say, "Aside from that, what is everything else that can come into that space..." That's a small break state.

In the Tiger pattern, if you have set the anchors properly, the relief that the client will feel at being able to move their hand away will be palpable. (*To student who did demo*) Is that not true?

Karen: Oh yes, as soon as my hand began to move away I said "I'm doing my yoga!"

Shawn: At the point the hand changes direction, guide them to create a break state. Something like, "aside from that..."

So now we will do an exercise. Working in pairs, find some behavior that your client wants to change such as exercising more, or eating less jelly doughnuts. Find the negative consequences and set some negative anchors.

(*Students do exercise*).

Shawn: Welcome back everyone! I saw people going way beyond the instructions, and that's a great thing!

Mercedes: We are overachievers!

Yuval: When I looked at the image I saw a picture of an old lady coughing and choking and that had an effect. If I just looked at a cigarette, it had no effect.

Shawn: So in that case you could take the image of the old lady and put it inside the cigarette.

Yuval: You put the old lady in the cigarette? And then you light it? (*Laughter*).

Lawrence: What do you do with a pipe smoker, who doesn't move their hand backward and forward, they're just holding their pipe?

Shawn: I have never worked with a pipe smoker, do they just keep it in their mouth? I would imagine they have to bring it to their mouth at some stage, at the start of the procedure? But feel free to modify it, for example you could put all the negatives in as they put the tobacco into the pipe, or whatever they do. I didn't even know people still smoked pipes!

Yuval: I know people who smoke pipes, but nobody complains about it because they don't inhale.

Lawrence: That's right, they just get jaw cancer rather than lung cancer.

Kristina: The emphasis is on the negative, right?

Shawn: Yes, we start with a negative because very often that's what they are focusing on... that's why they came to see you. But there is so much more than that to focus on, and moving their hand away allows all those good things to come in. So they think wow, I have all these options!

You can use the positive anchors, healthy breathing, clear skin and so on... but I like this idea of "what is everything else," all those possibilities!

Lawrence: Do you ever have a client who is comfortable smoking but is feeling pressure from other aspects of their life, and they come to you and ask you to relieve those other pressures so that they can enjoy smoking?

Shawn: No. As a provocative measure I might say, "All those other people want you to stop smoking and you don't want to, I can deal with that so you can be a happy smoker." I'd do that as a provocative measure so that they can accept that own desire to be smoke-free.

So now let's do the rest of the pattern. We have set the negative anchors, which we would normally do during the intake. We would also set positive anchors. After all, we might as well!

Because we want it to work in the outside world, we will get the client to hold a cigarette in their fingers and then induce catalepsy in the smoking hand. (We are going to be doing more with catalepsy later so if you're not used to working with catalepsy you'll get a chance to practice more then.)

Then put the negatives inside the cigarette, because that's where their attention goes when they smoke, so the negatives will be waiting there for them if they decide to smoke. Then we will anchor "everything else," as in "what is everything else that is not the cigarette." Obviously that will include the positives, but also a lot more than that.

Then we will get them to move their hand in as we fire the negative anchors, and you'll see them react appropriately, pulling away from the cigarette as it comes in. Then we will get them to move their hand away as we fire the anchors for the positives and for "everything else."

Jess: And you could also use the anchors that came out of the Perceptual Possibilities pattern. That's the way I do it.

Rita: How many times do you go back and forth?

Shawn: It's a judgment call. You do want to do it enough to condition it, but if you're doing it 30 times and it's still not working then you haven't got the anchors set. Even if you're doing it once and it doesn't work you haven't got the anchors set! You need to do it enough times so that you get the reaction. They pull their head away or they can't move their hand toward their face without you having to fire the verbal anchors. The cigarette itself has become the anchor.

Sarah: Very often, when they are in trance, they simply refuse to move it towards their face. Their unconscious mind says, "No, not anymore!"

Lawrence: It hadn't dawned on me that you are doing this in trance.

Shawn: Yes it is in trance. It doesn't necessarily need to be a deep trance, that's up to you.

Sarah: Smoking is itself a trance; you're hijacking their smoking trance.

Shawn: And after you've done it a few times, you are testing it. You're getting them to move their hand and the cigarette in towards their face without you saying anything. You want to make sure the cigarette itself has become the anchor. In fact this is a continuum where each time they move it towards their face you use less and less of the anchor. This is called "backing off the anchor" in NLP.

Then you can also do a future pace, by getting them to imagine doing it in all the times and places they usually smoke.

Shawn: So get back into your pairs and complete the exercise.

Jess: How was that, everybody? Welcome back guys!

Group: (*Excited chatter*)

Shawn: Obviously a transformative pattern…

Lawrence: Wow, just wow! In the final test she asked me to bring my hand back towards my face, and it didn't want to come back! I knew what was going on, but my hand was saying No! No! No!

Kristina: Yes, my hand just froze and there was nothing I could do!

Kristina: I have this idea, supposing someone comes in with anger issues, and if they were to see their own angry face on the palm of their hand, see themselves screaming, would that work?

Shawn: I would think so. Congratulations, you've just invented a new pattern! You just combine the Perceptual Positions pattern with the Tiger pattern, and a new pattern is born!

Sarah: The Angry Tiger pattern!

Shawn: It sounds like it would be a great pattern. Lets try it out! Everybody pick a context where you might get angry, or grouchy, or otherwise disagreeable to those around you. Because we all do that right? And put that on your hand, that picture of yourself on your hand, facing towards you. Bring that picture towards you only as quickly as you can double the intensity of what you're experiencing from the receiving end of that, with each inch that it moves closer... Yes, that's an awesome pattern!

Jess: Any other observations, questions, comments...

Lawrence: The challenge was to find negative anchors on the fly, and to find which would land with her, watching her reaction and saying "OK, more of that!" And as I did that I became more aware of Meta-Programs, whether she was more "toward" or more "away-from".

Shawn: The Tiger pattern tends to work better with an "away-from" person. The whole point of the pattern is that they think "I want to get away from that, but it's coming closer!"

Jess: When I do the Tiger pattern, I use a visual metaphor to close it by saying, "That's right, as you think of all the times in the future when you get to be smoke-free..." And I throw the cigarette onto the floor. That is an incredibly powerful visual metaphor for the client.

I will leave the cigarette on the floor, and at the end of the session when I am testing the entirety of the work, the first thing I do is to pick up the cigarette off the ground and say "Do you want this?" There are all sorts of nuances that you can add into the pattern, and is very very powerful. Ok everyone let's take a break.

THE DREAMING ARM PATTERN

Jess: How many people are familiar with the Dreaming Arm Pattern?

(one or two students raise their hands.)

Jess: All right! The Dreaming Arm utilizes catalepsy and arm levitation as well as a whole lot of suggestion and implication. This is where your Ericksonian language skills get to come out and play! We will spend some time going over catalepsy and arm levitation so we are all really comfortable with that, then we can build them into the full Dreaming Arm Pattern later today.

Catalepsy

Jess:

> *Now catalepsy and arm levitation are connected, but not quite the same. If you have arm levitation you have catalepsy, but if you have catalepsy you don't necessarily have arm levitation.*
>
> *A few months ago we were on a training in Amsterdam with Igor Ledochowski, our friend and teacher, and Igor asked for a volunteer to come up on stage to have a hypnotic experience. This was an Ericksonian hypnotherapy workshop, so the client comes up and sits on a high chair in front of everyone. And Igor starts to talk and because it is an Ericksonian course, Igor had to talk in a very specific kind of way, reminiscent of Erickson with a low gravelly voice, and as he is talking about trance and taking a few moments to go inside, this volunteer who was sitting up on the stage begins to relax and feel very comfortable. His physiology shifts, the color in his face changes and I can even see the shift in his breathing from where I'm sitting.*

And something very interesting begins to happen. As this man is going into trance he is no longer communicating with the hypnotist... verbally... But he is unconsciously communicating... and the primary way he is doing that is through tiny movements in his hands. First it starts with a finger twitching, then a hand begins to move, more fingers begin to move. And as I am sitting there watching this I was thinking back to a training that I had gone to a few weeks before in this very room, where we are now, with John Overdurf.

And John began to tell a story and I don't remember really what the content of the story was but I do remember that it began by talking about going all the way down... to the American Southwest...and how Erickson moved at one time in his life from a cold climate to somewhere that was warm. And as he went down to the American southwest he had to change many states...And as John is telling the story, I noticed that his hand begins to move in a very particular way, and as John does this was of course a nested loop...and it began with Erickson but then it shifted to a story about the Buddha who was giving a teaching...and to give his teaching he had to climb to the top of a very tall hill. And at first the journey was slow and he had to take one step at a time to get to the top...and he knew that when he got to the top of the hill there will be people there waiting to learn, to grow, to change...

And I am sitting in the chair and I can feel myself going into trance as he is telling the story, and I remember a time even further back when I was talking with Shawn...And Shawn is a phenomenal hypnotist, as is Sarah, and Shawn was talking about arm levitation at a practice night...And there was a question about how do you get an arm to lift...And Shawn began to do a demo about how to think about an arm almost like it's floating, like it's resting on a cloud, or on a hypnotic shelf, or perhaps being carried by birds higher and higher...And as he was describing this my hands began to lift up in a very characteristic unconscious way...

And as that happens he said to me "you know... you can think about all the times and all the places when you could use resources, and it doesn't matter if you consciously know when those times and places are... because your unconscious mind knows... That's right... Your unconscious mind knows where to place all those learnings...the things that you've learned today...the things that you learn last week...and the learnings that you've made even outside of this room...And your unconscious mind can fit those learnings into all the right places so that you can develop even more skills, skills and understandings that you won't even be aware of yet that can begin to happen...Because you are a complete person with a conscious mind, and with an unconscious mind. And the unconscious minds know so much more about creating positive change in many aspects of your life.

Because your conscious mind processes 7 plus or minus 2 pieces of information at any one time...while...your unconscious mind... that's right... there you go... processes everything else. So as that hand continues to lift and be comfortable...finding just the right height either in the outside world or in your imagination...you can rest...assured knowing that you can draw upon a lifetime of memories...dreams...hopes...experiences because the unconscious mind is a generalization machine that can take all those wonderful things and apply them in your presence and well into your future.

And eventually that hand can begin to drift down as it places all of those new resources into the points in your life where you can find them useful...and of course my hands started to drift down and John continued his story about how...at the end of that teaching, you have to go back down the mountain...going back down can be so

216

much easier with all the new learnings which have been put in place...and you simply get a chance to enjoy the rest... on the journey down...and I was in Amsterdam, and Igor was talking for a very very long time, with this volunteer...And when that volunteer found his hand returning...he reoriented back to the room completely transformed...I knew this because his physiology had completely shifted.

And when people in the room asked "what happened, what was this experience" he hadn't any conscious idea and yet something had taken place on the deepest unconscious level. And it was a profound shift.

Catalepsy is a naturally occurring phenomena. If you find yourself going out with friends for a drink, and engrossed in a conversation, just like we are now, and suddenly you realize it has been 10 minutes and your hand has not even moved, that's catalepsy. We are really good at it and we do it naturally, which means that your client, when they come to see you, already has all the resources that they need to do it.

How many people feel comfortable using catalepsy? Some of you. And for those who are, how do you induce catalepsy?

Group: Just notice it... Lift the arm up... Bring their attention onto the arm... A direct request followed by distraction.

Jess: For example?

Kristina: "Hold out this hand... And now hold out the other hand..."(*Demonstrates holding the left then the right hands out*).

Jess: Yes. And so to begin to build the Dreaming Arm, I'd like to you do an exercise, in pairs, and orient your client's attention to their hand.

(*turning to Shawn*) Shawn, can I borrow your hands?

Shawn: Sure.

Jess: Thank you. So I would like for you to pay attention to both of your hands, and have an awareness of the feelings in each of the hands. Notice how they feel resting on your lap, and as you do that, which hand right now feels lighter?

Shawn: Left.

Jess: Good…and which one feels warmer?

Shawn: Errmmm… Left.

Jess: That's right, left is lighter and warmer. And which hand for you is most comfortable?

Shawn: Right.

Jess: That's right! Now come all the way back.

We are looking for three specific things: which hand is heavier and which hand is lighter; which hand is warmer and which hand is cooler; which hand is more comfortable. A very quick two minute exercise. Stick to physiological experiences for now.

(*Students begin exercise, Shawn and Jess join in too as a pair.*)

Jess: (*to Shawn*) Shawn, which hand is happier?

Shawn: They are both happy in different ways.

Jess: Ah, they're both happy in different ways, and which of those happinesses draws your attention most…

Shawn: Left.

Jess: And what kind of happiness is that?

Shawn: The left is more gregarious, and the right is more self-contained…

Jess: The left is more gregarious and the right is more self-contained, and isn't it interesting that the hand that is more gregarious gets lighter? So there are different kinds of happiness, and different kinds of weight, isn't that cool? And which one of those hands is your trance hand?

Shawn: It depends on the trance.

Jess: It depends on the trance, and right now which of your hands is the trance hand?

Shawn: They are both in trance... the gregarious trance... And the self-contained trance...

Jess: That's right...there you go...that's right...

Coming back in your own time...

Jess: Welcome back everyone. Fun eh?

So let me ask you, at what point did you notice the catalepsy?

Lawrence: Right after "which hand is warmer." As soon as I have the answer to that question, my hand already has a slight twitch and is lifting up.

Jess: So you already had catalepsy, awesome! Did you expect that? Congratulations! And the thing with catalepsy is that every single person here has experienced it before, and not necessarily in the hypnosis world. If you have ever been distracted while holding your coffee cup or wine glass...that's catalepsy.

How about when you are on the phone? That is catalepsy too! It happens naturally and we can help our clients to experience it when they are in trance. I hope you're feeling really good because not only did you get catalepsy but you also got arm levitation right away. Well done!

Lawrence: My partner did something really sneaky and subtle, because right away before we started we were talking about how I'm very analytical and cognitive, and the pattern requires the presupposition that one hand is warmer than the other. She created space by saying, "If one of these hands is warmer than the other, which would it be?" And my conscious mind grasped on to that and said "oh I have a choice."

Shawn: Another slightly different way of doing this is if the client says "Oh, I think they are the same," you can say "are they exactly the same?" Obviously they can't be exactly the same, and that gives them the space to find a little bit of a difference.

Jess: And while maintaining rapport and with a twinkle in your eye you can also say, "That's right, you really think they are the same..." And they begin to doubt..."If I only think it, there must be something else going on..."

Rita: This hand was both cold and warm, the same hand, at the same time.

Shawn: So your hand was saying, "It's me, whatever the question is, it's me! Cooler, it's me! Warmer, it's me! Just pick me!"

Jess: For the next exercise we're going to focus specifically on a heavy hand and on a light hand. The people on the right side of the room, are you the heavy hand or the light hand?

Karen: Heavy hand!

Jess: That means the people on the left are the light hand. If you are on the heavy hand side, your job as the hypnotist is to wallow in the heaviness. Ask which hand is heavier, and then bring their attention to the heaviness. Layer on the implications and suggestions around heaviness. And for those on the light hand side, find out which hand is lighter. Find out whether it is lighter in the palm or in the fingers, and play with the lightness.

(*Students do exercise.*)

Jess: Coming all the way back... What did everybody experience? What did you notice?

Mark: I noticed that although one hand lifted, the other hand was actually in deeper catalepsy.

Jess: Wow, you guys skipped ahead to arm levitation? So you had one arm in arm levitation and the other in deep catalepsy. Interesting!

Lawrence: I want my membership card in the trance junkie society! I had arm levitation in the non-heavy arm, while the heavy arm was so heavy it pulled my leg over to one side (*Laughter*).

Kathy: My hand was twitching as if it was ready to go!

Jess: Shawn explained to me once that the hand twitches are a sign that the hand wants to go up! (*Laughter*).

Shawn: If you want to get levitation and your client is twitching their fingers then you can say, "Did you know that the twitching of your fingers is going to be followed by the raising of your hand..." This is pacing and leading, pacing current experience.

Let me ask you this, when you were the hypnotist were you speaking on the "in" breath or the "out" breath? Look at Jess with her hand out. Jess, I would like you to take a deep breath in... What happens?

Yuval: The hand went up!

Shawn: Right. The hand goes up because of the expansion of the chest, and the effect this has on the chest and shoulder muscles. So if you want to get arm levitation you should speak on the in-breath of the client. It's the opposite of what you would normally do, speaking on the out-breath to deepen trance.

Jess: So you won't always get arm levitation with the client, because they don't yet know what is expected. You will get catalepsy where the hand stays very still. And there are all sorts of techniques you can use to get the levitation, such as speaking on the in-breath. But there is also a cheat that you can do to help them to jump on board with the catalepsy and the levitation. And if you want to learn how to do that, I highly suggest that you come back in one hour, because it is lunchtime!

Arm Levitation

Jess: So this morning we practiced orienting the clients awareness to their hands...which hand is lighter?...which hand is warmer?...which hand's more comfortable? And you already got catalepsy and arm levitation. You are light years ahead! But we will be introducing another step because there will be times when we have catalepsy in the arm but the hand doesn't want to automatically move. So we have another step to this and it's the suggestion of arm levitation.

There are all sorts of different ways to do this. You may find in the orienting that it happens automatically. When that happens, you encourage it. You may find that as part of the trance process you notice that the clients fingers are twitching, so you encourage it. We call this utilization. This morning there was a lot of this going on when you were orienting.

And as hypnotists, coaches, NLPers, we have even more tools available. We can craft metaphors and stories around arm levitation without directly doing it. For example, imagine the arm is being lifted by birds.

While we were at lunch, Mercedes shared a beautiful metaphor. Before we begin let me check, how many of you have a dog or a cat? How many of you like dogs or cats?

How many of you are comfortable with a dog or a cat? Mark? I'm running out of yes sets here!?

Sarah: Who is a dog or a cat?? (*Mark finally raises his hand.*)

Group: (*laughing...*)

Jess: So if you've ever had a dog or been around a dog, they have this wonderful habit especially when you are just sitting there comfortably and just hanging out, maybe talking with someone or watching TV, they have this uncanny ability to get you to levitate you arm. And they do it by just coming up to you and just wriggling their nose under your hand and the next thing you know, their entire head is under your hand (*laughing*), and they are just waiting to be petted...has anyone had this experience?

Group: Mmmm, oh yeah.

Jess: It is naturally occurring arm levitation.

Sarah: So you can build a beautiful metaphor, especially if their hand or fingers are beginning to twitch and you know that they are a dog or a cat owner...

> And just imagine your dog Ginger gently comes and sits beside you and all of a sudden she is snuggling her little nose underneath your hand... and you feel your hand gently moving upwards as she nudges her nose under your hand...moving upwards...

You are building it in a story-like fashion, and just see what happens. Thanks Mercedes!

Jess: And I'm sure if you were to brainstorm you could come up with all sorts of different metaphors. A classic one I like to use is:

> you know that feeling, if you were to imagine that someone were to come over and comfortably tie a string around your wrist and just begin to pull up, could you imagine what that would feel like?

Anything that is not going to directly suggest the arm levitation but you are going to imply it. You're starting to build a resource for the client. So we've had utilization, metaphor, and there is one last piece.

The next element is suggestion and there are different types of suggestion you can use...of course it's all suggestion, but just for clarity I am going to give it it's own subheading. You can suggest that:

> *the hand is getting lighter and lighter and maybe that hand would like to lift, perhaps you could feel what it would be like if that hand were to gently float up, and up and up.*

You can also use physical touch. Indiscriminately touching the hand and very lightly, especially if you see the fingers twitching. If you see that someone's hand or arm is in catalepsy then there is a good chance that it will levitate.

So if you see it happening during the trance process then you can go ahead and just lift the arm and begin to tell a metaphor. Ask that hand to find a comfortable place to stay.

Rita: Even the touching is suggestion right?

Jess and Sarah: Yes.

Jess: Yes the touching is a very gentle, very light touch often under the hand and arm to suggest an "up" motion. So you're always implying the lifting. When the hand is in catalepsy and you pick it up it's going to stay pretty much where you leave it. That's the nature of catalepsy. So once you have the catalepsy you know that the arm levitation will be pretty easy.

So you've got metaphor, verbal suggestion, non-verbal suggestion, timing it with the in-breath and continuing to encourage the trance phenomena that you see. Ok?

So lets do an exercise, three minutes each, hypnotist and client, and play with these ideas. New partners, old partners, any partner will do!

(*Students do exercise.*)

Jess: How was that?

Lawrence: Uplifting!!!

Sarah: Oh Lawrence, you've been waiting all day to use that one!!!

(*laughing*)

Jess: So what did you learn...notice...observe?

Yuval: I had a wonderful experience and I realized that I am the one who is stopping myself...blocking myself from wherever I'm going. Do you have any exercise to help me to get out of my way?

Sarah: Is it your conscious mind that is coming in and talking and rationalizing to you?

Yuval: Yeah..and then I am saying, "get out of my way." I can see the limit and it's all inside of me.

Jess: Yes, it is all inside of you it absolutely is. Where else would it be? Even with all the conscious things going on, what was happening in your arm?

Yuval: My arm was going up very slightly, but I was blocking it from going any higher. For some reason, when we finished the exercise, and even before we began, I can see myself blocking it from smoothly going all the way.

Jess: May I make a suggestion?

Yuval: Yes.

Jess: You are absolutely free to block it or not block it and maybe you want to experiment with that. See how long you can block it. See how long you can block it before it goes all the way up.

Yuval: I can do that all my life!

Jess: And yet the arm was moving on it's own.

Sarah: And have you spoken to your conscious mind and asked it to just take a back seat for a while? Or you can allow your unconscious mind to speak to your conscious mind about unconsciously allowing things to happen.

Yuval: They probably do... but consciously I don't know what they are saying.

Sarah: Of course you don't. Sometimes when I have clients who are getting in their own way, and this happens from time to time, and I usually suggest a very simple thing that works well. I ask my client to just say "shhhhh" to the conscious mind when it begins to distract or chatter. And often something as simple as that can work. I've seen it happen many times.

Jess: I used to be highly analytical when it came to going into trance and I would say things like, "I wonder if I am going into trance;" or, "oh I like that phrase I'm going to use that." It used to drive me insane. So I had a conversation with John Overdurf when he was here in New York and he said to just stop caring, to just let it talk...and it stopped.

Sarah: It's ok to acknowledge that it is there, but that something else is going on too.

Secondary Gain

So let's continue on with our next building block for this Dreaming Arm pattern. We need to address the issue of secondary gain. Now with smokers, and with any problems in general, you have something called secondary gain. Every behavior is motivated by a positive intention. Every behavior.

The behavior itself may not be a positive thing, like smoking is not such a great behavior. However it is doing something for them and it's not the nicotine, it's not the chemicals, the smoking is doing something emotionally for them. It may be helping to let go of stress, or may be meeting an emotional need that was satisfied when the client first began smoking. There are issues around socialization, fitting in, or every once in a while you'll have a client who wants to keep people away. So, while the behavior is not good, the intention behind it is very valuable. If you recall last week we talked about the presuppositions which clients walk in with such as, "if I stop smoking, I'm going to get fat." If the secondary gain is not addressed, they very well may put on weight because they may substitute a new behavior, such as eating, to satisfy the secondary gain, whatever that might be. So to do a complete piece of change work, on one level we address the behavior, and on another level we deal with identity, and on another level we deal with the outcomes, and on another level the visual triggers, and on a deeper level, the emotions behind it.

Sometimes the clients may know consciously what the secondary gain is, and sometimes they may think they know, but it may be something else. We need to have something built into the session to address the secondary gain issues, so that when the client leaves the office, not only are they not smoking, but they do not need to begin any new unresourceful behaviors. The positive emotion behind the smoking, the thing that was driving the behavior has been satisfied in a new and healthy manner. And for the rest of today we are going to be focusing on exactly how do we do that. There are direct ways and there are indirect ways, and as long as the secondary gain is addressed you are ensuring a high level of success.

So how do we link this into the Dream Arm Pattern? We have the client in trance, their arm is cataleptic and levitating. I am sure that everyone is wondering what to do now that you have your clients' hand in the air! We can use it to meet issues of secondary gain because this arm levitation is unconscious.

The body is a direct link with the unconscious mind. If you think about it, your heart rate, your breathing, your blinking — when you don't bring conscious awareness to the breathing and blinking, it happens automatically. All of your body's functioning is at the unconscious level. So when we start playing with arm levitation and catalepsy we are interacting directly with the unconscious mind. We are not getting the conscious filters that we usually have through verbalizing what is going on. When it comes to secondary gain issues, even if it is outside the conscious awareness of the client, we can start stacking the deck in their favor so that those gains can be addressed in a way that is healthy.

Lawrence: So you don't have to have identified the secondary gains?

Jess: No.

Lawrence: You just assume they are there because the other behavior just wouldn't be there.

Jess: Anytime a client comes in with in issue, and this is not just for smoking, there is an element of secondary gain in it. If there wasn't then the client wouldn't be doing it. Through speaking with the client you start to get a sense. They probably won't consciously know or say, "Oh I have this secondary gain of X." You might come across that but it is pretty rare. You are more likely to pick it up through what they are not saying, and what they are saying just under the surface of the words.

With this pattern, the hypnotist doesn't have to know what the secondary gain is, because we are giving the unconscious mind the space to explore and change. It knows what it the problem is, and knows how to find ways of resolving it that are healthy and useful for the client. Good so far?? Fantastic.

So we already have the first 2 steps of the pattern:

Step 1: Orient to which hand is the trance hand/ dreaming arm.

Step 2: Arm levitation.

Lets move to the next step:

Step 3: Imply the arm is gathering resources for change.

So now that we have an arm in the air we need it to mean something other than just "an arm in the air." We are going to use implication to begin to address any secondary gains that may be there. First we imply that their hand is gathering all the resources necessary to make the change. We may say something like:

> *"So you have an arm that is going up and each and everyone of you here has a lifetime of experiences. You have memories, dreams, imaginings, learnings in many different situations and that means that your unconscious mind can begin to pull from all of those things to build for you a powerful resource, to change, to grow, to become more fully who you are."*

So we begin to imply that the arm moving up is connected with change. In issues of secondary gain this would be something like:

> *"...in the past you smoked and there were certain emotional elements to doing that and I'd like your*

229

unconscious mind to start going through your memories, your experiences, and your thoughts — all of the things that make up 'you' to find the contexts, the places, and the times when you have had resources that could meet that need so that you get to fully enjoy being who you are as a non smoker."

The idea here is that as the arm raises it is gathering resources. It is literally picking up resources from the unconscious mind. Eventually that hand will stop rising either because it has moved to a position where it is more difficult to continue to move — for example it is resting on the tummy or against the cheek or face — or it has found all the resources and has found a happy place to stop.

We are using the hand levitation as an outward metaphor for the process that they are going to do inside. We like this process to be outside of the conscious awareness so that the conscious mind isn't interfering and saying "oh yes...BUT..." So the conscious mind doesn't know the change that has happened because it is not the conscious mind that has created the link to the secondary gain. Therefore it shouldn't be the conscious mind that tries to solve it.

Step 4:

This pattern is called "The Dreaming Arm," so we obviously want them to "dream," and this is a good point. Suggest that when the hand stops there will be a dream, a sign or a symbol — something to let the conscious mind know that a change has occurred and that there has been a shift. Let them dream.

We may say:

"And dreams come in many different ways. They can come through imagery, symbols, memories, or a wonderful movie playing in your mind; it could be a feeling, maybe just a certainty, a determination, a

230

calmness or relaxation, a feeling of acceptance, openness, a part of a community. It could be sounds, it could be your mind saying, "yes, I've done this, I've made this change and I feel amazing."

So we are very broad and we imply that when the hand reaches its final point and it is ready to stop because it has gathered all of the resources, then the dream will occur. And then we start layering up the idea of dreaming in all of the different sense-modalities in which we can dream.

Anything the client is dreaming is exactly right. During this process I like to give the client time so I will be quiet and let them know that I am still there and just being quiet while they have the experience. In most cases, as you are calibrating their physiology you will see when it starts and you will see when it stops. You will see the expression in the face, the relaxation in the muscles, the normal things we calibrate for. When you get to the dream you'll see a distinct shift.

They don't need to share their dream or their symbol, they most likely won't tell you what it is anyway. So we just calibrate for their responses.

Step 5:

Finally, the last part is integration. They have the resources, they have a symbol that lets them know that change has happened. Of course, we don't want them to leave the office with their arm up in the air or on the side of their face (*laughing*), so we use the arm coming back down again as a sign of the integration happening. We might say something like:

"and that hand can come down as quickly as everything is put into place, all of those resources are put exactly where they need to be."

So if you think about it, in the beginning we are pulling those resources up. Then comes the dream where we are matching the resources with the situation, creating the shift. And then the resourced hand lowers as the unconscious mind is putting the resources into place.

Lawrence: Do you need to instruct the client to incorporate the solution of the dream into their behavior? Or is that understood?

Jess: You could. There's a lot of flexibility with this. You could do a lot of future pacing, getting them to mentally practice doing the positive new behavior in the future, as the hand is coming down.

This is really the bare-bones of it. The idea is to simply give the client a way of addressing whatever emotional needs are there on an unconscious level, and trying on new resources to meet those needs.

You have a lot of flexibility within this pattern as to how you set it up and use it.

So I will do a demonstration now, and for a demonstration I will need someone who really loves going into trance… Maybe even a trance junkie. Okay Karen, come and sit up here in the trance chair.

So Karen, is there a particular context, is there something small that you would like to work through? Or improve, or do more of?

Karen: Being more self confident.

Jess: Is there a particular context?

Karen: No pretty much everywhere (*laughing*).

Jess: All right, everywhere in life (*laughing*). More confidence. And when you have that confidence what will it feel like?

Karen: Ummmm…. It will feel… Light.

Jess: That's right...it will feel light. And when you have that confidence and are feeling light, what will you be believing about yourself?

Karen: That I can do anything I put my mind to.

Jess: Fantastic, because you can do anything you put your mind to. So is it okay if during the process I touch your hand, wrist, elbow and shoulder?

Karen: That's fine.

Jess: Okay, I like to get permission first. Alright, so I know that you are very skilled at going into trance, and you've been in and out of many trances already today have you not?

Karen: That is true.

Jess: All right.

> *So I would like for you to just have an awareness of your hands, the feelings in your left hand and the right hand... maybe the sense of the fabric underneath your fingers, a feeling of difference in temperature. Which one of those hands is warmer right now?*

Karen: My left hand.

Jess:

> *Your left hand there is warmer, that's right, and if you continue paying attention to both of those hands, noting the warmth in that hand, you may begin to have a sense of the space between your hands and your jeans where they are not quite touching and you can feel the movement of air in the tiny spaces in between. And as you do that, which one of those hands is lighter right now?*

Karen: My right.

Jess:

You're right, that's right, this right hand here, feeling lighter than the left-hand over there that's left right over there and is slightly heavier, because right now we are left with this right hand that can be lighter. So is it lighter in the palm or in the fingertips?

Karen: In the palm.

Jess: In the palm. Did you expect it to be lighter in the palm?

Karen: Mmmm…I hadn't really thought about it.

Jess: You hadn't really thought about it, and yet there it is!

Karen: Mmhmm.

Jess:

Lighter in the palm. So just focus on that lightness because the fact that this hand has a light feeling that starts in the palm means that it is ready to help you make an incredible change, so that you can fully know, from the inside and out, that you can achieve everything and anything you put your mind to. And you may even have a sense of how that feels when you truly know that. That's it (Karen's hand is beginning to twitch). And this hand here, is lightness, that's it, has it moved to the fingers yet?

Karen: Yes.

Jess:

That's right, that's it there you go (fingers begin twitching), and that pinky already knows so much about the change you are about to make on the deepest unconscious level, there you go. So I'd like for your unconscious mind to be centered here on this hand, because this hand is your trance hand. A chance to make a change in trance. That's it, there you go, so as that

234

hand begins the process of lifting, almost like it could be lifted under a soft comfortable cloud, that's it, as this hand lifts it is going to begin to gather resources. It's going to go through your thoughts, your memories, your learnings, your beliefs, your experiences everything that makes you, you. And it will collect those resources because at the unconscious level you know so much about having confidence, knowing that you can achieve anything and that this hand, oh that's it, there you go — (Karen's hand is continuing to lift), maybe the other hand wants in on the action too, collecting those resources. In a moment I am going to count from one to two and when I reach two I want for you to open your eyes and watch this hand here. Are you ready?

Karen: Yes.

Jess:

One, two, and you can watch this hand because his hand is going to continue to lift, and it really knows the right level for you to go, to collect every resource you need, that's it, and until then you can enjoy this process. And what's it like for you to know that you have a hand that is doing something that maybe you were not aware of?

Karen: It kind of freaks me out, in a good way.

Jess:

How charming to be freaked out in a good way by a hand that's developing confidence in all parts of your life where it's important for you to have that confidence, because I know that this hand really knows that because it is lifting in this way and gathering resources outside of your conscious awareness that it can help you to fully know that you can achieve anything you put your mind to. That's right, and as you continue to lift, gathering those resources, that's it, that's it, there you go... dreams, thoughts, memories, learnings, certainly, because I know the fact that you know what it's like to be confident means that you've had so many times in your life when you've had that experience…have you not?

Karen: Yes.

Jess:

So this hand is finding those times and collecting the learnings from them, the physiology, how you carry yourself when you are confident, there you go, the breathing, the emotion, the attention, your thoughts, that's it, and when that hand has reached the appropriate level it can stop and your eyes can stay closed and a dream will happen but not before then, until then you get to enjoy the process, because your unconscious mind as it's doing this is going to present to you a symbol, it could be a feeling a sense, maybe even an image, something that lets you know that it's on your side and helping to create this change. And how wonderful it is to have a dream, have you ever had one of those dreams where you've woken up the next day you know that something incredibly positive happened? You don't know what, but you just know.

Karen: Yeah.

Jess:

It's happened and you can cherish that dream, that's it, there you go, those fingers finding all of those resources. And I know that there were times in your past where you didn't feel as confident as you could, but now, and as this hand finds those resources, those other times can shift, because you are learning at an unconscious level that you can have the states, the behaviors, the attention, the thoughts of someone who's confident in any and every situation because you are someone who achieves anything when you set your mind to it, that's it, there you go…how amazing.

So what I'd like to happen now since you've had that experience is that this hand is going to begin to go down only at the rate and speed that your unconscious mind takes the feelings, those resources, and places them in all the times, all the places all the contexts where you just know that you can totally and completely enjoy being confident, that's it. I remember when I was little and I would go somewhere like the mall or a restaurant and they would have that crane game that would go and pick up the stuffed animal and the little crane machine would come and pick it up and then you would have a prize. In the same way, the changes that are taking place at the deepest unconscious level can begin the process of integration for you, that's it...there you go and you can take all the time you need for that, genuine unconscious processing. That's it, and when that hand reaches your lap again your eyes will open and you'll reorient to the here and now feeling refreshed, relaxed, alert, and confidently fantastic, from the top of your head all the way down to the tips of your toes really revealing in that open feeling, that big expansive feeling, that certainty, because you are achieving so much even beyond what you suspected on the conscious level you are achieving so much more because you have a conscious mind and you have a phenomenal unconscious mind, always there protecting, helping creating amazingly good states for you. There you go...that's right. You did a great job, what a amazing unconscious mind. Fantastic work, how was that for you?

Jess: You did a great job and you have an awesome unconscious mind. That's fabulous. Thank you.

Group: (*applauding*)

Jess: Any questions?

Yuval: When you are touching the hand, does it matter if you are saying something positive or do you just touch?

Jess: Either way. I tend to be saying lots of positive things so mostly I will be touching and saying positive things at the same time. And you can just do the touch. When we are in trance your senses are amplified so this gentle, very light touch, along with the hand moving all by itself is a very pleasant feeling all on it's own. So either way.

Any other questions?

Rita: I want to ask Karen, "Are you feeling more confident now?"

Mark: Yes!

Sarah: Well, Mark is!

Karen: I am feeling confident that Mark is feeling confident!! I am feeling really good and I feel really positive…I can't really say.

Sarah: She is probably still processing what happened.

Karen: I feel great like I always do when I come out of trance.

Jess: So as you are feeling great, and you are just coming out of trance and things are processing, think about a time where you would like to have that confidence…what's happening?

Karen: I feel fine and I don't feel any of that gushy-ug…

Jess: And when you're not feeling that, what are you feeling?

Karen: I am feeling calm and powerful and strong and confident.

Jess: Awesome.

Yuval: If I was doing this with a client I would probably create an anchor that she can use when she wants.

238

Jess: Yes you could do that…there are lots of ways to use this. This is just a demo of the "Dreaming Arm" pattern, that's all.

Kristina: What happens when we have used the lifting arm for the negative in the Tiger Pattern, and now we use it for the positive…how does that work?

Sarah: Do you use your arms for different things??

Kristina: Ahhh….yes.

Jess: And when you think about it the hand will be in a different orientation for the Tiger because they will be holding a cigarette and so their arm/hand will be turned towards their body as they mimic smoking.

Shawn: Or you could do it with the opposite hand if you want to separate them.

Jess: Or you could put an entire metaphor around it as we did before about the smoking hand now becoming the resourceful hand…it's creating an unbelievably powerful future for them.

Mark: Do you ever get people complaining of shoulder problems?

Jess: Not really unless there was something there to begin with. When you are in catalepsy there is a balancing of the muscles so it is much easier to hold a hand up. You can also position the elbow for more comfort. Ok are you ready to have a go?

Kathy: We are all still in trance.

Jess: That's right and what a wonderful place to work from! States are contagious!

So you'll work for 10 minutes each and you may want to get a context, an idea of what your partner would like more of, so you have a frame to work around. Or you could do it content free. Either way is better.

Recap and Review

1. Orient the hands.

2. Establishing the hand levitation through utilization, metaphor and suggestion.

3. Implying the gathering of resources as the hand moves up.

4. Suggesting that when the hand stops there will be a dream, a sign, a symbol something to let them know a change has occurred.

5. Let them dream and then...

6. Integrate suggestions for the hand to come back down and the resources being put in place.

(Students do the exercise)

Jess: Welcome back everybody. How was that? Anyone like to share?

Kristina: I didn't know what resources I wanted, but as soon as my partner suggested that I gather the correct resources my hand began to move. I know my past is oriented on my left and my hand began to move over to the left. I still don't know what the resources that it gathered from my past but I trust my unconscious mind to know what it is doing.

Sarah: I think that is important for our clients to know also that the unconscious mind may not share changes, or resources with the conscious mind and that's okay. Also because we are working in the unconscious mind it doesn't always give us the answers in a concrete understandable way. We understand that the unconscious mind will communicate to us with symbols and images and feelings. Sometimes a client wants to know the "answer," the one thing that is the solution to the entire issue. And they want this in a word or a phrase. I usually mention something during my hypnosis pre-talk about the unconscious mind making the change and sometimes keeping it to themselves. And all of that is OK and they will probably get a sense that something shifted.

Jess: And something will shift, problems just don't stay the same especially during this type of work. With any piece of change work you may not get the big shift right away. Every little shift is moving them closer.

Mercedes: It's interesting how sometimes your unconscious will show you resources, almost like a chain effect. It builds up and it builds up and it builds up. And as you see the resources, you know that your unconscious is beginning to integrate inside. It's like a whole chain reaction and when you come out of it you say, "Oh yeah, OK I got it."

Lawrence: I am amazed that I seem to learn more when we make mistakes — where we leave a piece out or it doesn't seem to go exactly right, or as smoothly as the demonstration.

Jess: We have wonderful demos and we have wonderful clients, and things aren't always going to go as planned.

This entire quit smoking protocol came out of me working with a lot of clients and learning something from each of them.

The Perceptual Possibilities pattern came out of me trying to do a standard "fork in the road" pattern and it not working. Those are our best learning opportunities. There are no rights and wrongs. It is all feedback and experience.

I saw some wonderful, wonderful arm levitations going on today. There will be times with clients where it doesn't happen right away. So would it be useful to have some skills in case the arm isn't moving or for when you don't have catalepsy? There are things we can do. The very simple answer is if the hand is not going, then to just do something different.

But if you are totally keen on having the arm levitation there are ways that we can help. One nice way is to get the client to begin by raising their arm consciously and then switching that movement to the unconscious. Would you like an experience of that?

Ok if you will all put your feet on the floor, put your hands on your knees and I would like each and every one of you to pick one hand that is going to be your trance hand.

Everyone have your trance hand?

Great.

So I would like for you to focus on that hand whichever hand it might be, and begin to lift it one centimeter at a time, moving it as slowly as humanly possible. In fact as you lift that hand you can have an awareness of all of the tiny muscles in the hand that are connected to the arm, connected to the upper arm, the muscles that are connected to the shoulder as that hand lifts centimeter by centimeter, connected into the shoulder and those muscles around the shoulder connected to the back. And when you lift your hand something very interesting happens because you may have a thought to lift the hand, one centimeter at a time and that thought goes from your brain into your spinal column and through a series of electrical impulses and that signal is sent from the muscles in your back and into your shoulder and from your shoulder down into the arm, from the arm into the elbow, into the forearm, into the wrist, into the hand and as you move that hand centimeter by centimeter as slowly as humanly possibly you may begin to find, there you go, you may begin to find that eventually that hand starts to move on its own...and you don't have to know consciously when it happens and until it happens you can continue to move that hand one centimeter at a time. Centimeter by centimeter until it feels like you're not moving it at all. That's it. And when you're ready you can reorient to the here and now, shake the trance off and come all the way back.

How was that?

Mark: That worked!

Jess: Yeah…this is a wonderful way of getting arm levitation. Here you are placing responsibility for the levitation on the client's conscious mind. You are giving them very direct suggestions. Because you are asking them to move it just one centimeter at a time consciously…look when I do it, what does it start to look like?

Karen: It's a bit jerky, like unconscious movement.

Jess: Yeah unconscious movement. It will reach a point where it happens on its own. So that's one way of doing it, but that's not the only way. We have other methods. Sarah may I borrow you?

Sarah: You may.

Jess: So there are times when you pick up someone's arm and it will just drop and you can use this dropping to suggest that the client "dropping deeper into trance." If you do this 3 or 4 times they will have dropped into a nice deep trance. If we want to go for catalepsy and arm levitation we can do it through verbal metaphor again, and through suggestion.

So Sarah I want you to go ahead and imagine that you can find a hypnotic shelf, somewhere for this arm to rest.. (*Gently moving Sarah's arm back and forth*) That's it, somewhere for this arm to rest, there you go, and you can come all the way back to the here and now.

So moving the clients' arm and ambiguous touch confuses the conscious mind. Through touch the conscious mind is guided to a different area. We are engaging the imagination and as we are moving the arm, the person loses touch of where it is going and eventually it becomes unclear as to who is holding the arm up. And then you have catalepsy.

For the NLPers or the CHPHers when we do the Reintegration or Visual Squash pattern we get catalepsy the same way. Both hands are extended and we ask the client to focus on one palm. While they are focusing on one hand they have "forgotten" about the other; yet it is still staying in the same position. The unconscious mind has taken over the "forgotten" hand while the conscious attention is focused on the other hand.

There are many different ways of getting catalepsy. So you can feel what it is like to have an arm that is not in catalepsy, kind of in catalepsy, and fully in catalepsy. Let's do an exercise and practice not getting the levitation right away.

So in pairs just practice. We don't want you to completely resist and refuse to have catalepsy, just to give your partner the experience of knowing the difference between a non cataleptic arm and being able to notice when it starts and when it is fully there. Let's just take 2 or 3 minutes each.

(Students do the exercise)

Jess: Welcome back everyone. How was that?

Mark: That was great. Somehow I used the idea of resisting the desire to not move the hand up and it worked really well. I am not quite sure what I did!

Sarah: Wonderful, sometimes that happens. As the hypnotist, we go into trance too and maybe you went so far into your unconscious that you don't even remember exactly what you did.

Mark: I think that's what happened. I should do that all the time!

Lawrence: I had an interesting experience with Rita. I had her arm up and resting on an imaginary bar. I was tapping her arm in the same place and she was definitely holding it up. Then when I tapped in a different place that she wasn't expecting it suddenly went cataleptic.

And then we started having fun with her hand resting on the bar. I said "and now the bar is moving up." "And now the bar is moving down." After a couple of moves like that she started playing along consciously and I could feel a change in the muscle tone. That was really trippy.

Sarah: Yes… it is quite obvious when you have experienced it. It is important for us as hypnotists to have this kind of experience, and to know what an arm feels like when it is not cataleptic, when it is going into catalepsy, and when it is entirely in catalepsy. These can be subtle differences but once you are aware of them it is easy to be able to tell exactly where the client is.

Karen: Even the feeling of their skin is completely different when they are cataleptic. It is really weird.

Jess: Have you had the experience when you are in catalepsy that there is a little bit of dissociation?

Group: Yes

Jess: My favorite way to do that is to ask a client "can I borrow your arm?"

With that question dissociation begins right from the start – because it sets up that this arm is kind of a part of me, and yet it is not.

Sarah: Before you want them to go into catalepsy, a nice metaphor that I like to use which expands upon the idea of the bird flying is:

You've seen a bird just floating, hovering and gliding in the air haven't you? Well what they are doing is riding on waves of air, these shelves of air, that's what they are doing, they are resting on these shelves of air.

Sometime during this I will have picked up their wrist and be gently moving it around. I am waiting to feel when their unconscious mind takes over and their arm begins to find its own "shelf of air" and I will continue by saying:

*So now, I wonder where your shelf of air is going to be?" and they usually find their **own** shelf of air.*

Mark: So what about a client whose arm is resting on the shelf of air and they suddenly bring themselves out and begin to talk about something else?

Sarah: Yes that can happen. There is some kind of conscious / unconscious dissociation going on. I had a client last week who was in the hypno-chair and was going into trance. I asked her which hand was most relaxed and she said her left. As soon as she said that I asked her which finger was going into trance first and her index finger began to twitch. She opened her eyes, looked at me, and said with a smile, "I didn't do that." This happened for all the fingers and her thumb. She was fascinated that her hand was going into trance and yet she could still communicate quite easily with me. She said her hand was going into trance but really it was all of her. As soon as I suggested that she close her eyes, she dropped into a nice deep trance.

Jess: From time to time you will come across a client who does this and becomes a little unnerved by the experience because it is a complete dissociation. So you have to calibrate to the physiology and you can also ask, "how does it feel to see a hand moving all on its own? "Sometimes they may say that it is weird or freaky, and so we would begin to reframe the experience focusing on the positive. You could say something like, "how wonderful it is that you have an unconscious mind that protects you to the extent that it can do things for your benefit outside of your conscious control."

So it is something to just keep in mind especially if you ask them to open their eyes. I like to ask my clients to open their eyes if we are doing the Dreaming Arm because it is a really cool experience.

Sarah: And it is a huge convincer that trance is happening. You can say something like, "as your body remains deeply in hypnosis I would like you to open your eyes." Most people will do so and are completely amazed to see that their arm is levitating.

Jess: And you can use this as really good leverage by saying something like, "and your eyes will close only when your hand reaches your face" or wherever it is going. So there is some leverage to keep the unconscious movement going so that the rest of them can go back into a wonderfully deep-eyes closed trance. So really play with this. This is just a scaffolding and what you put on it is your choice that it may change with every client. In fact, I hope the way you do the Dreaming Arm changes with every client, and I know it will.

Okay is it time for a break, let's take 10 minutes and if you would like to know what to do aside from the Dreaming Arm to squash that secondary gain into a resource, then you'll have to come back in 10 minutes.

Sarah: Welcome back everyone. So we have been using the Dreaming Arm technique in order to deal with secondary gain issues which may be very unconscious and unknown to the client. This is a vital part of any smoking protocol. There is going to be some secondary gain for the client, some unconscious positive reason for them to be maintaining the behavior and this positive reason needs to find an alternative behavior in order to make a real and lasting change.

If the intention is not satisfied in a positive and healthy way then the client may either not make a lasting change, or may begin another behavior which is equally unhealthy. This is very typical for smokers. All too frequently a person quits smoking and begins to eat too much and gains weight or maybe begins to bite their nails. The one behavior has been replaced with another, equally negative behavior. When this happens the secondary gain hasn't been addressed and dealt with sufficiently.

The Dreaming Arm is a wonderful way to do this. You are asking your client to gather all the positive resources, all the ways that they can find new and healthy behaviors to satisfy whatever lies beneath or behind their smoking. And then to process and integrate these new ways that will manifest in positive behaviors. This happens totally on the unconscious level for the client.

THE SIX STEP REFRAME

Sarah: Anyone recognize this pattern?

1. Identify the issue.

2. Establish communication with the unconscious mind.

3. Ask the unconscious mind for the positive intention.

4. Generate alternative ways to satisfy the positive intention.

5. Select one new behavior and obtain commitment.

6. Ecology Check.

Group: The Six Step Reframe pattern.

Sarah: Yes, it is the classic Six Step Reframe pattern from NLP. It is something that I will inevitably put into a quit smoking session. This pattern has six steps, hence the name, so on the face of it, it is pretty simple. And of course, there are subtleties which make this pattern even more elegant, and more powerful.

Whenever I am going to do this pattern I will always talk with my client about the concept of positive intention. It can be as brief as just mentioning the NLP presupposition that "behind every behavior there is or has been a positive intention"... whether they know that consciously or unconsciously, it is there somewhere. Most of the time that's just about all I will say because I am calibrating that my client is agreeing. I want to know that they understand on some level their smoking habit is doing something else for them. We may have had a glimpse of what that might be from our discussion either during the intake or some other time in the session. The client may have an idea of what the positive intention is on a conscious level or they may not — it doesn't really matter.

The first step of the Six Step Reframe is to identify the behavior. This is usually pretty easy with a smoker because the issue is... that they smoke! The second step of the Six Step Reframe is to establish communication with the unconscious mind. If you are doing this pattern towards the end of the session, do you think that your client may have already established some kind of communication with their unconscious mind?

Group: Oh Yes!

Sarah: Exactly, their unconscious mind has come out to play! However for this step we really want them to focus on finding their unconscious signal for "yes" and "no." This is because there will be a number of questions that we will be asking the unconscious mind and we need to know if the unconscious mind is agreeing or not. So what I normally do is to just ask the client to go inside and ask their unconscious mind to show you a "yes." I don't know what that might be as everyone is unique and individual.

Lets do this as a group so that you can find your own unconscious "yes."

Okay, put everything down, settle yourselves in, put your feet comfortably on the floor, take an easy breath in and out, just go inside now and ask your unconscious mind to show you a "yes." Ask, "What is my unconscious "yes" today?" It maybe a sensation, a movement, a knowing, an image, and when you have got a "yes" you can open your eyes and come on back to the room.

How was that? Everybody got a "yes." That was pretty quick, probably because we are all very used to going into trance and we have been in and out of trance numerous times today. You may find that you need to spend a little more time when asking your client to do this, or not! You may ask your client to find the agreement, the yes, the positive. There are a number of ways to phrase it and I usually go straight to the "yes." What kinds of things did you get for your "yes" signal?

Group: A smile... movement...a quiver in my upper lip...I found my inner balance.

Kristina: I didn't get one.

Sarah: That's OK...just allow it to happen as we go forward.

Karen: It was kind of weird because I was thinking that I was going to get a signal from my hand but I actually got a sensation in my heart center. It was a little hug.

Sarah: Awww...that's adorable. So we don't know what the client is going to get. They could be physical things, images, sounds or words or anything else!

As hypnotist I will also be watching for any kind of physical movement, often a finger will twitch or there may be a movement in the body somewhere that the client is consciously unaware of. I usually ask a couple of times for the "yes," and if I see the same movement each and every time then I know that the unconscious mind is communicating. And it is perfectly okay if the client is totally unaware of the signal.

After this I will ask the client to ask their unconscious mind for a "no" signal, and I will spell this out "n - o." The unconscious mind is very literal and could possibly confuse the word "no" with the word "know" and we have to make this a clear distinction. So let's play with finding your "no" signal.

Take a breath and drop inside... ask your unconscious mind to give you a "no" signal. What is your "no" signal "n - o." What is a "no" for you today? "n-o." And when you have it, you can open your eyes and come on back to the room.

Kristina did you find one this time?

Kristina: Yes and I found my "yes" too.

Sarah: Great, I knew you would! So you all got some kind of sensation, signal, sign, feeling for your "no" today. I usually say "for today" because the sign can change from day-to-day.

So you have really established an easy way to communicate with your unconscious mind.

Step three of the Six Step Reframe is to identify the positive intention behind the behavior. If you have forgotten to talk with your clients about the positive intention — and it can happen — this would be the time to do it. Again it can be just a very quick sentence such as, "you know that behind every behavior that is or has been a positive intention" — something as quick as that.

We then ask the client to go inside and ask their unconscious mind if it is willing to share with them what the positive intention is. There are a couple of possibilities here. The unconscious mind may share exactly what the positive intention is, or it may share that it knows what the positive intention is, and yet is not willing to share it with the conscious mind. Either way is okay.

As long as the unconscious mind knows what the positive intention is, we are able to move forward. This is why we set up a clear yes and no signal. Your client might go inside and get a "yes" from the unconscious mind and come back out and say, "well I got a yes but I don't know what it is." This is still okay.

Other times the clients may come back from this inquiry and say, "I know what it is, it is: safety/protection/comfort" etc.

Lawrence: Are you asking the unconscious mind if it knows what the intention is, or are you asking it for the intention?

Sarah: Yes, either of these. I'd usually phrase it as, "go inside and ask your unconscious mind, 'what is the positive intention behind this behavior?'" I find that the client will come back either with a "yes it knows what it is," or they will come back and tell me the name of what it is. And either way really is fine.

So now they have established communication with the unconscious mind, and they have found the positive intention of the behavior — or at least they have an understanding that their unconscious mind knows what it has been doing.

Step four is when we asked the unconscious mind to come up with alternative behaviors that will satisfy the positive intention. These are alternate healthy ways for the client to satisfy whatever was driving the other behavior — but this time in a positive way.

Yuval: So you are looking for a new behavior?

Sarah: Yes, let's think of it like this. The client has been behaving in a certain way which they are now ready to change. Even though the behavior, the actions, the things they are doing are now negative or unhelpful, the behavior has been satisfying them in some way or form.

The client may be aware of these reasons — maybe smoking is a stress relief, maybe it helps them to socialize. But there may be unconscious reasons that the client is unaware of that are driving the behavior. We want to keep the positive and just redirect the behavior. So in this step we ask the unconscious mind to come up with alternative ways to fulfill what ever the positive intention is.

We will ask the client to come up with quite a few alternatives — 20, 25, 32. A high number like that. Why do you think we do this?

Group: To screw them up (*laughing*)...to take over the negative behavior...to give them more choices.

Sarah: If we only ask for two or three, then we are asking the conscious mind to get involved and as John Overdurf says "the conscious mind has no business getting involved in an unconscious process."

How many of us can carry 20 or 30 things in our mind at any one time? We can't, we can usually only hold a few things...maybe 5 or 6. Remember the 7 plus or minus 2 rule? So by asking for a large number, we are intentionally asking the unconscious mind to do this work. The unconscious mind works very fast, and can pretty quickly come up with a lot of alternative ways to satisfy the positive intention that lay behind the behavior. This is really utilizing the unconscious processing here, does that make sense?

Group: Yes.

Sarah: So you would say something like, "go inside and ask your unconscious mind to come up with at least 20 new behaviors, positive and healthy behaviors that will satisfy the positive intention."

Karen: And will they be listing these?

Sarah: Could you list 20 or 30 things in just a couple of moments? Probably not consciously — but your unconscious mind is able to do this quickly.

Karen: Ah yes, I get it, we are asking them to do this unconsciously.

Sarah: Absolutely. If we just ask for two or three we may get a conscious answer like, "well...I could...go get a

manicure ...or...I could go and read a magazine...or..."
and that would be very conscious.

Karen: They've probably done that before.

Sarah: Right, and that may be why they haven't been able
to quit.

Lawrence: Do you give a certain amount of time for this,
or do you wait for the unconscious mind to give a signal
that it is done?

Sarah: Yes, I will usually say, "and let me know when that
is done." I will then be looking for their "yes" signal or
waiting for them to come back. If it feels like it is taking a
long time – and this is a judgment call – the conscious
mind may have got a little too involved. I might say
something like, "Ok just allow that to continue to process
as we move on." Got it?

Group: Yes.

Sarah: Step five...we are getting there...we are going to
ask the unconscious mind to select one of the behaviors to
"try on" for a period of time. Now again this has two
possibilities. Sometimes a client will know exactly which
behavior has been selected, and other times they just have
an awareness that the unconscious mind has selected one
but they do not know consciously what that is.

You are also asking the unconscious mind to commit to
taking on this new behavior for a period of time –
something like 2 weeks and that, if it is working out well,
to continue the behavior. If the behavior isn't working out
then it will select another one.

Lawrence: What if it can't make that commitment?

Sarah: Great question. We want yes and no signals so that
the client can track the decisions that are being made.
What would you do if your client says yes, they have

picked a behavior, only to find that the unconscious side is unwilling to commit to following through on the new behavior?

Kathy: Do something different!

Sarah: That's right, you can ask about the time period…maybe two weeks was too long or too short. If it is not connected to the amount of time, then you would ask the unconscious mind to go back to the list it had generated and select a different alternative behavior. Does that make sense?

The sixth and final step is the ecology check. We want to make sure that every part of them is completely satisfied and aligned with this new change. And that is exactly why we will ask, "go inside and ask your unconscious mind to check if every part is completely satisfied and aligned with this new behavior." Again, your client will get a "yes" or a "no." If the client gets a "no" what do you think you do?

Group: Go back and pick another one.

Sarah: Right, you will cycle back to step number five and ask the unconscious mind to select a different behavior from its list of alternatives, ask for commitment to change and do another ecology check.

Sarah: This is a classic NLP pattern. Something I didn't understand when I first learned the pattern, and have come to realize since studying hypnosis, is that this pattern utilizes a tremendous amount of fractionation. You all remember what fractionation is right? Fractionation is a hypnotic phenomena which relies on dipping someone into trance then bringing them back out, and dipping them back in again. Each time your client goes in to trance they will go deeper. How many times do you think we can bring the client in and out of trance with this pattern?

Group: Six.

Sarah: Yes, that is the minimum. We will also find every opportunity to ask the client to go back in and say "thank you" to the unconscious mind. This more than doubles the amount of times the client will be going in and out of trance. For example we say:

> Go inside and ask your unconscious mind to find a "yes" signal." When the client comes back with their "yes" we say "great – now go inside and say thank you to your unconscious mind for providing you with the yes.

See how we double up on the effect? It's brilliant isn't it? You have a minimum of 12 opportunities to fractionate your client, knowing that each time they are going deeper and deeper into trance. Isn't that nice? You are satisfying secondary gain by finding positive and healthy new ways to behave. This is such an important part of the quit smoking protocol. Everybody good with this one?

Yuval: Quick question, in the ecology check do you only check inside yourself if it is okay, or do you check with your family and your wider circle?

Sarah: Within this pattern the client is checking within themselves, making sure that every part of them is onboard and supportive of this change.

Yuval: There maybe other ecology issues around the client quitting smoking that may need to be addressed.

Shawn: Yes, let's say the spouse also smokes and is not giving up.

Kathy: How would you deal with that?

Shawn: It's really the future pace that would catch this one.

Sarah: You would have to do a very big future pace because they know they are going back into the environment when their spouse is smoking and possibly tempting them to return to the previous behavior.

Kathy: Is this something that you would bring up during the intake discussion?

Sarah: Yes, it is there in the intake questionnaire.

Jess: It is also important if they know they are going back into a household where someone else is smoking, that they can be a non-smoker and still maintain the same relationships. They are making this change for themselves knowing that they can have a healthier and stronger relationship with their spouse or family member.

Shawn: Right, and this also goes for personal friends and coworkers.

Lawrence: So the ecology check is performed with the unconscious — do you also run it over the conscious mind?

Sarah: Yes you can, but it is not usually part of the classic Six Step Reframe.

Shawn: Here's the thing. The client comes into your office and says, "I smoke when I get stressed at work." That's a secondary gain you would specifically address. They may also say something like, "all these people have been on me for ages to quit, so I guess it is time for me to give up" — so there may be resentment. They feel they are being pushed into it. And that is a secondary gain for smoking, right? They are being a rebel, they are being their own person, and they are telling you that.

You don't need to say, "oh I see that in your case a secondary gain of smoking is that you are a rebel." So you could say something like, "ah, they thought that you couldn't quit, so when you leave this office smoke free you will have shown them." You are turning this around so your client is able to keep their rebellious side. The

Dreaming Arm and the Six Step reframe are intended to catch the non-obvious ones.

Sarah: Yes, this is like the "clean-up" pattern.

Shawn: So they might say something like, "yes my unconscious mind says it is because I am stressed at work." Well we knew that already but we don't need to do the Six Step Reframe in order to get that. This is really when they have a circuit in the brain and what is that circuit going to do when they don't smoke?

The classic example is the client of Bandler who comes in with a frozen arm — he can't move his arm, and there seems to be no medical reason. Bandler transfers the inability to move into the client's fingernails and the client leaves his office complaining and saying, "you've frozen my fingernails... I can't feel them anymore." His arm is fine (*laughing*), and yet he is still complaining. There was some secondary gain in having a frozen arm — who on earth knows what that might be, but this way the client was able to keep the secondary gain and the only price he had to pay was to have frozen fingernails.

Group: (*Laughing.*)

Shawn: So this pattern really is the catch all pattern, to change those things which are not obvious. Not obvious to the client and not obvious to you.

Sarah: And remember, the Dreaming Arm is also a version of the Six Step Reframe. You already know what the issue is, you are definitely getting communication with the unconscious mind, you are finding all the resources and new ways of behaving and then integrating. And you can do the ecology check while the hand is moving down. So you now have two ways of working with the unconscious secondary gain issues.

Lawrence: You wouldn't do them both though?

Sarah: You might.

Jess: You could also do them in combination, using the raising of the arm as the "yes" and then changing that to lowering the arm as you integrate and do an ecology check. Have fun with it, play with it.

Sarah: Ohhh...the "Six Step Dreamer."

Sarah: So as most of you are familiar with this pattern, how about you just dive right in and see what happens. Lets say 10 mins each?

(*Students do the exercise*)

Jess: Bringing it all back around. How was that?

Sarah: Any questions? How many of you remembered to bring your client back up and then to drop them back in to "thank" their unconscious mind. It is a lovely little piece to constantly be thanking the unconscious mind, and it is something that we don't tend to do too often. As hypnotists we know that we are doubling the potential of the fractionation. So it may appear to be kind of cute AND we know that we are intentionally using it to create a very powerful effect.

Jess: If everyone can just close your eyes for a moment. You can get a sense of where you are sitting, and that each and every one of you has been here both as a conscious mind. Both parts of each and everyone of you have been learning, and the unconscious mind has really helped in that process of integrating this knowledge on a deep unconscious level. So why not take a moment, inside, and thank your unconscious mind and notice what happens when you do. And when you're done just open your eyes and come on back.

What were your experiences?

Kathy: Relaxing.

Karen: I had a thought. When someone thanks you, you have a greater intention and desire to help them the next time.

Sarah: Yes, you are deepening the relationship.

Kathy: I felt gratitude, which goes along with what Karen was saying.

Jess: How many of you had some sort of pleasant kinesthetic response or a feeling...(*hands going up*) ...Yeah...it feels good! It is a wonderful thing to thank the unconscious mind. By this stage, the client has gone through a lot of different processes and their unconscious mind has stuck with them through the entirety of it.

Yuval: And as you acknowledged yourself, it's a good feeling.

Sarah: Yes it is.

Jess: Exactly. So by thanking your unconscious mind once you got a good feeling, imagine thanking your unconscious mind 10 or 12 times in the Six Step Reframe. What a positive powerful feeling your client will have when they come out of it. What a resourceful state they will be in.

Shawn: When we do any kind of validation, if we see a sign of trance, or an unconscious response, the traditional thing to say is "that's right." Another way to say that is, "thank you."

Sarah: There were some questions as to whether we would do both the Six Step Reframe and the Dreaming Arm, so let me make it perfectly clear for those of you who asked. The answer is ...yes! (*laughing*).

You can let the client actually choose. Let's say that I have layered up the lovely metaphor of the birds gliding and the idea of finding the shelf; I have picked up their arm and am waiting for them to find their "shelf"... and they are not finding it! So I am holding their wrist up, giving them suggestions of catalepsy and it is not working.

What to we do?? You are holding their wrist, and can feel the weight of their arm and they haven't transitioned into catalepsy...what do you do?

Karen: Use it as a deepener?

Sarah: Absolutely, use it as a deepener and say something like, "and in a moment I am going to gently drop your hand into your lap and when I do you will go into a nice deep trance." I usually do this 3 or 4 times, each time suggesting that they are going deeper and deeper. It takes any pressure off.

From here I will now probably go into using the Six Step Reframe as opposed to the Dreaming Arm. It's all utilization. So whatever the client does is absolutely right.

Mercedes: And they won't feel like they have failed or done something wrong.

Sarah: Yes. Really both these patterns are serving the same purpose, just in slightly different way.

Mercedes: That's what happens when you have a lot of tools.

Sarah: Exactly. Whatever the client does is right and we can use that.

Jess: Throughout the session, we are giving them as many opportunities to succeed as is possible. It is a big, "yes set." The more they succeed at the little things and we congratulate with the simple "that's right," the more you are priming the unconscious mind for success.

Sarah: The Six Step Reframe is a very nice pattern. Any questions?

Mercedes: I guess I just keep going back to the tools and the protocol. There is a big difference between using a script and having tools and a protocol. Last night at home I was going through some papers and I found a script for quitting smoking. I was looking at it, imagining if I was a hypnotist who just used scripts. What would happen if the script didn't work or if something went wrong? Then you would be stuck, and not know what to do.

We know that so much of our communication is non-verbal and the client may well pick up through your tone of voice that things are not working and you don't know what to do. This is so much better, to have real tools and a structure to use.

Sarah: Yep. And we all know that "one size doesn't fit all" — so a script limits not only the flexibility you need to address the client's individual issue but also inhibits the rapport between you and the client. And it is a physical barrier that makes "holding the space" impossible.

Jess: So all of this is a scaffolding upon which you can build your smoking cessation palace. And it will change with each client. The structure will change, and what you put on the walls will change — but you have all of the moving parts.

So you'll begin to have a sense of what fits where and when. And as we said before, we are presenting this protocol to the extent that you are willing to be flexible with it. So with some clients I will use the Perceptual Possibilities and the Smoking Destroyer. Then a future pace and a little bit of the Six Step Reframe, other times, maybe just the Six Step Reframe to the Dreaming Arm.

Sarah: Alrighty, so what we thought we would do for the last half hour is for you to find a partner and to practice one of the patterns. Lets take a look at the protocol and remind you of the patterns we have covered. Ok so we have EFT, the Backward Spin, the Perceptual Possibilities Pattern, the Smoking Destroyer, The Tiger Pattern, the Dreaming Arm, the Six Step Reframe and even some Provocative. There are a lot of things we have covered. Remember if you are going to do the Perceptual Possibilities or the Smoking Destroyer and you want to role play then we have some "fake client profiles" up here for you. Ok everybody cool? Lets take 15 minutes each.

(*Students do the exercise*)

Sarah: Nice to have an opportunity to practice? So you have a very powerful set of tools for helping clients to quit smoking

Jess: And with tomorrow's pattern you'll be able to neutralize environmental triggers for the smoking behavior and you can do it at the beginning of the session, in the middle of the session, or at the end of the session. It fits in everywhere. But that is tomorrow which means you will have to come back.

Group: (*laughing*)

Jess: So are you beginning to get a sense of how these pieces fit together?

Group: Yes.

Jess: Is everyone's brain feeling a bit full up?

Mark: Will we get a chance to do a whole practice session?

Jess: Yes, there will be an opportunity to have a longer "practice session" with someone in the class. A regular session with a quit smoking client is likely to be initially two hours. We will probably have around an hour per person tomorrow, so you will be able to go through quite a lot of the protocol. But that is tomorrow and we still have the rest of the day.

Shawn: …the rest of the day…

Jess: *... The rest of the day... To the wrap up... So we've reached the end of the day... End of day three of the "QUIT workshop for hypnotists and change workers." ... And I would like to thank the best parts of each and every one of you for coming this far along the journey and continuing the journey with us tomorrow... And I would like to thank your unconscious minds for sharing these experiences today... For coming out and playing... Having fun... Learning... Growing... changing on the deepest unconscious levels... Because the learnings that you've begun to make here can continue to generalize out... Today... Tomorrow... Next week... Next month... Next year... still learning in ways that are comfortable... Easy... Natural... And it's so very easy to learn when you take a few moments to just make yourself comfortable... And maybe close your eyes...*

Shawn: *...Or maybe not...*

Jess: *...Either way...*

Shawn: *... Is better...*

Jess: *... Because some people go into trance with their eyes closed... And others go into trance a different way... And it all leads in the same direction...*

Shawn: *... And we've talked about when somebody is focusing on one thing... Consciously... Their unconscious mind is able to focus everything else... So whilst you've been sitting here... In this class... With your conscious mind... Focusing on that thin stream of information... 7+ or minus 2 bits of information at any one time... You can rest ...assured.... that your unconscious... Has been paying attention... To everything... Else...*

Jess: *... And I wonder what everything else is that you weren't aware of about feeling comfort and relaxation... That maybe you can begin to have a sense of now...*

Shawn: *... Learning about and having the experience of the dreaming arm... And yet while your arm was dreaming... Were you paying attention... To what the rest of you was doing...*

Jess: *… And who knew that an arm can dream… And if an arm can dream…what does that mean for the rest…of you? For changing and growing…*

Shawn: *…because certainly a songbird can dream…many dreams…*

Shawn: *… In fact they do say that songbirds learn to sing in their sleep…*

Jess: *..it's true…*

Shawn: *…it is true…*

Jess: *…I know the man who knows the woman who did the research…*

Shawn: *…and I met her…there she was…a client of mine and I said…*

Jess: *…did you know that songbirds learn to sing in their sleep?…*

Shawn: *…and she said yes I do, I was the one who did the research…*

Jess: *…what they do is take the young songbirds and put them together with a master songbird…*

Shawn: *…and the young songbirds sit and listen…. And as we know they are paying attention consciously to only a small piece of what the master songbird is doing…*

Jess: *…and unconsciously they are paying attention to so much more…*

Shawn: *…to everything else…*

Jess: *…and I wonder what is everything else a songbird is aware of that they don't know… That they actually do know…*

Shawn: *…how could we know… What they are paying attention to… and what they are not…*

Jess: *...we do know that when those songbirds sleep... They dream...*

Shawn: *...because they track their little avian brain waves... As they listen... And as they sing... And as they sleep... And they see the patterns of the songs... As they sleep...*

Jess: *... And dream comfortably... Learning... Mastering a new skill... A new song... In ways that consciously those little songbirds had no idea they were doing...*

Shawn: *... Now of course... We don't know what a songbird dreams about... How could we... Know consciously...*

Jess: *... And though we don't know consciously... Just what it is those songbirds are dreaming about...*

Shawn: *... Because when you are a songbird... And you tuck your little head underneath your wing... And you sleep... And you dream...*

Jess: *... Comfortably... Relaxing...*

Shawn: *... Now you may have Technicolor dreams...*

Jess: *... You may have black and white dreams...*

Shawn: *... You may have exciting dreams of flying and singing...*

Jess: *... You may have boring mundane dreams...in your nest...*

Shawn: *... And that's okay... You may have dreams of a cast of thousands... Of songbirds...*

Jess: *...or just a few of you may think that you've had no dreams at all...*

Shawn: *...and let that be a sign of the changes taking place...*

Jess and Shawn: *...on the deepest unconscious level.*

Shawn: *...so you can wake up now...bright eyed and bushy brained...ready for Saturday night in New York City...the most exciting city on the face of the earth...*

Group: (*Clapping and cheering*)

Jess: Thank you so much guys...great work today. We will see you tomorrow!

Day 4

Sarah: Any thoughts, any questions, any observations? This is our open frame.

Kristina: Lots of dreams but I only remember fragments, even though I asked my unconscious mind to help me remember.

Sarah: Did you get a yes or no from your unconscious?

Kristina: I guess it was a no! (*Laughter*).

Sarah: It's saying "I'll give you a little teaser!" That's what happens, the unconscious mind comes out to play and continues into our dreams at night. Anyone else?

Rita: Isn't the protocol a lot to do in one session?

Sarah: Yes. Remember the first session is a two-hour session, with a follow-up session of an hour to reinforce the change. However it is not necessary to do every piece of it. For example you might only do the Dreaming Arm and not the Six Step or vice versa depending on which one you want to use to address the secondary gain. You're going to mix and match of course within the main structure of the protocol.

Shawn: And some of the patterns can be really quick. If you have your anchors set then the Tiger pattern is really quick, five minutes perhaps.

Mercedes: Yesterday when we did the Six Step Reframe, and we got the positive, I have to say that as soon as I stepped through my front door I started with the new behavior! I was so surprised at how easy it was to change! Usually I would be dropping things on the floor as I came in, and I found myself tidying up instead, and putting things away!

Karen: Mine was for exercising. My hotel room is very small so I can't exercise there but I found myself planning what I was going to do as soon as I went home!

Sarah: It is powerful stuff!

Shawn: This is not a course where we aim to change you, but sometimes a shift happens! You have been warned, you may get unexpected and beneficial changes from being here!

Kristina: One of the things I was working on was being more healthy and I found myself eating a healthy dinner!

Lawrence: I was talking last night with a hypnotist who is organizing a festival for the second year in a row and she's not sure what she should do. And I said to her, "You may not know that you know, but if we ask your unconscious mind if it knows, you don't even need to find out what the solution is but we can set it in motion." This seems like Jack's magic beans...How far do you take Erickson's ideas about the wisdom of the unconscious?

Shawn: As far as we can! And I love your pattern, "You know, you may not know, but your unconscious mind knows, you know?" That's a great language pattern. Did you know that you did that about you know?

Lawrence: ...Yes... it just seems wide-open! It's the hammer in your toolbox! It's such a beautiful hammer!

Sarah: And the thing is, when you're going through it you get the sense of the yes or the no, you get that feeling of a shift. You can't put your finger on it but that's the unconscious speaking.

Mercedes: When I was doing the dreaming arm I got an answer that my conscious mind didn't want to hear. But last night when I was dreaming I dreamt, "this is what you need to hear."

I consciously I thought that was not the answer I wanted, and the conscious part of me in the dream state said "no, that's not what I want to hear!" But I guess my unconscious mind is sending me a message!

Sarah: Absolutely.

THE SWISH

Shawn: And talking of the unconscious mind...Who here has heard of Milton Erickson? Everyone! He would say to his clients, "I don't know when, and I don't know where, but some time in the course of the day you will see a flash of color..." (*Shawn flashes a red pen each time he says the word 'color'*).

And everything would change for the person. They would become the person they always wanted to be. And if you were to imagine that standing right here is the person you want to be, your idealized self, that's right... The person who is everything that you want to be, everything that you want to have in your life, everything that you want to manifest is standing right there.

And you could see the person and the only thing that you have to do is to stand up and step into that person and it would all be yours. Everything that you want is yours. And of course Milton Erickson didn't say that in exactly those terms because he had his own strange voice so he would say, "I don't know when, I don't know where but sometime in the course of the day you'll see a flash of color..."

And what he would really mean is that you can see right here your ideal self, the person that you want to be, the person who has all the abilities, all the beliefs and all the values, the person who is your ideal self is standing there. And so when you see a flash of color, what you're really doing is seeing the person that you want to be, is it not?

It's a metaphor, so each time you see a flash of color what you're actually seeing is the person that you want to be. Each and every time you see a flash of color. So the question for you right now is, what happens when you see this? (*Showing the red pen*) (*Laughter*).

And this brings us to the Swish pattern. The Swish pattern is a classic NLP pattern. If this is the only pattern you know in the entire world, you will fix every smoker that you meet!

Mark: So the last three days have been a waste? (*Laughter*).

Shawn: Belt and suspenders! The great thing about the Swish is that it's flexible so in terms of the protocol you can do the Swish in three minutes. It automatically involves the unconscious mind — the right brain if we make that sort of distinction. It cements the changes that you're making in a different modality than the ones that we've used so far.

Or you can spend an entire session on the Swish pattern and if you do so it becomes completely generative, it will change their life, it will transform them, it will transform who they are. It is probably the most generative pattern that we have in NLP. And as a pattern, you can do it in three minutes or you can take an entire session and transform a person's life. You can do it in trance, or you can embed it in your trance work when you're doing the dreaming arm.

You can do it conversationally. As they say in England this is the "bees knees" of patterns!

Kathy: We say that here too!

Shawn: Really? Do bees have knees?

Kathy: Yes, six of them!

Shawn: Bees with a lot of knees! And who here knows the Swish pattern? Not everyone, okay. We'll be going through it in a little bit of detail.

The Swish pattern basically has three parts — because it's the meta-pattern! The Swish is a visual pattern. One part includes a visual-external picture, which is to say what the person sees in the outside world, in the real world.

And part of the pattern involves a visual-internal, seeing a picture inside your head. And seeing a picture inside your own mind is typically a right brain activity, so you automatically get unconscious involvement in the pattern.

A visual pattern involves simply chaining two pictures together, so it's really really easy. The first pictures is going to be an external picture, and the second picture is going to be an internal picture and we're simply going to chain them together: "See the external picture, see the internal picture"…"see the external picture, see the internal picture"… "see the external picture, see the internal picture"…like that.

And so on until it becomes a chain, until it becomes automatic, until it becomes unconscious.

In the case of smoking, the first picture is an external one, something your client is actually going to see in the external world. What do we know that they are going to see before they smoke?

Yuval: The cigarette pack!

Shawn: Right! The cigarette pack! They're going to see that… (*shows pack of cigarettes as if offering to audience members*)… They see this… So this is going to be the first picture typically, it's going to be what they see right before they smoke. This is what the picture is going to be, the first picture. It's not going to be a picture of a person smoking a cigarette, or reaching for a cigarette. It is going to be a picture of their own hand reaching for a cigarette.

In NLP we call this an associated picture, we are looking out of our own eyes.

Then on the back-end of that picture we're going to chain another picture, so the two pictures run in sequence. The second picture is going to be internal, it is inside their mind.

And it's going to be a picture of themselves, it's going to be as if they are looking at themselves. This is what we call a disassociated picture. So the first picture is associated, seeing out of their own eyes, and the second picture is dissociated, seeing themselves. And all we are going to do is to attach those two pictures together.

Mark: So the second picture...

Shawn: (*Puts his arm around an imaginary Mark*). Mark, do you see 'Mark' here?... Do you see his blue shirt?... Do you see his hat? What's the ideal hat for this Mark to be wearing?

Mark: A Knicks hat!

Shawn: So you see Mark here in his Knicks hat. This is the ideal Mark! This is the Mark who "goes first," this is the Mark who has that ability to go first, to speak his thoughts. This is the Mark who has every potential... And this Mark doesn't smoke, that's no surprise to you because you don't smoke, but it would be if you were for a smoker!

And because this Mark doesn't smoke he has clear skin, clear eyes, good breathing. And this Mark is a Mark who goes first!

(*Shawn was borrowing various anchors which Mark has, including "going first," "obligation," and "witness."*)

Mark: That's so powerful.

Shawn: And here's the thing, let's do this... I'll take my special invisible cape and cover this Mark up. And I will drop the cape each time you see red, and when I drop the cape you will see this Mark who goes first...(*Shawn flashes* *the red pen, and lowers the imaginary cape which covers the imaginary and idealized Mark).*

There he is, do you see him? I'm covering him up again...there he is... and if every time you see red during the course of the day... you will see this Mark who goes first... who is more than just a witness... who is not under obligation... but goes first...

Mark: I'm in trance! So in a smoking version...

Shawn: We haven't got there yet, we're just playing! We don't use a magic cape in the smoking version! Here is the pattern for smokers: they have that pack of cigarettes, they actually hold it, they don't have to imagine that they're seeing it, because they brought their pack of cigarettes with them. They don't have to imagine that they're seeing it, they can actually see it. (*Shawn is playing with one of the students who has said that she can't see pictures in her mind. He alternates holding out the pack of cigarettes, and holding out his empty hand as if it contains a pack of cigarettes, inviting her unconscious mind to create the image. Laughter*).

And somewhere in this pack there is a spot, a point, a detail, maybe it's the 'O' of Marlboro, or the small red shield on the front of the pack... Whatever it is. Then we are going to take that picture of the ideal self and shrink it down and embed it in that point, say in that tiny shield on the front of the pack.

And then we are going to do something to stimulate their unconscious mind, by having fun with the picture. So what we might do with a smoker is to have the picture of themselves expand out of the spot, so it leaps out of them like a girl jumping out of a cake! (*Demonstrates.*)

Let me show you what that's like, and I'm not going to do it with those (*dropping the pack of cigarettes on the table*) because those are dirty and disgusting.

276

(*Picks up a quarter from the table*). We can all use change occasionally, right? Here we have a quarter, and in this quarter (*show's it to students*) if you look at it you will see an eagle, and what I want you to do is to take this picture of your ideal self and shrink it down until it's the size of a postage stamp or even smaller, and put it on the quarter. Do you see it there? Do you see your image on the quarter, your idealized self? Do you see that? Do you see that Kyle...? Do you see that Mark...? That's the Mark who goes first!

In a moment, (*showing coin to Kathy*)...but not yet, I'm going to tap the back of the coin and when I do that picture is going to leap out life-size, is going to leap out of the coin. It's going to be your idealized self, but now life-size, big, bright. Ready? One, two, three... There she goes!

Now it's shrunk back down on the coin. Are you ready? One, two, three... There! (*Kathy laughs*). Shrunk back down... Ready? There she goes!... Shrunk back down... Ready? There she goes!

Kathy: She's getting taller! (*Laughter*)

Shawn: So all we are doing is chaining those two things, in this case seeing the quarter, then seeing the picture of her idealized self. Quarter, self. Quarter, self. Just like that.

(*Shows quarter to Kathy*) And what happens when you see that now?

Kathy: I see the big one!

Shawn: That's right! You see the big one!

Kathy: My ideal self.

Shawn: Your idealized self! So that's the pattern, and it's really easy because it's just visual pictures which for 99% of the people is very easy.

So what they see is going to be the pack of cigarettes, and then somewhere in that is going to be a small picture of their ideal self, and then you're going to lead them to have the picture of themselves leap out of the pack of cigarettes.

So we are doing this Swish with what are called submodalities, which are just the qualities of the picture. In the one that we did the picture got bigger. The picture starts off very small... And then it gets big. Very small then big, very small and big. But for some people size isn't everything! For some people, distance is where it's at, like in the Tiger pattern. And what we can do is to use distance...

(*To Kathy, showing her the quarter*) Do you see that? In a moment, but not yet this image is going to shoot off into the distance... far away... and getting very small... and that is going to come back again and when it comes back it's going to be the picture of your ideal self, life-sized, big, bright, okay? Shooting off into the distance, far away... Coming back... Whoosh (*Kathy laughs*).

And we see that doing the Swish in this way is more effective for her. I am getting a bigger response with the distance one, than using just size...

(*To Kathy*) In a moment it's going to shoot off into the distance... Whoosh...(*Kathy laughs*)... One more time, are you ready?...Whoosh! That's good huh!! I like it!!!

(*Shawn uses theatrics during the above part of the demo, miming throwing the picture into the distance then having it return with a 'whoosh' sound. Each time he runs the pattern Kathy laughs more and "lights up."*)

Mark: I like it too!

Shawn: ...Whoosh...Whoosh... Now close your eyes for a second, see that quarter in front of you and when I click my fingers you'll see it shoot off into the distance, and when it comes back it is going to be life-size, big, bright, idealized you! Ready? (*Clicks fingers, Kathy head snaps back and she smiles*)... Blank that screen! See the quarter again, ready? (*Clicks fingers, Kathy's head snaps back and she smiles*)... Blank that screen! See the quarter? (*Clicks fingers, Kathy's head snaps back and she smiles*)... Blank that screen! See the quarter... (*Clicks fingers, Kathy's head snaps back and she smiles*)... Blank that screen! One more time, see the quarter...(*Clicks fingers, Kathy's head snaps back and she smiles*)... Blank that screen!

Kathy: (*Opening her eyes and smiling*) I feel... It's like... It's a reverberation...all over my body...

Shawn: Oh my God, a reverberation all over your body!! And what happens when (*shows her the quarter*)...?

Kathy: I see myself!

Shawn: That's right, you see yourself! And that's the Swish pattern, do you want a demo?

Mark: Yes!

Shawn: I just gave you three demos, you're not getting another one! Are there any questions before you practice?

Mercedes: When I try and do the Swish I get in my own way...

Shawn: So the picture bumps into you when it comes back? (*Shawn mimes throwing the picture into the distance but then being hit by it as it returns*).

Class: (*laughter*).

Mercedes: (*laughing*) Yes that's basically how I feel! (*Class continues laughing*)... I can't get the mechanics... So after the first few times I always ask myself "Why am I feeling it and the client isn't?"

Shawn: Are you doing the distance one?

Mercedes: Yes.

Shawn: Try the size one, maybe that will be easier for you.

Lawrence: Is that an indicator as to which submodality will work with a particular person?

Shawn: There are ways of finding the best submodality. However, if you do the slingshot then you are working with distance, size, and potentially brightness. The slingshot pattern is the one we just did where the picture moves off into the distance, because it's like on a piece of elastic — as it shoots off into the distance the elastic is stretched and then it's pulled back. And because this deals with distance, size and brightness it will work with 95% of your clients. That's why we recommend it.

If you just do the size Swish then it will work with most people but not everybody, and the effect may not be as great, like we saw in the demonstration the slingshot version was much more effective.

Now if you got the state, you got them excited about the picture of their ideal self, and the slingshot doesn't work then you can play around with submodalities to find the best way, but for now we recommend that you stick with a slingshot.

Mark: With reference to the other day to the muffin demonstration, you can really dream into that one...

Shawn: That's the idea! Mark, you are exactly right. You remember we talked about the muffin, right? The reason people have these desires and compulsions is because their attention is pulled into the object and therefore the rest of them, their hand, is pulled towards it as well.

If their attention is put into another object then the first object is no longer attractive, it no longer pulls them closer. So they have their attention inside the cigarette, and we give them something else which they would much rather have their attention inside, the picture of their idealized self. So it's got to be attractive!

If they just say "Yeah, I guess it's attractive..." then that's not it. It's got to be "Wow, I WANT that!!" Is got to be something more attractive, something that has more pull than the cigarette.

And you have some flexibility on time — you can do it quick, like we just did or you can spend some time and really get them revved up about the picture. "Yes, yes, I really want that!!!" And if you do that it becomes more generative because you can put more things in the picture.

Karen: Can you do that with a feeling too?

Shawn: Yes of course, but with a picture it's easier for people who are visual.

Karen: If people do this with me I go straight to the feeling...

Shawn: Exactly, for you why put in the middleman? You go straight into feelings. But for many people they are more used to seeing pictures in their minds than accessing their feelings, so for most people the Swish is very easy. The key thing for you as the hypnotist is to make sure the feelings get attached to the pictures.

Karen: So you would use their pack of cigarettes?

Shawn: Yes you would use their cigarettes. People become very attached to their own brand. Cigarette companies do not like to change packaging because the pack becomes an anchor for smoking.

Lawrence: Are you saying that Kathy will no longer have an interest in quarters?

Shawn: (*laughing*) No, what I am saying is every time she sees a quarter she is going to get in touch with her ideal self and feel herself drawn towards her ideal self. A quarter is not going to hold a fascination for her, it's just going to be a quarter.

Lawrence: Presumably seeing your idealized self would be a good thing... So wouldn't you seek out quarters? Wouldn't you seek out cigarettes so you could see your idealized self?

Shawn: No! But that's an interesting idea thought. As long as somebody wants to get a pack of cigarettes and look at them just so they can see their idealized self, then that doesn't concern me too much. As long as they don't smoke them!

But once the unconscious mind has access to the picture they don't need to see these (*waves pack of cigarettes*). It's a generative pattern because both the conscious and unconscious mind help to construct the image of their idealized self, saying in unison, "Yes we both want this!"

Kathy: So the quarter isn't necessarily an anchor...

Shawn: It becomes an anchor, but it's not the only anchor — it's not the only way they can access it. Each time they see the new self-image they become a little more of their idealized self.

Mark: How would you do this in other modalities? Could you do this with sound?

Shawn: Yes, we just did and it would sound (*snaps his fingers*)...Hear your ideal self Mark, because when you go first that's auditory, you hear the sound of your own voice. The feeling, and the sound of your own voice lets you know that you're going first. So when I click my fingers you will feel and hear the sound of your voice...(*click - click - click*). There you go...so you can do this auditorily!

Mark: And kinesthetically?

Shawn: No more demos! Are there any more questions on the pattern? Let's review the Swish specifically in the context of quitting smoking.

Step 1: Pick a spot on the pack of cigarettes.

Step 2: Create picture of the client's ideal self, shrink that picture down and put it in the spot on the pack of cigarettes.

Step 3: Have them look at the pack then imagine the pack shooting off into the distance and coming back as the picture of their ideal self life-size, three-dimensional.

Step 4: Blank the screen.

Step 5: Repeat a few times (*See the pack of cigarettes shoot it off into the distance, and it comes back is the life-size picture of their ideal self.*)

Remember we blank the screen each time because we only want the chain to run one way, from the pack of cigarettes to their ideal self.

Kristina: I was told at another training that in the Swish we create an image of the problem and then the image of the way they want to be... I was confused about that, but I guess I just answered my own question!

Shawn: Right! The first image is what they see with their own eyes. The only reason you would create the image in the session is if you didn't have the actual image there — for example, if it was the face of their boss and they didn't bring him along to the session!

So they would have to imagine the boss because the boss was not there in the session, but in this case that boss *is* the pack of cigarettes and the pack of cigarettes *is* in the session.

Jess: You have the problem right here when they bring that pack of cigarettes in.

Rita: Does it have to be fast?

Shawn: Its calibration. Generally the faster you do it the better, so what we typically do is to give them a little more time at the start so they can get used to the process. But the visual sense fires off seven times a second, that's how fast your eyes work. They basically take a picture seven times a second.

At the end of the Swish pattern you can go really fast...(*click - click - click*), especially if they are in trance you can snap your fingers and you will see that head snapped back as the new picture jumps out, that's what you're calibrating to.

Rita: So it's important to do it many times?

Shawn: I would typically do it a little more cognitively at the start, so you show them the pattern and you do it a little more slowly, and then maybe you ask them to do it in their own mind a little faster.

Then when they are in trance later on, you can run it as many times as you want because it's really fast once it's set up. So when they are in trance you can just say "Every time you see a cigarette...(*snap*)" and you'll see them snap their head back as they run the pattern on their own. And then you can do it as many times as you want. Conditioning is a good thing, and single shot change is possible.

Lawrence: Would you generally say when I snap my fingers you'll see the cigarette and it will fly into the distance a comeback as the idealized you?

Shawn: What I would usually say after I have set the pattern up is, "When I snap my fingers, you know what's going to take place right?...Whoosh... When I snap, right? (*snap - snap - snap*)... And you can see her move her head back as the picture flies towards her, then close your eyes please...(*snap - snap - snap*)... And you can see she's doing it inside. So we have the slow version, see the pack of cigarettes... And in a moment but not yet... Flying off into the distance... Further and further.... Smaller and smaller.... Coming back.... Bigger and bigger... Your new self... Big and bright...Whoosh!

This is the theatrical version, and theatrical is good because you're giving them a big state by being theatrical. Once they've got it you can be quick, snap, snap, snap! This conditions it. So for the first few, be more theatrical and give them a big state. Then get faster to condition it. Got it?

If you're doing the Swish and say (*to Jess in a low energy voice*), "so, you have your pack of cigarettes... and... errr...humm... In a moment...errr...hmmm... It will shoot off into the distance...errrr...so...there it goes...hmmm... Coming back...errr... here... yawn (*Jess is unresponsive*).

Class: (*Laughter*).

Shawn: There is no pop because there is no energy. The change takes place in the space in between you and the client and you have to put the energy into that space, especially in patterns like the Swish.

Sarah: States are contagious! We're going to give you 10 minutes each, that's loads of time.

(*Students do the exercise*)

Shawn: How was that?

Group: That was good!

Shawn: The Swish is an awesome pattern. Remember when you are doing any pattern, there are two patterns being run, that is the pattern the coach is doing, and the pattern the client is doing. The job of the coach is to make sure that both those patterns are running at the same speed.

So when you think about where you are in the pattern as the coach, what you are really asking is "where is the client?" As the coach you may be ready to got to the end of the pattern, but if the client is still on step one then you have a timing issue.

And a big part of the Swish pattern is that the outcome picture has to have emotional content. If the outcome picture is just a picture, then the pattern will not be very effective. They have to say, "Oh, I want that!" They have to transform their lust for the cigarette, into a lust for themselves... for the new them.

Mark: They have to fall in love with it!

Shawn: Yes...emotional content. Are there any questions on the pattern?

Kristina: Do I have to be hypnotized to get into the pattern?

Shawn: Remember the energy at the start has to come from the hypnotist. At the start of the pattern all the energy comes from you, the hypnotist, and as the pattern goes on you should be able to fire it off very easily, just by snapping your fingers, because by that stage the client has to be putting the energy in. That's why theater is really really important!

Sarah: You, the hypnotist, has to go first. It's the same as any pattern.

Shawn: You may think that trance work is all about, "Now...you are going in...to a wonderful state...of relaxation..." But it's not. Some patterns take a lot of energy, and the Swish is one of them.

Rita: Is it more effective if the client is in trance?

Shawn: It's very effective as long as you have set it up before they went into trance. If you have to try and explain this to a client who is in a deep trance, then good luck. Of course you can say, "Every time you see a cigarette you can think about how wonderful you are as a healthy non-smoker."

But the Swish pattern is much easier to set it up before they go into trance.

Mark: The pattern has its own built-in test — the cigarettes are the test, but can you take that further...

Shawn: We take everything further, we take them as far as we can!

Mark: Would you stop with a cigarette? The pack of cigarettes?

Shawn: You want to attach it to the trigger. We know that one trigger will be a pack of cigarettes, but we also know there will be others. If they smoke when they are stressed and they get stressed when they see their boss, then ideally we would like to do the Swish on their boss's face. The pack is one — but only one — of the triggers.

Lawrence: If one of the triggers was their spouse smoking at home, could you use that as the trigger picture, could you do the Swish on the sight of their spouse smoking?

Shawn: Yes. Here's the thing, if those are the facts then you have to make sure that built into the outcome image is tolerance.

Lawrence: The tolerance of the spouse?

Shawn: No, the tolerance of the ex-smoker, the tolerance of your client. The last thing you want to do is to have them go home and start to lecture their spouse on why they should stop smoking. There's nothing worse than being lectured by an ex-smoker on why you shouldn't smoke.

Well there are a lot of things worse than that, but you know what I mean! You don't want the client to build up this self-image of being smoke-free, and having no smoke around them, and then they go home and their spouse is smoking and they say, "How dare you smoke around me! Don't you know who I am! I am smoke-free!"

Jess: You may also find in the spouse situation that the client desperately wants their spouse to quit, but the spouse isn't ready yet. Tolerance becomes really important.

Yuval: How do you get the tolerance?

Jess: With the Swish you build it into the ideal image. Tolerance, or patience, becomes a value which is built into it. For example they could see themselves in the presence of their spouse not reacting to the smoke, being calm and peaceful. "It's not yet her time to quit."

Lawrence: Neither Kristina nor I could engage that state. Could you take the client into trance and before you do the Swish say, "Now picture your ideal self..." And build that up, reference it, during the Swish?

Jess: Yes, you can do that. I like to set up the Swish cognitively and then run it later on when they are in trance, during the Dreaming Arm. If you do the Perceptual Possibilities pattern you already have the image of their ideal self.

Lawrence: I guess the issue I'm having with this is setting it up. If they're not engaged right away, it seems like you're not going to get any effect...

Shawn: They have to be engaged! There is a difference being not engaged and not in trance...

Sarah: There are questions on the intake form about how you will be as a person when you are a non-smoker. Take that opportunity to begin to build up their outcomes state.

Lawrence: So it's just in the artificial environment of this the class where I had no engagement. If she were a client walking into my office I would have some level of activation? Some level of investment?

Jess: As change workers our business is state elicitation, getting the client into the right state. We built states, that's how the change comes. In all these different patterns, the key is to build the states. Because we set the pre-frames, and we've gone through the steps in the intake, we have an emotional investment in realizing this. Your clients will be invested in the change.

Lawrence: Where in the protocol do you set up the Swish?

Shawn: I would do it after the EFT. The pack of cigarettes is just the trigger image, so you don't necessarily need emotional attachment to that, you can tap away the desire. Of course you can use the desire for the cigarettes to transform into a desire for the new self, but I do it after the EFT and show them there is no power in the pack of cigarettes.

But I would set up the Swish before the trance. Jess is absolutely right, as change workers we get paid for state elicitation, for state-control. That's what we do!

If you have rapport with the client, and you become attached to their outcome then they will become attached to their outcome. That's what rapport is. It's state matching. They follow you when you pace and lead.

Lawrence: So you establish rapport, then go to the state, and they will follow?

Shawn: Yes! If you feel attached to the picture then they will feel attached. If you say to them, "Build a picture of your ideal self and let me know when you're done..." Then you don't have state control, you're not managing your own coaching state, so you don't have control of the client's state.

When I see the picture of my client's ideal self, I become attached to that! I have attachments to this ideal Mark, this Mark who goes first! Can you feel that? Aren't you feeling somewhat attached to this ideal Mark, and it's not even you!

Mark: It's congruency. If you are congruent you control you're client's state...

Mercedes: So that's why we make a picture of the client as a resourceful non-smoker as soon as they walk in the door...

Sarah: That's right, the first thing we do as coaches is to make a picture of the client as they want to be and we hold that in our attention. We place that representation in the space between ourselves and the client. And as a coach you'd better be attached to that! It doesn't mean that it's your responsibility to make the client into that, but you better be attached to it if you want your clients to be!

Jess: In holding that image you will be able to feel a kinesthetic response when your client is moving towards it, rather than moving away from it...Then you know where to go and where to take things. Holding that image of them as a non-smoker frees you up as a change worker. It takes a lot of pressure off you because you now have your ideal client in front of you! All you have to do is to calibrate whether they are moving in the right direction.

Shawn: And when you say, "My client doesn't seem to be attached to the picture," you're really talking about yourself as coach.

Jess: When I started doing change work, I didn't fully understand this. My change work was technically sound but I didn't have that sense of passion for the outcome, so the theater wasn't there. When you have that passion for their outcome than both you and they will be drawn towards it, like the muffin.

When your client walks into your office their attention is inside the cigarette and they are pulled towards it. Our role as a coach is to help them to put their attention inside their ideal self so they will be pulled towards that.

Shawn: Bear in mind that they may push back against their ideal self — to overcome that pushback, and get them moving in the right direction we do the provocative work or the metaphor work.

Mark: What about actual client beliefs?

Jess: The question is, how are those beliefs attached to the smoking? By doing the provocative change and the metaphors we at least loosen the ties between the beliefs and the smoking. If you want to change all their limiting beliefs that becomes a longer-term process.

Shawn: If they have a belief which is going to lead them to replace the smoking with something equally destructive, that is a concern. That's why we do the Six Step Reframe or the Dreaming Arm, so at least any replacement behavior is not damaging. There is no point in replacing the cigarettes with doughnuts!

Jess: The Smoking Destroyer can be an identity level change and can lead to positive changes in beliefs. Are there any other questions?

Kristina: I asked my partner whether he wanted anything else in the picture, and he said no, it's fine. So I'm wondering if I went more into that, maybe he'd be getting more attached?

Shawn: One way of approaching it is to find an archetype — a character from a book, or history of somebody they know. That archetype is going to bring all sorts of positive things; an identity, beliefs and values, capabilities and resources, as well as behaviors. It's a package deal and it saves a lot of time asking what capabilities and skills, what beliefs and values, would be in their ideal self. And for most people the right archetype is going to automatically have some attraction.

Mark: So you mean a historical figure?

Shawn: Historical, fictional, mythical, biblical... NASCAR racer... Was that lady called?

Sarah: Danica Patrick...

Shawn: Right, Danica Patrick, the first female NASCAR racer to have pole position at Daytona, the Super Bowl of NASCAR. And this woman has pole position! She's in number one position! Danica Patrick!! Isn't that awesome! Isn't she self-actualizing as a woman!!

If you can imagine the qualities... You may not be into NASCAR, in fact I'm sure most the people in the room are not... But the quality she must have as an archetype, the raw courage that you need to have to drive that car around that track 250 miles an hour, or whatever ridiculous speed they drive at, around that narrow track and you're just gunning that thing!! Isn't that fucking incredible!!!

She's a woman, she doesn't have all that male testosterone stuff, but she has DRIVE, just pure "go for it" DRIVE. Now isn't that something you could use more of? And when you think of that time in your life when you would normally say to yourself (*whiney voice*), "I don't know if I can do this..." (*Laughter*)... or the thing you see when you look at your client, and maybe you see they're not attaching to that image, and they say (*whiney voice*), "I don't think I'm attaching to this..." And suddenly a picture appears in your mind of Danica Patrick and you feel that DRIVE, that energy, there may be cars in front of you but you go "I'm gunning it!!! I'm gunning it for that line!!!"

And that's the Swish. Are you getting some emotional attachment now? (*Laughter*).

Mark: Does doing the Swish with somebody count as a Swish for you as well?

Shawn: Of course, because you go first!

Sarah: And look at how much Shawn built that up...

Kristina: Wow, and I didn't even know who she was!

Sarah: And he got in touch with the energy of it and the passion of it. If he just said "Think of Danica Patrick... Swish"... (*Laughter*)... And then he got up at his seat and embodied the energy of it, and that's the theater!

Shawn: I didn't even know her name. You don't even know who she is!

Kristina: I didn't, but I do now! (*Laughter*).

Shawn: You have to put the energy in, and that's why we're saying "where are you in the pattern?" Not, "how many steps have I done," but "where is my client?" So you know there is a pack of cigarettes, and the next step is for them to get a picture and for the picture to have a pop, to have emotional energy and you're calibrating that, and doing whatever you have to do to get that pop. Whatever it might be!

DIRECT AND INDIRECT SUGGESTION

Jess: You have a client come to see you because you're a hypnotist, and they want the magic, and they have specific expectations about what hypnosis is. And you do a lot of pre-frames in your pre-talk, about what hypnosis is and what it's not.

And they are still thinking of the stage guy on TV who goes "SLEEP... do this, feel amazing." The Scooby Doo trance. So why not give it to them?

Last week Shawn told a story about a client who just needed to be told "Stop smoking!" and it got the change. So let's move into the area of direct suggestion. How many of you have studied classical hypnosis? The Elman induction?

Direct suggestion has a place, and is really valuable. So far we have done indirect hypnosis, but when we have them in trance — maybe during the Six Step, maybe during the Dreaming Arm — it's a wonderful time for you to layer in more direct suggestions.

The deeper someone is, according to Erickson and others, the more direct you can be. The less indirection is needed, and there are all sorts of ways to do this. Sarah was talking about a technique earlier, would you like to share that?

Sarah: It's called the no suggestion suggestion, and I found it in a script book by Drake Eastburn. Not that I ever use scripts with clients but occasionally I read them to get a couple of ideas. And this is a really nice one. It goes something like this:

> In a moment I'm going to give you a suggestion, and this suggestion is so powerful that it works 100% of the time, and I know from the work we have done up to now

that you're completely ready for this really powerful suggestion that I'm going to give you, and what you might or might not realize is that your unconscious will be able to track exactly what the suggestion is, and when your unconscious likes the suggestion it's going to embrace the suggestion, and because your unconscious mind is going to embrace this suggestion fully and completely, the changes which you are going to make about being a non-smoker and living a healthy life are going to be so powerful that you will automatically change when I give you this suggestion...And a side effect of this suggestion is that you won't consciously remember what the suggestion is, but your unconscious will...

Do you see where I'm going with this? I keep telling you that I'm going to give you a suggestion and in the meantime I am layering up the suggestions!

So this is a very nice way to begin to layer in direct suggestions. It's also very nice for those A-type people who want to track everything is going on, and are thinking "When is it going to come, when will they say the suggestion...?" And in the meantime the suggestions are coming thick and fast...

Shawn: So rather than an open loop, this is more of an open-ended loop! You're saying in a moment... but not yet you're going to do this amazing thing...and in the meantime you're giving them suggestions for all these amazing things while they are waiting for the amazing thing!

And their conscious mind is going, "Come on, get to the suggestion!" but in the meantime all the rest of the suggestions are going in.

Jess: And one of the things I like to do, generally after the Dreaming Arm, is to go through the entire session as direct suggestion:

You've come in to change, you've experienced what it's like to see that ideal you, you walked the path finding the amazing things that lie ahead of you as a non-smoker, and sharing those with the people you care about and who care about you, you have reformed who you are from the inside out, knowing how to say no over and over and over again, in a way that is healthy and completes you as a person, you've developed skills and you know how to increase relaxation, to have a sense of socialization (and whatever other needs were satisfied by the smoking). *You had this experience of your unconscious mind creating resources for you. And you have a dream and because you have a dream this means you are now the non-smoker that you always were...*"

So that's one of the ways I like to do it. And I will be even more direct than that in deep trance: "You are a non-smoker! You are a non-smoker! You are a non-smoker!"

I like the blackjack rule, say it 21 times! And when they're in trance, it feels good to hear it!

Shawn: Some people say it's only 15 times, and some people say it's 21 times, so why not say it 36 times and cover your bases! (*Laughter*).

Jess: And when they're in trance, after going through the various processes or even in between the processes, there are other ways you can play with language. You can layer in more direct suggestions, because the unconscious mind may very well have the expectation that, "I've come to see a hypnotist and they need to tell me to stop smoking." So why not tell them! Remember we're using ALL our skills to create change.

Rita: Could you throw direct suggestions into other parts of the session?

Shawn: What we do is to use indirect suggestion throughout the session. Here's the difference:

I may say to you, "You will fully and completely access your ideal self, and feel that sense of confidence rushing through your body, as soon as...it's coming up for lunchtime." So you're making the suggestions conditional.

Or I could say directly, "You are amazing, you are feeling confident, you are feeling a sense of joy running through your body, flowing through your heart, flowing out of your heart into the room like love."

The problem with direct suggestions is that if somebody is a polarity responder, or is strongly internally framed, they will go inside and say, "That not true." So we can make it conditional upon something else, like it being lunchtime.

Or we can use extended quotes and say, "I had a client who came in last week, and I said to her, 'You are amazing, you have amazing skills, you have unlimited potential!'"

They can't argue about it because I'm talking about somebody else, and they weren't even there. But the suggestions are still going in. So we use indirect suggestion all the time during the session.

Direct suggestion is no messing around, no use of quotations, just give it to them straight. And we do this when they are in a deeper trance, when their critical factor is more likely to be down.

Jess: There is another version of direct suggestion called forcing, which goes something like this: "In a moment I'm going to count down from 3 to 1, and when I reach one you will know from the inside out that you are a non-smoker and feel amazing three, two, one..."

Once again you are being very direct and as Shawn said, using that type of suggestion earlier on, you run the risk of them saying "no, that's not true." The critical factor checks everything being said: "is this true?" The conscious mind makes a decision as to what information to let in, it says yes or no. Once the conscious mind has stepped aside, the unconscious mind can begin to create and generate the conditions for change.

Direct suggestion is more valuable once you have established a pattern of "yes" using yes-sets, and a pattern of success with hypnotic processes.

So now, in groups of three, formulate some direct suggestions that you can use with smokers. You have a smoker in deep trance. What direct suggestion are you going to use to confirm to them that they are a non-smoker?

(*Students do exercise*).

Jess: How was that guys? What were some of the suggestions you came up with?

Group: Directly working on the trigger situations…

Jess: Aha, can you give me an example?

Kathy: The next time you are in a bar with your friends, you have no desire to light up a cigarette, and you will be enjoying a pint of beer even more because you can taste it…

Jess: Good. Within the field of NLP and hypnosis there is the idea that the unconscious mind cannot process negation very well. There are some hypnotists to say don't ever use negation because the unconscious mind cannot handle it. While that's not entirely true, there is a two-level process that has to happen with negation.

So the unconscious mind first has to form the image — in this case, an image of the "desire to smoke." And then it has to negate it in some way. That doesn't mean it can't be done, and I've seen hypnotists brilliantly use negation but there is a another level of cognitive processing which has to take place. This is something to keep in mind,

Sarah: So for example, if you say "you won't want a cigarette" the unconscious mind may hear "I want a cigarette."

Rita: How about, "The more you see someone smoking, the less of a desire you will have to smoke…"

Sarah: Or "the more you fully embrace being a non-smoker…"

Jess: For many people, one of the reasons they want to quit is the smell of the cigarettes, which does not sit well with most people. When they are ready for a change, most smokers will say, "I don't want to smell bad, and when I am around people who smoke it smells awful." So you can play with that and say, "The more you're around people smoking, the more you realize how it smells."

Kristina: The longer you are smoke-free, the more money you will save… the more…the more…

Lawrence: If you use that language game, the more…the less, does that activate the inverse? So for example, if you say, "The more you are around smokers, the less you will want to smoke." Does that activate, "The less you are around smokers, the more you want to smoke?"

Sarah: I tend to do the more…the more. The more you are around smokers, the more you realize the stench, and the more committed you are. So you are always building.

Kristina: The more committed you are to your health, the more you'll be smoke free…

Shawn: We very often do the "more-the more-the more."

Group: The more time you'll have for others to enjoy you… The more time you'll have for your hobby.

Karen: What about the tense? Do you want them to already be a non-smoker?

Sarah: Yes, and you want to generalize it to the future. You are a non-smoker and you will continue to feel wonderful. So a mixture of tenses.

Mercedes: Continue to remember, as you are walking up the steps, how easily you're breathing...

Kristina: What's a good metaphor for somebody who was a smoker but who became a non-smoker?

Sarah: I would use a client story. "I have a client and she recently came back to tell me how wonderful she is continuing to feel..." And you could say, "And I said to her 'you have already achieved this, you are living the life of a non-smoker!'"

Mercedes: "And her skin was looking so nice..."

Sarah: "And I said to her 'you are looking fantastic!'" I am changing the pronoun to direct it toward my client.

Lawrence: Don't you need to make an explicit reference like "and that client was just like you!"

Sarah: Don't go that far. You're unconsciously communicating it through gestures and pronouns.

Jess: When I am setting the pre-frames for the session I will tell them about the client I saw the previous week or the previous month who achieved the change. And this does a couple things, it allows you to use the pronoun shifts and embedded suggestions with extended quotes: "And then I said to my client, 'you're awesome!'". It also normalizes the change, because they think "If this other person with the same problem can change, then so can I!"

Kristina: When we were training before, I was working with a partner and she said to me "let me try something I used with a client, and it worked really well." So I have this big expectation, and I was all in!

Karen: I have been using it on myself, because I used hypnosis to stop smoking as well...

Jess: That's really powerful! You should definitely use that! You should put that in with your pre-talk. It gives you a whole bunch of credibility that I don't have because I've never been a smoker, and it allows you to explain the power of the techniques on a first-hand basis. You are the living proof that they can achieve this!

FUTURE PACING

Jess: Now we have some more pieces to wrap up our work. It's not done yet!

We have done all this work and we want to make sure they will continue to use the resources we have helped them create. So we are going to do something called a future pace. We do this both in the trance and also after the trance. "Think about tomorrow. You are having your breakfast, and what happens? What about those cigarettes?"

"They are not there."

We want to encourage them to start thinking in the future, to start generating the future outcome, and their future memories. So you can start by suggesting that the cigarettes are gone, but at some point you want to ask them as part of the test. Perhaps you say, "You are at the bar with your friends, there are a couple of friends over here who are smoking and they offer you a cigarette, what happens?"

"I smell the cigarettes and they're gross...but I'm cool with them smoking because I'm a non-smoker..."

Sarah: Because of the work we've already done, we know their environmental triggers. We know when and where they smoked and we're going to future pace each of those occasions, each of those places, each of those events, each of those cigarettes, in a positive way. The unconscious mind does not differentiate between what is very strongly imagined, and reality.

Jess: There was a study that came out about a year ago, and they did fMRIs of people imagining doing things while they're in trance. And they found that the centers of the brain that were associated with visual recognition were the parts of the brain that were activated. The brain was actually seeing the pictures as if they were real.

This is really powerful stuff, they are actually going through the experience in the future of being a non-smoker and we are creating a future memory.

Lawrence: If in the course of doing this, they say "I'm reaching for another cigarette," do you loop back through one of the patterns?

Sarah: It might happen, and if it did, then yes I would.

Jess: If it is going to happen, you would catch it much earlier in one of the other patterns.

Sarah: And we use future pacing for any issue, not just smoking. We are testing and future pacing on numerous situations. Although we will always do a big future pace at the end of the protocol, you may do a few after any of the patterns. Loops inside of loops inside of loops inside of loops.

So lets have a quick example of a future pace. Someone give me an example of a time when their fake client might have smoked...

Mark: Playing cards.

Sarah:

> Now I would like you to imagine in your mind's eye seeing yourself sitting down and playing cards as a non-smoker. And make this picture big and bright and absolutely perfect in every way. See yourself healthy, see yourself completely as a non-smoker. And when you are ready step into that picture, see what you see, hear what you hear and feel what you feel. Feel how fabulous it is to be healthy, playing cards, having fun, and being a non-smoker.

And next week you're going to go and play cards with your friends, and you're going to be sitting there with the cards, and your friends, drinking, what are you doing? What are you noticing? What about the cigarettes you used to have? They're gone? Isn't that interesting…

If it's a recurring event, you can use the same event numerous times. So you can say, "And then in three months you go to play cards again…" Or you can choose a number of different situations from the past where they smoked.

Rita: Is this in trance or not?

Sarah: Yes. It could be straight after the Dreaming Arm, or perhaps right after the Six-Step Reframe…

Jess: And if you want, you can take them into the future and have them look back:

"Imagine being 50 years in the future, looking back at your life at all those times you got to breathe easily, and smell good, and feel confident."

You can go all the way to the far end of the timeline so that in between you have a lot of the generalization happening for that success. Play with it, be creative!

TESTING AND THE REALITY STRATEGY

Jess: ...and now that we have the future pace in trance, it's time to reorient them to the outside world, and have an experience of success there and then in your office. What a wonderful opportunity to let them accomplish the final goal right then and there. And once more we want to make sure that the pieces are in place, and most importantly, if something is not in alignment, we prefer that they fail in front of us, rather than after they leave our office. Because we can work through it, we can reframe and set the groundwork for the next session.

There are a couple of ways that we test. If you remember, the cigarette has been thrown on the floor. I will pick it up and say to them, "Would you like a cigarette?" That's test number one.

Test number two. I offer them their pack: "Would you like a cigarette?"

"No."

"Would you like to throw the cigarettes out?"

"Yes."

The final ritual is throwing the cigarettes out. That's a behavioral test but it's also a state test. (Thankfully, it's a lot easier than the one they use to torment public school kids.)Because we don't want the clients to simply go through the motions, then leave your office and buy another pack! We want to continue to reinforce the change which has taken place.

Rita: When you ask them if they want to throw the cigarettes out, do you hand them the box and ask them if they want to put them in the trash?

Jess: Yes. It's far more powerful if they do it. You will see clients who will also empty out their matches or their lighter. And then we begin the final loop this is called the Reality Strategy…

Sarah, will you role play for a moment?

Sarah: Sure.

Jess: So let's imagine that Sarah has just thrown out her cigarettes and I will say:

"You mean you've changed?"

Sarah: Yes, I guess I have.

Jess: Really? Are you sure you changed? Really?

Sarah: Yes.

Jess: How do you know?"

Sarah: I feel it.

Jess: Are you sure?

Sarah: Yes!

Jess: You mean in the two hours we spent together you changed a 20 year habit?

Sarah: Yes I have!

Jess: Really? You're not just saying that are you? I can give you your cigarettes back if you'd like?

Sarah: No I don't want them back!

Jess: Really? How do you know?

Sarah: It's just a horrible feeling…

Jess: You mean you've really changed!

Sarah: Yes!

Jess: Congratulations!

This is all done with a twinkle in your eye. We want to tease them. We want to push the client to the point where they getting a little tired of us asking, until they're like, "Yes I've changed, leave me alone!"

Sarah: We cycle through the these three questions quite a few times:

- Really?

- How do you know?

- Are You Sure?

What does that do to the client? What do they have to do in order to answer the question?

Kathy: They have to go inside and check.

Sarah: Yes! "Really?... (*Go inside and check*) "Yes"... How do you know?...(*go inside and check*) I feel it...Are you sure?... (*Go inside and check*) Yes!!

Jess: And you can combine this with the future pace, "Are you telling me that tomorrow, when you go to the bar, you won't want those cigarettes?"

Sarah: No!

Jess: So during this cycle we also retest the future pace by introducing the triggers again.

Sarah: It's a nice powerful tail-ender for any change. This is based on John Overdurf's work, and each time you cycle through the loop you put more energy into them having to convince you as the hypnotist that they have changed. So you start gently and then each time you push them a little harder.

Jess: And you will actually see the state build in the client, it's very cool. So we've talked a lot about future pacing, the reality strategy and testing. I'd like everyone to get into pairs and have a go at future pacing and testing.

If you would like to run the role-play as the client who has just had a huge change, this will give the hypnotist the chance to play and experiment with how the future pacing might go, as well as the reality strategy.

Sarah: So the client should give the hypnotist a couple of places where in the past they would've smoked so that the hypnotist has something specific to future pace. Is that clear? Then bring them out of trance, ask them how they are doing, then pick up a cigarette from the floor — that's their first test. Then offer them the pack "what do you want to do with these?"And they can put them in the trash. Now the reality strategy loop, "So you've changed? Really? How do you know? You sure? Really?"

And realize the testing for the smoking is so easy because you have the cigarettes there in the room. If someone has a fear of penguins is much more difficult to test that unless they bring a penguin with them.

Karen: If there are a number of different instances in which they smoke — say they play cards a lot — is it useful to get just one of those occasions?

Sarah: Yes. For example if you know they're going to go play cards on Thursday, I would say "And I know that you're going to go play cards on Thursday, imagine walking into the room...." If you know there is actually an event, then it's wonderful because you can lead him through that specific event. And you might want to do it slowly, preparing to go to the event and being so proud of themselves for quitting, arriving at the event as a non-smoker, and future pacing through the entire event. With a smoker you will have so many times they would have smoked. And then you may wish to get more general and say, "Think of sometime when in the past you might've smoked, but now you're a healthy non-smoker..." And get them to run through that. You're leaving it open for the unconscious mind to really generalize to other times.

Ok everyone, let's go and do this!

(*Students do exercise*).

Sarah: How was that guys? Nice to have an opportunity to practice a little future pacing, testing, and reality strategy?

Jess: The reality testing, the future pacing, the testing, the ritual of throwing out the cigarettes is a really powerful moment for the client. They have been through a lot of powerful experiences in the session and this is the moment for them to really claim that outcome, to claim their identity as a non-smoker, to claim the strategies to meet those needs in new, healthy, and productive ways. So really layer this up; once again think of this is theater.

This is the pinnacle of all the small successes that they've had — each step of the process has led to this moment. Congratulate them, really congratulate them. Take this opportunity to have them leave your office in such a powerful positive state that it continues on. Their life is different, and you helped to save it. And that's amazing!

Lawrence: If in the future pace testing you discover that they are not really there, you obviously want to offer them the opportunity to throw out the cigarettes because they'll fail and you don't want that, so what might you say?

Sarah: I would review the changes they have made, and the progress they have made. Point them out very strongly, go through the different experiences which they've had, remind them of those, and layer up that the unconscious mind is changing, because all we are is changing. I'll probably do a big loop about change, that some people change in a snap, and for other people it's more incremental, it takes more time.

Mark: If they relapse, they may do so incrementally…

Sarah: And also, with a smoker it is often black and white. They have one more cigarette and suddenly they are back to being a smoker.

Jess: This can happen. Sometimes they will decide to test themselves. They will say, "I can have just one." And this comes back to the issue of identity.

I may tell my clients, "Look, if I have one cigarette that doesn't make me a smoker, that's not what makes someone a smoker." If I have a feeling that they may want to test this, I will out frame it. Sometimes I'll just tell them "don't test it! Why would you do that to yourself!"

Mercedes: Even if they are not totally changed at the end of one session, it is inconceivable that they could go through all of these patterns and not have experienced some change which they are aware of. And you can point out that change and say, "the changes are ongoing and we will address this in our next session."

Jess: There will be change. Perhaps they're only smoking one cigarette less, perhaps they'll be smoking only one pack a day as opposed to two. And I may take this opportunity to Task. Tasking is really great because it puts responsibility on the client in a real concrete way. And what I do is, for every cigarette they smoke they have to put it in a jar. And for every pack they buy they have to put the monetary equivalent into that same jar. So now they are paying double for packet of cigarettes.

For their session they can leave the money at home because that's often a lot of money to be carrying around! But they need to bring in the jar with the cigarette butts so that I can add water to it. And I say, "there, do you want to smell?" And you start to link them to a very visceral experience. If you do this, keep an air freshener in your office, because it stinks!

Rita: How do you know when to do that?

Jess: I do it in between the first and the second session if the change isn't quite there yet. It depends upon the state. Some clients may be highly cooperative and they will throw out their cigarettes because they think that's what you want. You are looking for the energy behind it, the state.

Lawrence: How much time between the first session and the second session?

Jess: A week.

Lawrence: And if you are done after the first session, but you sold them a package...

Jess: I'll do one hour of pleasant trance with lots of self-esteem and confidence building, lots of future pacing of those resources.

Lawrence: What do you tell them they are coming back for?

Jess: Reinforcement.

Lawrence: Even if as far as you're concerned they're done?

Jess: Yes. Also you want to get testimonials for your practice and I do that in the second session, as a closing to the whole thing, either video or written testimonial. I say "You've made this amazing change in your life, and there are a lot of people out there who don't know just how powerful hypnosis can be to make a change. And they don't know how resourceful they can be in their lives to become a non-smoker. And as part of the work of getting the word out is to have testimonials from non-smokers like you, would you be willing to give me a testimonial?"

I give them two options, either a video testimonial or a written testimonial, although you will have some people who tell you they will do it later and it will be three months before you get it, if you get it at all. I have also had people who didn't turn up for the second appointment because they got the change so they think why should they bother to show up. Sometimes they call and sometimes they don't, so I'll call them or email them and they'll say "oh, I'm fine, I'm not smoking anymore."

Rita: When do they pay you?

Sarah: Upfront! I send them a PayPal money request and I tell them that once I receive their payment then they'll have a confirmed session with me. If you don't do that, and this has happened to me before, they'll book the appointment and then they simply won't show up, and I'm sitting in the office wasting my time.

Jess: And paying in advance gives them a financial investment in the change, it's financial leverage. They're making a commitment toward the end result.

Kathy: What kind of release to you have them sign?

Sarah: Our release is included in the appendix.

Lawrence: Do you film your sessions?

Jess: You can film them, or audio record them. You will need a secure place to store the recordings. And you will need to get that permission which is included in the release — and we also inform them.

Lawrence: Do you give them a copy of the recording?

Sarah: I don't. What can happen is that people tend to pick it apart, the conscious mind becomes involved and they start undoing the work.

Shawn: If you're seeing a client who you have seen a number of times before, and they want a recording of the induction, that I would give to them.

Jess: You can also make an audio CD for them to take home to reinforce the work.

Lawrence: Can you sell that?

Shawn: Yes you can sell it if you want to. And if you are doing a Living Social, or some other voucher program, you may be able to include it in the package, a session plus a CD. This will give you a higher base for the cost of the package. Obviously you have to be genuinely selling it at that price!

REVIEW AND RECAP

Jess: So now you have the complete "QUIT" protocol... from soup to nuts and from nuts to bolts, from beginning to end, and everything in between. Now all you have to do is to wait for the check to clear!

Lets see how everything fits together:

Step 1. Initial phone call

The client calls you and you have your initial phone call.

Step 2. Intake process

They arrive and you do the intake. During this time you are looking for the context and the triggers, the Meta-Programs which the client is using, noting the client's presuppositions, time line organization, and gathering leverage for the change You may use the coaching pattern and you will be looking for the client's map of the world.

Step 3. Provocative and Metaphors

We will start to get into the more formal change work, using metaphors and provocative language to lay the pathway for change and overcome any obstacles which the client may raise.

Step 4. Craving Busters

Using EFT or the backward spin to deal with any cravings. EFT and the backward spin are very powerful tools not only to manage the craving then and there, but the client can also take them into the future and use them in all different scenarios as well.

Step 5. Hypnosis Pre-talk and convincers (*if it is the client's first time in trance*)

Now we will do the hypnosis pre-talk, perhaps with a formal convincer, such as the twist around, you may not need this because, remember, EFT and the backward spin are also powerful convincers.

Step 6. Induction

Any formal or informal induction will do. Whichever one you prefer and whatever works in the context for the client. So now we have the client in trance.

Step 7. Perceptual Possibilities Pattern

We begin to provide the clients with leverage for change and we do this by kindly supplying them a reality check, using the Perceptual Possibilities pattern, a sense of cause and effect essentially. This is enormously powerful for creating leverage for change, as well as the change itself.

Step 8. Smoking Destroyer

And then we move on to the idea of identity, reshaping their identity as a non-smoker through the Smoking Destroyer.

Step 9. Tiger Pattern

From there we go on to the Tiger pattern, transferring a negative anchor onto the cigarettes so they are no longer an enjoyable experience. In fact it becomes quite the opposite.

Step 10. Swish (*this could go anytime after the Craving Busters*)

Now we move on to the triggers and associations using the Swish pattern. We create an intensely positive strong state so that every time they have a visual cue of their trigger, they automatically respond with an image and a state of who they want to be, who they are as their ideal self. And although we have the Swish a little bit lower in the protocol, we like to do it more cognitively earlier on, after the EFT and before the induction. We are then repeating it in trance, so that it reinforces and builds upon itself and becomes highly generative.

Step 11. Dreaming Arm/Six Step Reframe

Then we have the Dreaming Arm and the Six Step reframe. You can do either, they are actually the exact same pattern just dressed up a little differently.

Step 12. Future Pacing

You will want to layer up suggestions throughout this, perhaps with a few future paces as well.

Then we will end the formal trance process, and bring them out. And during this you can introduce the idea of a forgetting loop, or conscious forgetting. The idea that the problem (*smoking*) existed in a trance.

This is true...they had been in the "smoking trance." And what we've done here is to create a new trance, a better trance and we're applying the new trance to the old trance — we are collapsing the trances.

You see, throughout every waking moment a client isn't necessarily thinking about the cigarette. They don't think about it until it is time to have a cigarette, or in this case know that they have quit. And we don't want them to consciously pull apart the entire session for the next three days. So, we are equating this new resource state with what they were doing before. You are building a lot of self-esteem as they are coming out of trance and putting in a lot of congratulations.

Step 13. Testing and Reality Strategy

Then end the formal trance. And test your work with the cigarette on the floor and throwing away their pack of cigarettes. Use the Reality Strategy to help the client check inside themselves and to be certain of the change...How do you know?....Are your sure?...Really?

Step 14. Congratulate the new Non-Smoker

Then "Thank you, you did a wonderful job. Congratulations on your new life as a non-smoker!" And you have a non-smoker.

If not you may wish to pre-fame the next session, and give some tasking, still congratulating the client on the steps they've taken in the direction of their goal.

Sarah: So that's the entire protocol, and it's a protocol only to the extent that you can be flexible with it and every client you have is a unique individual who is smoking in their own unique way, and the time spent during the intake gives you vast amounts of information to know the direction to take during the session.

Rita: Do you do one big trance? Or a different trance for each of the patterns, and bring them in and out of trance several times?

Jess: I tend to do one trance but this is personal preference. There is a lot of value to bringing them up and down especially in terms of fractionation, as we saw with the Six Step reframe. But because it can be a little bit awkward to go from one pattern to the next, I break it up and say, "In a moment, I'm going to be quiet, and when I'm quiet your unconscious mind can drift and float comfortably as the changes you've made through this experience integrate at a deep unconscious level." So that in between each trance I'm creating space for integration, and also to break the state they had been in before.

Rita: So you go from one pattern to the other while in trance?

Jess: And Sarah does it a little bit differently...

Sarah: Usually I bring them out a little, and then we go back in. Sometimes they're in a deeper trance than others, in the patterns. It's personal preference really. Experiment!

Rita: So do you do a full induction in between, or just say close your eyes and go into trance?

Sarah: We all know when somebody "comes out of trance" they're not necessarily all the way out. You may be able to say "close your eyes" and they'll go straight back in without needing a big induction. They are hovering on the edge of being in hypnosis, so I may say go back inside and go straight into another pattern.

Other times I'll bring them back a little bit more and say "How was that?" And I know that they are still in trance and that the hypnosis is going on. So I'll say, "Something really is happening isn't it? And now what I want you to do is to close your eyes..." and then I'm into the next pattern. So for example if we are moving into the Tiger pattern I want them to be holding the cigarette, so I'll bring them out a little bit more and say "Now you're going to be doing an amazing pattern..."

Jess: And you can do a combination of the two. For example when I get to the Tiger pattern and the Dreaming Arm and get them to open their eyes and look at their arm in catalepsy, it's a great convincer and is the type of pattern that provides a visual link to the negative anchor you're setting. So play and experiment. Either way is better.

So now we're going to give you about 45 minutes, and we realize that the entire protocol could take up to two hours, so you'll have the opportunity to do some of it. This is role-play and it is for you as the hypnotist to learn the protocol — rather than as a piece of change work. Skip the induction, no formal trances.

Sarah: Welcome back everyone. That was really quality work.

Jess: You guys are already much more skilled than the vast majority of the hypnotist working out there with smokers. You guys are light years ahead!

Kristina: I wish to make a comment. When I first saw you guys were having this workshop I thought it wasn't for me, or I don't want to deal with smokers. They are all the same and they can quit smoking by themselves! (*Laughter*) But this has been so beautiful, I'm so glad I signed up.

Sarah: Well thank you all so much for bringing your energy, questions, thoughts, your wisdom and enthusiasm...

Shawn: Thank you for bringing both your conscious and unconscious minds with you to learn and to play...

Jess: And thank you most of all for the work you are going to do in helping to save lives. That is truly amazing!

Now go out there and save lives!

Appendix

INTAKE FORM

Date:
Name:
Address:
Phone Number :
Email:

Are you currently under psychiatric or medical treatment? If yes, describe

Have you ever been treated for: epilepsy/ heart problems/Diabetes?

List any medications you are taking:

Are you pregnant?

Do you have any fears/phobias?

Have you ever been hypnotized? If yes please explain.

How long have you been smoking?

Age when smoking began?_____

How many per day?_____

Did you ever stop smoking? If yes what worked for you?

When do you smoke? (Specific times a day, rituals)

Where do you smoke? (Specific locations house, car, work?)

What are some circumstantial triggers? (Arguments, pressure, state of mind?)

What are your physical symptoms? Are you experiencing shortness of breath after climbing stairs etc? (List all ailments and discomforts.)

Is there anyone else in your household smoking?

Why did you start smoking? Did you like smoking right away?

What are some of your favorite pastimes/Hobbies?

What are the benefits to being smoke free? In what way will your life change?

Who else will benefit most when you stop smoking?

How will you spend the money you save by not smoking?

Who will you be as a person once you have stopped smoking?

RELEASE STATEMENT

I understand that _____is not a
Physician, does not practice medicine, and does not
diagnose or treat any medical condition.

I affirm that I am not currently being treated for any
medical condition related to my requested behavior
modification program. Hypnosis can be used as a
complementary care to most medical conditions, however
a referral from your physician or licensed mental health
counselor is required if requesting this type of hypnosis
treatment. I understand hypnosis does not constitute
Psychiatric treatment, Psychotherapy or Psychoanalysis

I also understand that hypnosis is not a replacement for
traditional medical or mental treatment and should not be
used as such. I understand that Hypnosis is not a
replacement for my doctors care nor is it to be used for, or
is it a replacement for any medications, diagnosis or
treatment of a licensed medical doctor.

I hereby authorize _____to
hypnotize me for the concerns we have discussed and/or
that I have indicated on this intake form.

I give _____ permission to
use hypnosis for any issues that have been outlined in this
intake form and for any future purposes that I may
request.

I understand that the success of my hypnosis sessions
depends greatly on my own ability and desire to affect
change in myself and the results depend greatly on my
own serious participation and follow through. I
understand that although hypnosis can be very effective
and has a high success rate,_____ does
not offer a guarantee, as my own personal success depends
on my own ability and desire to create change in myself.

I hereby consent to being recorded (audio/visual) by
_____I understand that if audio
recordings are made during these sessions that
_____holds the copyright of these
recordings.

I am aware and understand that in some cases it may be
necessary for the practitioner to respectfully touch my
shoulder(s), hand, wrist, or forehead in order to assist me
in relaxation. I give the practitioner permission and
consent to do so in order to help me establish a beneficial
state of hypnosis.

I understand that matters discussed during a session will
be kept confidential except in the following circumstances:
I sign a release of information giving permission to release
information to a specific individual or agency; child/elder
abuse; client is in imminent danger to self or others;
subpoena of records.

In addition, _____may from time to time
discuss aspects of my case with other colleagues (the client
would not be identified by name) who will likewise
maintain confidentiality.

I understand that there is a strictly enforced 48 Hour
Cancellation Policy and I agree to pay in full should I
cancel an appointment within 48 hours.

Signature: _____

Date: _____

BIBLIOGRAPHY

Barber, Joseph. (Jul 2001). "Freedom from Smoking: Integrating Hypnotic Methods and Rapid Smoking to Facilitate Smoking Cessation." *International Journal of Clinical and Experimental Hypnosis*, Vol 49(3), 257-266.

Craig, Gary. Emofree.com

Eastburn, Drake. (2007). *Power Patter: A Script Book for Hypnotists and So Much More!* D. James Publishing 2007.

Farelly, Frank. Brandsma, Jeff. (1981). *Provocative Therapy.* Meta Publications 1981.

Overdurf, John, Silverthorn, Julie. (1995). *Training Trances: Multi-Level Communication in Therapy and Training.* Metamorphous Press; 3 edition (November 1, 1995)

Schmidt, Frank. Viswesvaran, Chockalingham (October 1992). "How One in Five Give Up Smoking." University of Iowa, *Journal of Applied Psychology.* and *New Scientist,* October 10, 1992.

Tiers, Melissa. (2010). *Integrative Hypnosis: A Comprehensive Course in Change* (2010).

photo by Caroline Bergonzi

Sarah and Shawn Carson are founders and co-directors of the International Center for Positive Change and Hypnosis. They are both NLP/HNLP and hypnosis trainers and run a thriving training center in New York City. They are consulting hypnotists and work with private clients for trance-formational change. Both originally from the UK they live in Manhattan NY.

Jess Marion is a trainer with the International Center for Positive Change and Hypnosis and founder and director of Philadelphia Hypnosis. She is a hypnosis trainer, NLP/HNLP trainer, and consulting hypnotist. Jess runs a busy private practice in Philadelphia and lives and works in New York and Philadelphia.